D0323153

Ngoma

*Discourses of Healing in
Central and Southern Africa*

John M. Janzen

UNIVERSITY OF CALIFORNIA PRESS
Berkeley · Los Angeles · Oxford

University of California Press
Berkeley and Los Angeles, California

University of California Press
Oxford, England

Library of Congress Cataloging-in-Publication Data

Janzen, John M.
    Ngoma: discourses of healing in central and southern Africa /
John M. Janzen.
        p.   cm.—(Comparative studies of health systems and medical
    care; no. 34)
    ISBN 0–520–07265–0
    1. Folk medicine—Africa, Southern.   2. Folk medicine—Africa,
Central.   3. Healing—Africa, Southern.   4. Healing—Africa,
Central.   5. Rites and ceremonies—Africa, Southern.   6. Rites
and ceremonies—Africa, Central.   I. Title.   II. Series.
GR358.J36   1992
398'.353—dc20   91–43703
                                                                      CIP

Printed in the United States of America
1 2 3 4 5 6 7 8 9

Contents

Contents

Figures

Photographs

Preface

Discourse is central to the construction of knowledge about misfortune and healing. In Central and Southern Africa, discourses of healing take a number of forms: the evocation of distress and hope before others; prayers to God, ancestors, and spirits; songs both out of the cultural stock at hand as well as original compositions from the wellsprings of individual emotion; highly codified dress; instrumental accompaniment and dance; the creation and use of materia medica. All come together in the "doing of ngoma" that is the subject of this book. Discourse is the descriptive term of choice for this action "doing" because at issue is the mutual expression of feelings and ideas and the marshaling of knowledge and social networks required to bring about an acceptable solution to the range of ills addressed by ngoma-type movements and institutions.

The subject has been much examined in Central and Southern Africa by many authors under rubrics as diverse as divination, healing, health care, religion, epidemics, magic, ritual, cult activity, dance, song, folklore, and more. This book explores for the first time the possibility that some of this activity may in fact be a unique historical institution. Such a proposition is suggested above all by the presence, over a vast region, of similar words, names, procedures, and types of behaviors—discourses, in short—around the interpretation of misfortune and the treatment of affliction. For some time the use of language history has been a tantalizing vehicle for the study of the history of cultural domains. Where the compilation of lexica and grammars has progressed far enough, it is possible to single out for special study terms and structures in language around particular domains. In the present survey work this analysis is applied in a relatively simple manner to some cognate terms of health and healing that are widely used in ngoma. The rigorous analysis needed awaits further collection of detailed local vocabularies and the identification of practices; this has not been done very widely.

However, as this book goes to press, the horizon of new research that will supersede it is already apparent. Great strides have been made with the use of linguistic history as applied to the history of selected cultural domains. The paragon of such work is J. Vansina's recent *Paths in the Rainforest* (1990), on the evolution of political institutions in the rainforests of Western Equatorial Africa.

New research on ngoma is already in progress, including fieldwork of ngoma in Tanzania, the documentation of revivalist ngoma in the aftermath of the civil war in Zimbabwe, and the mapping of the institution in terms of layers of historical language formation. The result of this work will take its place within a growing body of self-conscious literature on the subject. The present project is the first comprehensive study of the discourse on misfortune and healing in Central and Southern Africa in connection with the institution Ngoma.

I must acknowledge many and varied individuals and agencies who made possible, and facilitated, this project. The University of Kansas sabbatical fund permitted me to take a leave from teaching for research travel in Africa. A senior research fellowship from the CIES-Fulbright Program made it possible for me to travel to the four cities that the research plan suggested would be opportune. The University of Cape Town invited me to its distinguished professor series, which opened doors and made contacts possible that I otherwise would not have been permitted.

Research in Zaire, Tanzania, and Swaziland was greatly facilitated by CIES sponsorship. In Kinshasa, this included such necessary privileges as being picked up from and taken to the Njili International Airport and being helped in a variety of other ways by the people of the Cultural Affairs Office at the U.S. Embassy, Acting Officer Phyllis Oakley and Nsumbu Ndongabi Masamba. Nsiala Miaka Makengo of the National Research Office, and Mabiala Mandela of the Centre de Médecine des Guérisseurs granted me much hospitality, time, and attention, as did Father Joseph Cornet and Lema Guete of the National

Museum of Zaire. I am also indebted to Kamanda Sa Cingumba and Nzimbi Nsadisi for their friendship and assistance.

In Tanzania, Emmanuel Mshiu and Dr. I. A. J. Semali of the Traditional Medicine Research Unit at Muhimbili Hospital were my formal sponsors. The National Research Council authorized the project, for which I am grateful. E. K. Makala, of the Music Division of the Ministry of Culture, and his colleague Yesia Luther King assisted greatly in making a number of contacts and by sharing their understanding of the research topic. Professor Ernest Wamba and Fidelis Mtatifikolo of the University of Dar es Salaam were friends to me while I was in Dar.

In Swaziland I had an excellent introduction and accompaniment to my stay from Ted Green, who was at the time working with the Ministry of Health and collaborating with Lydia Makhubu of the university in research on indigenous health-care resources, including *tangoma* (plural for *sangoma*: "healer"). Harriet Ngubane, a South African anthropologist who has worked with Zulu diviner-healers in Natal, introduced me in a marvelous way to many individuals in Mbabane and provided extensive interpretative help for my research. I am deeply indebted to these two friends.

For my survey research on ngoma in the Western Cape I am indebted to many people, including Professor Martin West, head of the Department of Social Anthropology of the University of Cape Town, and the members of the university administration who helped me during my time in Cape Town as a visiting distinguished professor; Janet Mills, whose acquaintances with numerous *amagqira* helped me to make quick contact; Adelheid Ndika, *igqira* (*igqira* is "healer"; *amagqira*, "healers" in Xhosa), who graciously invited me to the *nthlombe* (feast) sessions of her cell, encouraged me to photograph and record the events, and explained what was occurring.

Following a policy begun in earlier writing, I have used the names of healers and other public figures associated with the rituals and subjects of this work, insofar as they granted permission for this. However, although the therapy sessions described are often open to the public, and in that sense very different from the confidential character of Western healing, I have used pseudonyms for the sufferer-novices of the ngoma therapies. Because they were sick or deeply troubled at the time of my encounter with them, they were often not in a condition to consider the question of permission.

Parts of this work, or perspectives forwarded in it, have had the benefit of reaction from a variety of scholarly publics. The section

"Lexicon of a Classical Sub-Saharan Therapeutics" in chapter 2 was first put forward in a paper prepared for the Hamburg, Germany, conference on "Ethnomedicine and Medical History," May, 1980, organized by Joachim Sterly and Hans Morgenthaeler, and subsequently published as "Towards a Historical Perspective on African Medicine and Health" in *Ethnomedizin und Medizingeschichte* (1983). The present interpretation of the Bantu lexical data benefits from an additional decade of important new analysis. The perspectives presented in the section of chapter 2 called "Social and Political Variables of a Complex Institution" were presented in two papers. The mandate to sharpen the ontological identification of ngoma came from Stan Yoder's discussion of my paper "Cults of Affliction: Real Phenomenon or Scholarly Chimera?" in Tom Blakeley's conference on African Religion at Brigham Young University, October 23, 1986. Another perspective in that section was aired in a paper entitled "How Lemba Worked, or, the Trickster's Transformation" at the African Studies Association, New Orleans, November, 1985. Ideas from this paper also appear in chapter 5, "How Ngoma Works: Of Codes and Consciousness." Some of the material in chapter 4, "Doing Ngoma: The Texture of Personal Transformation" was first given on February 9, 1987, before the Department of Anthropology at the University of Chicago, in a Monday colloquium entitled "Words, Beats, Tunes: The Fabric of Personal Transformation in Ngoma Ritual Therapy." The relationship between kin, or lineage-based, and extra-kin strategies of health seeking were explored in a presentation to the Health Transitions conference organized by the Rockefeller Foundation and the Health Transitions Centre at Australian National University in May, 1989.

The nucleus for the book was set forth in a set of unpublished papers called "Indicators and Concepts of Health in Anthropology: The Case for a 'Social Reproduction' Analysis of Health" and "On the Comparative Study of Medical Systems: Ngoma, a Collective Therapy Mode in Central and Southern Africa." These were circulated in various ways as "Two Papers on Medical Anthropology." Chapter 6 grew out of the first of these papers, and further collaborative writing and thinking on the subject of the basis of health with Steven Feierman in preparation for an edited volume, *The Social Basis of Health and Healing in Africa.* The reader will find echoes of the perspective put forth here in several published articles, including: "Changing Concepts of African Therapeutics: An Historical Perspective," in *African Healing Strategies,* edited by Brian M. du Toit and Ismail H. Abdalla, 1985; "Cults of Affliction in African Religion," *The Encyclopedia of Religion,* edited by Mircea Eliade, 1986; "Health, Religion and Medicine in Central and Southern African Traditions," in *Caring and Curing: Health and Medicine in World Religious Traditions,* edited by Larry Sullivan, 1989; "Strategies of Health-Seeking and Structures of Social Support in Central and Southern Africa," in *What We Know about Health Transition: The Cultural, Social and Behavioural Determinants of Health,* edited by John C. Caldwell, et al., 1990.

I remain indebted to numerous others who have listened to my arguments or pointed out important issues as this work has progressed. Special thanks go to Nels Johnson, who reminded me of Mary Douglas's use of Bernstein's analysis as it appears in chapter 3; Thembinkosi Dyeyi of East London, South Africa, who interpreted the intricacies of the "doing ngoma" session presented in chapter 4 and translated its text into English; Stan Yoder, Richard Werbner, Terence Ranger, Henny Blokland, and several other anonymous readers who offered constructive criticisms; Sue Schuessler, who discussed ngoma in many conversations, and whose own work on this subject has helped me understand some of the issues in the literature; Gesine Janzen, who drew the maps and figures; and Linda Benefield, who copyedited the manuscript.

Finally, I am, as always, indebted to Reinhild for her critical encouragement of my research and writing, and to Bernd, Gesine, and Marike for their enduring interest in their father's seemingly endless project on African health and healing.

Introduction

That which was a stitch of pain,
   has become the path to the priesthood.
             Lemba song text,
             Kongo society, 1910

An important feature of Sub-Saharan African religion and healing, historically and in the twentieth century, has been the interpretation of adversity, paradox, and change within the framework of specialized communities, cells, and networks. In Central Africa these communities have come to be called rituals or cults of affliction, defined by Victor Turner, a major author on the subject, as "the interpretation of misfortune in terms of domination by a specific non-human agent and the attempt to come to terms with the misfortune by having the afflicted individual, under the guidance of a 'doctor' of that mode, join the cult association venerating that specific agent" (Turner 1968:15–16). In some circles these communities are called "drums of affliction," reflecting the significance of their use of drumming and rhythmic song-dancing, and the colloquial designation in many societies of the region of the whole gamut of expressive dimensions by the term *ngoma* (drum). The drumming is considered to be the voice or influence of the ancestral shades or other spirits that visit the sufferer and offer the treatment.

This work is concerned with institutions carrying the designation *ngoma* and related terms. By entering African religious and therapeutic expression through its own language, we are identifying some important underlying, and possibly historic, commonalities and connections. We can also establish the basis for variants and transformations more intelligibly.

A number of modern scholars have looked at this institution in Central and Southern Africa, although not always through the indigenously labeled categories. For example, Hans Cory, in the thirties, studied the constellation of ngoma groups among the Sukuma in colonial western Tanganyika and on the Islamized coast. His work for the British colonial government was concerned with the potential of these groups for social unrest. This work today provides a useful cross section of ethnographic and historic interest at one moment in time (Cory 1936).

The reference point of scholarship on African rituals or "drums of affliction" continues to be Victor Turner's work among the Ndembu of northern Zambia in the fifties; he introduced the term as a translation for the indigenous word and concept *ngoma* (Turner 1968, 1975). Turner's in-depth studies on several of the twenty-three Ndembu cults of affliction showed their inner workings and social contexts, intricate ritual symbolisms, therapeutic motivations, and societal support systems. At the same time, although he put forth the Ndembu as universal persons with believable aches, pains, and expressions, we now see that his account of them was largely ahistorical, localized in its coverage to the villages in which he did fieldwork, and presented in a largely static analysis characteristic of the prevailing structural-functionalist paradigm of the time. It was not clear in his work how widespread this genre of institution might be, nor whether it was particular to the Ndembu of Zambia on the Southern Savanna.

A variety of authors, researching and writing about the central and southern regions of the continent, described similar features in connection with the verbal cognate *ngoma,* but they usually did not make the connection between their own work and that of other scholars in other regions. In the era of structural-functionalism and colonial domination, the local "tribe" was the unit of study. Rarely were comparisons, or concerns for historical directions, articulated. However, useful work was accumulating which would make the task of historical comparison possible later on.

J. Clyde Mitchell (1956), a colleague of Turner's, followed the Beni-Ngoma movement into the migrant labor camps of the copperbelt. Terence Ranger found, in coastal and historic trade-route Tanzania, that the revivalist and dance dimensions of ngoma had followed the trade routes and population movements between early colonial settlements (Ranger 1975). Marja Lisa Swantz (1970, 1976, 1977*a*, 1977*b*, 1979) and Lloyd Swantz (1974) studied ngoma and related ritual healing on the Swahili coast in connection with social change and development. Wim Van Binsbergen, Gwyn Prins, and Anita Spring studied ngoma in Zambia. Spring's work added comparative ethno-graphic data from the "ngoma mode" of healing among Luvale women (1978, 1985). Prins and Van Binsbergen contributed to the history of western Zambian ngoma, the first to the cognitive framework of ngomalike therapeutic ritual (Prins 1979), the second to the linkage between numerous cults in the history of a region as an expression of differing modes of production and forces of historical change (Van Binsbergen 1977, 1981). Monica Wilson (1936), Harriet Ngubane (1981), and others studied the therapeutic ngoma settings in Southern Africa, where it was perceived as having largely to do with divination (especially among the Nguni-speaking societies).

Despite the value of these authors' writings on the subject of the cult of affliction, none has looked at the larger picture. They do not tell us how far-reaching the institution, as a culturally particular institution, might be. Luc de Heusch and Jan Vansina have been among the few to attempt broader surveys of possession cults in Central and Southern Africa. DeCraemer, with Vansina and Fox (1976), offered a summary profile of Central African religious movements, which they suggested were part of a cultural expression reaching back a millennium or more. But this article, suggestive in its general lines, did not provide a lexical or structural handle on how to study it further. De Heusch (1971) established a structuralist comparison of types of possession cults and relationships throughout the West African and Central African region that had far-reaching ramifications in such scholarship of the area. He emphasized, for example, the important contrast between possession cults, which entailed healing and exorcism, and cults that venerated shades and spirits, on the one hand, and cults that utilized mediumship for the interpretation of misfortune, on the other.

Ian Lewis, with a scholarly focus in the Horn of Africa, has offered important hypotheses on the nature of African cults and religions, first with his "peripheralization" or "deprivation" approach (1977), more recently with emphasis on the extent of "controlled" and "uncon-trolled" power in society, and the relationship of witchcraft patterns to patterns of possession (1986). Most recently, DeMaret (1980, 1984) has used archaeological and linguistic findings to attempt an overview of Central and Southern African religious and social features. I will have occasion to come back to these authors and their work.

This brief review of some of the scholarship relating to healing in community settings in Central and Southern Africa suffices to demon-strate that the field is not well defined, nor is it clear where one begins.

Current scholarship tends to break down into a distinction between religion and healing, but this distinction is not so useful in the present setting. A fundamental ambiguity that will need to be worked out in this study is that between the indigenous categories and terms, on the one hand, and the analytical models we devise for such an institution as the rite, cult, or drum of affliction, on the other hand. The term *ngoma* has been identified as the indigenous word for an institution. And yet, in many regions it is not necessarily used, nor exclusively used, to describe collective rites of healing. In the course of this study, therefore, the layered ontology of the "unit of study" will need to be clarified and variations around themes explained. This will be done ethnographically or contextually, culture historically, ethnologically, and analytically, in sequential chapters.

My own concern for the understanding of the shape and character of African therapeutics began, like that of other scholars, with very local work—in Kongo society of coastal Zaire (1969, 1978*a*, 1978*b*)—and has gradually moved to increasingly expansive coverage of institutional arrangements (1979*b*), therapeutic dynamics (1986, 1987), and historical processes (1983, 1985). Following intensive fieldwork in Kongo society on the "quest for therapy" and the structure of local institutions, I looked at a major historic cult, Lemba, which had emerged in the context of the coastal trade in the seventeenth century, and which had mediated the disintegrative mercantile forces of the overland caravan routes in that trade with the local lineage-based communities (1982). It became clear that local descriptions and explanations made little sense of the continuities and variations in Lemba. One had to take both the regional view of the cult phenomenon and a long-term historical perspective of the economic, political, and social climate to understand its emergence and duration.

After extensive reading in connection with my own local fieldwork and after historical study, it has become apparent that the cult of affliction and the ngoma designation of it is widespread throughout Central and Southern Africa, although there are many institutional and terminological variations. The scholarly task of the present moment, therefore, is to situate this work in wider regional, societal, and subcontinental context, and in the process to ask how widespread this institution might be, whether its many manifestations are transformations of an underlying common institution, why particular forms of it rise and decline, and how it relates in a dynamic relationship to other features of society and religion. A major lacuna in studying the wider phenomenon of the cult or drum of affliction across its appearance in Central and Southern Africa has been the absence of a set of comparable studies. Scholars have either done local ethnographic studies with careful attention to the structure of customs and languages and have done little to seek broader generalizations, or they have attempted broader generalizations without careful attention to the cultural particulars.

In 1982–83 I undertook to remedy this situation for myself with an extensive field survey of ngoma manifestations in four settings of Sub-Saharan Africa where the literature suggested it occurred. I was especially interested in how ngoma impulses and organizations were represented in major urban settings. The sites I visited in this work were Kinshasa, a hub of Western Bantu societies, including Kongo, in the Zairian national capital; Dar es Salaam, where Eastern Bantu and national Tanzanian cultures come together, with a strong Islamic presence; the Mbabane-Manzini corridor in Swaziland, at the northern end of Nguni-speaking societies, in a strong traditional kingdom; and Cape Town, in whose black townships all Southern African traditions merge in the underside of a society torn by apartheid.

Why were urban settings selected, which tended to feature immigrants to cities and transplanted practitioners from home areas in the countryside? First, the urban capitals studied offered much more accessibility to regional traditions than single rural areas. Indeed, one could find all regional traditions represented in these cities. Further, it was easy to identify ongoing local scholarship on these traditions and to converse with scholars and practitioners about the unfolding direction of the therapies. Ongoing practice in the urban setting would demonstrate continuing life, although changing, of the institution. Finally, it was virtually impossible for me to do justice to the subcontinental survey short of visiting a selective set of points on the map, such as Kinshasa, Dar es Salaam, Mbabane-Manzini, and Cape Town. Of course, other capitals could have served equally well, including Harare in Zimbabwe or Lusaka in Zambia.

The comparative survey emphasized eight points regarding the therapeutic dimension of cults of affliction: (1) the names of principle rites, their regions of origin, and terminologies; (2) modes of affliction (following Turner: symptomatological signs) and etiologies (spirits, social forces); (3) the characteristic therapy of a rite; (4) the social scale of the affliction (whether individual, group, or combination); (5) the sociocultural context—class and status, ethnic group, gender—of the afflicted and of the healer; (6) characteristic devices and musical instruments, dances, and songs of the rites; (7) profile of individual(s) in charge of the therapeutic rite—family, diviner, other specialists, association members; (8) perceptible changes in the last decade. These queries provided the underlying thrust of the investigation and were answered in each of the four regions, insofar as possible.

Although this work will address a particular type of institution in concrete historical settings and is in many ways simply a straightforward attempt to understand and to portray this institution, the framework of the inquiry is intended to be universally applicable. In other words, there is a theoretical subagenda to this work, for which ngoma is the case study. I present this agenda in the form of three issues—health, healing, and efficacy. They must be approached, theoretically, in this order. This order may seem reversed to some; however, it stems from a growing concern in medical anthropology that this field is not effectively applied to health issues (Harwood 1987:4). I contend this is the case because of a lack of concern for the ways in which healing, or medicine, affects health, that is, the subject of efficacy, or how the therapy "works."

Increasingly, in social science and medical writing, definitions of health provide the point of departure for the analysis and action of specific interventions. This gets us squarely into the debate on conceptions of health, which authors approach from a variety of viewpoints. Most of the time we use the negative "absence of disease" definition of health, or the demographer's profile of mortality, natality, and morbidity. However, definitions of health may also be philosophical (e.g., Boorse 1977), ecological (Dubos 1968), political economic (Doyal 1979; Savage 1979; Morsy 1981), sociological normativist (Parsons 1951; Freidson 1971; Zola 1966), or ritualistic, discursive, and interpretative. Exploration of definitions of health suitable for the analysis of African ngoma therapy will be addressed in some length in the final chapters of this work.

The application of a concept of "social reproduction" seems particularly suitable here. Given the widespread network relationship building that goes on in ngoma, "health" may be seen as a society or social unit's ability to regenerate itself (i.e., socially reproduce). This approach is inspired by the work in Southern Africa of Colin Murray on labor migration in Lesotho and the outflow of labor capital, resulting in a crisis of social reproduction (1979, 1981). Other authors who have developed a social reproduction analysis include Pierre Bourdieu (1977). This approach overcomes the chronic problem in classical medical anthropology and other disciplines of not being able to completely explain the deterioration of health in a society or a sector of society and the way in which members of society cope with this situation. The perspective of health as social reproduction will set the stage for an analysis of the collective therapies of Central and Southern Africa.

Establishing the character of the conscious therapeutic intervention as the basis for the comparative study of medical systems and traditions is the second major theoretical issue in this work. What will be the framework with which to analyze, in common terms, varied phenomena? What are the criteria of the "common," the "comparable"? Are they that which is labeled in indigenous practice and parlance? Or do they have to do with behaviors? In the case of Central and Southern Africa, do the common cognates of Bantu languages play a major role in determining what is the core of the historic and contemporary therapeutic system? Then there are the "institutional" questions, having to do with the primacy of the individual versus the collective, or societal. Central and Southern African therapies such as ngoma are so different, and differ in so many ways, from Western therapy, that we must first ask how the boundaries of researchable reality are to be drawn to identify this as medicine, or as healing, in order for it to have anything in common with the institutions the Western industrial world identifies by these terms.

Criteria of efficacy in therapy will need to be formulated, both in terms of specific therapies and interventions found in ngoma and in terms of the more general question of whether, and how, they may contribute to health. Both individual (psychological, symbolic, pharmacological, musical) as well as social mechanisms (entering and extending a network, creating support groups and redistributive chains, social competence) need to be studied as therapeutic mechanisms that may have generalizable qualities. Many of these measures enhance the ability of individuals and societies to contain trauma and to deal appropriately with difficulties, thereby contributing to social reproduction in the marginalized, alienated, or stressed sectors of a society, which ngoma therapeutics appears to address.

In order to accomplish the basic ethnographic-historical task of presenting ngoma and to open the theoretical discussions raised above, this book has the following structure. Chapter 1, "Settings and Samples," is a straightforward comparative study of four regional settings: Western Bantu, as found in Kinshasa, Zaire; eastern Africa, as found in Dar es Salaam, Tanzania; southern Africa, focusing on Mbabane in Swaziland, which is one of the North Nguni-speaking societies; and the townships of Cape Town, South Africa, predominately Xhosa, or South Nguni, but also a cosmopolitan synthesis of all of Southern Africa. This survey is largely a presentation of my field research of 1982–83, and thus it has all the strengths and weaknesses of a single scholar's work: limiting, in that it is only one individual traveling vast distances; enhancing, in that a trained eye can see much and make connections that a casual observer misses. In the western setting (Kinshasa, Zaire) I concentrate on the particular cults of affliction called Lemba and Nkita, of Lower Congo origin; Zebola, of the Equator origin; and Bilumbu, of Luba, or Kasai origin. Most of these are couched within the lineage setting or are designed to buttress the lineage. In East Africa (Dar es Salaam, Tanzania), because of the early work of Hans Cory on historic Sukuma ritual organizations, it is possible to offer a profile of both western Tanzanian ngoma and coastal Swahili, Islamized society, and ngoma expressions. From Southern Africa (Mbabane, Swaziland, and Cape Town, South Africa) come some of my best full accounts of ngoma, partly because of fieldwork luck and also because the institution may be less specialized there and may represent a more generic manifestation.

Chapter 2, "Identifying Ngoma: Historical and Comparative Perspectives," raises the possibility that ngoma is indeed a classical manifestation of Central and Southern African ritual. This chapter situates the book's subject in the context of research on the origins and dispersions of Bantu languages and cultures and the distributions of cognate lexica for ngoma and other African therapeutic-religious institutions. What is the evidence for culturally homogeneous domains beyond the linguistic tags? How do we account for the immense variations around the linguistic commonalities in this vast subcontinental region?

Chapter 3, "Core Features in Ngoma Therapy," develops a description of the main characteristics in ngoma therapy underlying the myriad manifestations of the institution throughout the region. These features include a phased rite of passage in which the sufferer, following identification of a sponsoring healer, moves gradually through the therapeutic initiation to membership in the order; a similar pattern of defining and interpreting misfortune through the invocation of, and possession by, ancestor shades, nature spirits, and other spirits; a common symbolism defining the status of the sufferer-novice moving through "the white," the ritual status of being "in process"; the role of sacrifice and exchange; and the empowerment of the novice through the transformation of the self and the composition and use of medicinal substances.

Perhaps the most important core feature, however, is the subject to which the next chapter is devoted.

Chapter 4, "Doing Ngoma: The Texture of Personal Transformation," moves beyond the behavioral and symbolic features of therapeutic initiation to the conscious, verbal dimension found in the ngoma sessions. A single session is described and analyzed in depth. It provides the basis for a wider comparison with other examples. The centrality of song to ngoma becomes apparent here. The variations in communicative structure of ngoma provide important clues to the understanding of the institution.

Chapter 5, "How Ngoma Works: Of Codes and Consciousness," proceeds with a presentation of the indigenous theory of this form of healing. From there it moves to the application of several academic analytic evaluations of ngoma, including the role of metaphor shaping, of consensus, and of the range of manipulations that shape affect of sufferer and therapists alike.

Chapter 6, "The Social Reproduction of Health," looks at ngoma from the standpoint of its contribution to society's fabric, attempting to answer the question of ngoma's contribution to health as understood in today's world. This chapter, of necessity, opens with a discussion of various health definitions, to determine which set might be appropriate for an understanding of ngoma's contribution to health in a contemporary context.

A project such as this is at once audacious and precarious. It is an attempt to demonstrate something that has not heretofore been known, essentially a mapping out of the core feature of a classic civilizational healing system in Central and Southern Africa, or at least a major feature of it. It is precarious because the assumptions that must be made in attempting this are not well validated. Working with linguistic reconstructions and variations around core behaviors often leads to interpretations of local evidence collected by others. One scholar, looking "over the shoulders" of others, is bound to be wrong some of the time in others' ethnographic backyards. To make matters more complicated, my ethnographic "home territory," Lower Zaire, in the Western Bantu-speaking region, fits the generalizations on ngoma least well, in some respects.

However, it will have been worth the risk if the end result, if only through criticism, provides the stimulation of new ideas and better research, especially that which goes beyond the confines of tribe and territory in Africa.

1
Settings and Samples in African Cults of Affliction

Do you intend to spend your sabbatical in airport waiting rooms?
A skeptical colleague

Lagos airport, awaiting night flight to Kinshasa: It's 34 hours since I've slept. I wonder if there are any kola nuts to be had. How would one find a kola nut in Lagos airport? Is this still Nigeria, or Africa? In the souvenir sales area I approach a group of gathered men and tell them I've been traveling a long time and need to stay awake—any kola? Several reach into their robes and pull out kola nuts. One shares with me, biting off the end of a nut and handing it to me. They are delighted; I feel at home, officially, in Africa.
Field Journal, July 2, 1982

At a "washing of beads" in a Cape Town township: A cross section of black Cape Town, showing great kindness and hospitality toward us. Indeed, it seemed they were seeking approval of the outside world. We heard unusual statements such as "we're not cannibals, drunkards, and uncivilized people" as the government would have everyone believe. They urged us not to be afraid of them. We assured them we weren't, otherwise we would not have come. They kept asking us if we were happy, and offered us chairs, drinks, food to welcome us . . . the men sought constant physical contact, to touch, hold or shake hands, as if to indicate their humanity through vicarious recognition.
Field Journal, November 14, 1982

This ethnographic survey is intended to sketch an impressionistic picture of cults of affliction in Central and Southern Africa, particularly in the contemporary urban settings of Kinshasa, Zaire; Dar es Salaam, Tanzania; Mbabane-Manzini, Swaziland; and Cape Town, South Africa. These national capitals represent the urban syntheses of four major regions of Africa respectively: the Congo basin, particularly Western Bantu-speaking societies; East Africa, particularly the Swahili-speaking setting; the northern Nguni-speaking setting; and societies influenced by Nguni, Sotho-Tswana, and Khoisan and by South African urban societies of the Western Cape. In each setting some attention will be given to the historical backdrop of cult-of-affliction origins in these regions.

The impressions assembled here can hardly be expected to be systematic. However, they are firsthand authentic portrayals of the subject of the book. Through the conversations with healers and patients, officials and scholars, they reflect some of the thinking on the role of Central Africa's affliction cults in bearing the load of the caring vocations.

THE "GRANDS RITES" OF KINSHASA

Kinshasa, Africa's largest city below the Equator, with about 3.5 million inhabitants, covers over two hundred square kilometers on the banks of the Zaire River. Local scholarship speaks of "les grands rites," representing numerous regional and ethnic traditions from around the Congo basin.

The local society of Kinshasa, and approximately half of its inhabitants, are of the Kongo-speaking (or Kikongo) society, of Lower Congo, or Zaire. From its beginning as the village of Kinshasa, then as the capital of the Belgian Congo, and after independence in 1960, as the capital of Zaire, Kinshasa has drawn residents from the entire region. The civil wars of the postindependence era and the deterioration of rural infrastructure and standard of living, together with the lure of the city, have led to the migration of many people to the city to seek their livelihood. Population expansion far beyond the ability of the city to provide an infrastructure of electricity, sewerage, and even water, has given rise to enormous suburban villagelike settlements. These population movements into the capital have brought with them the religious, therapeutic, and social forms of the regional cultures. From the Luba area of the Kasai region, one finds Bilumbu; from the upriver Mai-Ndombe region of Bandundu, Badju and Mpombo; from upriver in Equateur Province around Mbandaka, Zebola and Elima (or Bilima); from the Upper Zaire and Kivu, Mikanda-Mikanda; from Bas-Zaire and Bandundu provinces, Nkita; and from East Africa and Kivu, Mizuka.

BUTTRESSING THE LINEAGE IN
WESTERN BANTU SOCIETY

Of the major cults of affliction represented in Kinshasa, the most characteristic of Western Bantu society—coastal Kongo, eastward into

Bandundu—is undoubtedly Nkita. Not only is the focus of its therapeutic ritual, the lineage, at the core of the society, but it is ancient. It is mentioned in early historical documentation on the Congo coast, as well as in accounts from Haiti, where it has become an element in the *loa* system. Nkita is associated with *bisimbi* nature spirits, and, as a lineage cult, is often involved in the regeneration and maintenance of lineage government. The *bisimbi* invest, or validate, lineage authority, which in many regions is embodied in powerful medicinal and religious compositions, the *minkisi*. Nkita concentrates on the dynamics of the matrilineage and the individual affliction believed to originate from lineage problems. The cult cell is within the lineage itself, frequently originating in the crises of segmentation and the need to renew leadership (Bibeau et al. 1977; Janzen 1978; Lema 1978; Nsiala 1979, 1982; Devisch 1984).

The history of lineage and public cults of affliction is significant in coastal and Western Bantu society. Given the prominence of fairly fixed settlements, landed agrarian lineages, and of markets and trade, and of—especially coastal and Southern Savanna—chiefdoms, this is not surprising. However, few of the early institutional forms have been adequately studied. The close articulation of emblems of authority, social renewal, and healing is common. My work on the historic Lemba cult that emerged in the seventeenth century in the context of the great coastal trade bears this out (Janzen 1982). Lemba represented a ritualized concern for several dimensions of society: the maintenance and protection of alliances between landed and prominent lineages; protection of the mercantile elite from the threat of envy by their subordinates due to their accumulation of wealth; the maintenance of trade routes overland between the Atlantic coast and the big markets of the interior; finally, the resolution of contradictions that resulted from the social upheavals caused by the great trade. There will be occasion to return to Lemba as an example of a public cult of affliction later in this book.

As in many cults of affliction, *nkita* is at once the name of the illness, the spirit behind it, and the therapeutic rite. The sign of affliction in Nkita is frequently expressed in diffuse psychological distress, dreams, and fevers, or threat to the continuity of the lineage in the form of children's illnesses or deaths, the barrenness of women or couples, or lingering sickness of male leaders. These problems are often associated with the suspicion of inadequate leadership, or at any rate a loss of contact with the *bisimbi* or *nkita* spirits in which lineage authority is vested. An individualized version of Nkita therapy concentrates on particular cases that, if cumulative and serious, may trigger a collective therapy that seeks to renew leadership through the resolution of conflicts and the reestablishment of harmonious relationships with ancestors and nature spirits.

The Nkita rite, following the identification of the individual or collective diagnosis of the cause of the misfortune, requires the "quest for *nkita* spirits" in a river at the outset of the seclusion of the sufferer. These spirit forces are usually represented in smooth stones or lumps of coral resin found in appropriate streambeds, and they become the focus of the identification of the sufferer with the spirits. The seclusion of the sufferer-novice and instruction in the esoteric learning of Nkita is the first stage of teaching by the Nkita leader. The site or domain of this seclusion, a common feature of all ngoma initiations, is in Kikongo called *vwela* and refers to the forest clearing or the enclosure of palm branches, set apart and sacralized for this purpose.

Because of the lineage focus of Nkita and *simbi* spirit mediation, the rites attendant to Nkita have a close connection to, or are done concurrently with, other rites that perpetuate collective lineage symbols, such as shrines bearing ancestors' mortal remains (nails, hair, bits of bone), leopard skins, chiefly staffs, sabers, or other signs considered to bear the spirit and office of past leaders. In some of these parallel rites, ceremonial couples, such as the Lusansa male and female priests, provide the personification of the continuous spiritual line. Instances of sickness or infertility in lineages associated with these rites may precipitate the nomination of new priestly couples.

In urban Kinshasa, according to psychologist Nsiala Miaka Makengo, who surveyed Nkita extensively in the mid–1970s (1979, 1982), there are an estimated forty to fifty "pure" Nkita practitioners, a figure that does not, however, include those whose practice is limited to their own lineages. The full rites, done with a full-fledged *nganga Nkita* are expensive and complex, thus beyond the reach of many families. Cost and availability of drummers, musicians, supporting personnel, transport to the site, and coordinating the whole ritual have become problematic. Thus, Nkita practitioners have tended to become generalized therapists for Kongo and non-Kongo people, in which non-kin join the seances, and the rituals become generalized for a range of conditions. Nsiala found that these Nkita healers receive on average five cases per day that require hospitalization, either in their compounds or another hospital, and up to a dozen cases that can be treated and released (1979:11). Of these, 40 percent were male, 60 percent female. They came in all ages, distributed as follows: Children from birth to five years (15 percent), youths up to sixteen years (50 percent); adults (35 percent). Despite the apparent trend for the Nkita healers to become generic urban healers, their work continues to reflect the dual levels of the individual and the collectivity. Although the majority of cases are individuals, unique family or lineage therapies have evolved in the urban setting. These include mutual confessions, the group confessing to the sufferer, lifting the potential harm of malefic medicines, and holding veritable "psychopalavers" to vent the aggressions that exist within the group. These mechanisms of group renewal are frequently interspersed with divination to seek further understanding as to the internal group reasons for misfortunes.

GOD, JESUS, THE ANCESTORS, AND JANET IN LUBA DIVINATION

Bilumbu, of Luba-Kasai origin, reflects the same emphasis on the core points of the social structure, in this case the patrilineage. Like Nkita, it has experienced significant changes with the urbanization of its clientele. The *kilumbu* (singular of *bilumbu*) is a medium of the spirits who interprets the misfortunes of others. Bilumbu mediums enter this role after having their own possession or disturbances, and having been told by diviners that they have *bulumbu*, that is, the gift of prophecy or divination. The bilumbu, as well as the chiefs (*balopwe*) in Luba society, are the individuals who legitimately interpret *buvidye*, the quality associated with *bavidye*, the founding spirits of the Luba nation (Booth 1977:56; Roberts 1988).

Observation of a Makenga variant—"to work for those who need it"—of the Bilumbu rite in Kinshasa in 1982, however, makes very plain that the urban rite, at least this one, has changed significantly from what it was earlier. After many generations of male mediums in a particular patrilineage, a woman had become the central medium of this particular cell. The "generalization" of divination and therapeutics, which has already been mentioned in connection with Nkita healers, was also evident in this instance of Bilumbu.

Kishi Nzembela, a woman of about sixty years, mother of eight, grandmother of twenty-two, carried on her lineage's Luba divinatory and therapeutic tradition. Zairian psychologist Mabiala ma Ndela, who accompanied me on this visit, had known Nzembela for some time and regarded her work as somewhat atypical within this tradition.

Nzembela "owned" or "managed" the spirit of her deceased daughter Janet, although all *buvidye* holders within the Nzembela line of mediums and spirits had been males for at least four generations before her.

Nzembela prefaced our discussion of her ancestors, and her daughter Janet, with emphatic affirmations that she was a devout Catholic and believed in God and Jesus, and that these must be named before any ancestors in an invocation. The walls of her small chapel featured two painted portraits, one of the Christian Trinity, the other of her daughter Janet.

Nzembela's entry into this work had begun in 1956, eight years after the death of her daughter Janet at age eighteen. Janet, a cripple, had been a talented, dynamic person and a leader, having been elected to head a group of handicapped children. She was also a gifted singer and had wanted to pursue a career as a singer. She had been possessed by spirits and claimed the gift of spiritual healing, as well. At eighteen, in the course of a pregnancy that seemed to the family to go on interminably, she died of complications. The family had also at that time had trouble with the police at the market.

Janet's spirit visited the family in 1956, when her brother, a soldier in training in France, was possessed following a sickness he could not overcome with help in hospitals. In his dreams, Janet instructed the family to give her a proper burial, to construct a beautiful tomb. Her brother did not wish to become a medium, so Nzembela, the mother, offered to do it for him. In a family celebration, a beautiful tomb was dedicated (in the *byombela* rite with the ngoma drum), and a feast was held following the sacrifice of a goat and four chickens. Having done this, Kishi Nzembela received a vision in which her mother, Madila, told her there was no conflict between the work of Janet and membership in the Catholic church. She was instructed to continue attending church, although on hearing of her possession, the church threatened her with excommunication. She went to the priest with her dilemma. After her presentation of her visions, and the priest's affirmation of how beautiful they had been, she received his blessing. If her work was evil, it would destroy her; if it was good, she would be blessed.[1]

She has continued working with the spirit of Janet and has had many mostly Luba clients from within and outside the family, including a few whites. Nzembela does not divine and heal on Sundays, the days she prays and worships. Weekdays, she is very busy. Some clients enter into trance quickly, others need *pemba*, white powder, sprinkled on them to achieve it. Nzembela offered that her own behavior may affect the degree to which Janet will come to clients. If, for example, she has done wrong, Janet will hesitate. Sometimes Janet journeys to Europe to visit her siblings, in which case she will not respond to singing and chanting in Nzembela's seances.

As we arrived to visit Nzembela, she was singing and shaking two rattles. Five other persons were seated on the floor inside the chapel, either singing or in trance (fig. 1). Nzembela had already taken care of one healing case earlier in the morning. Mabiala and I were invited to join those seated before her. All present were given white powder to put on their foreheads and at each temple, so as to be able to "see clearly" the things of the spirit. Nzembela and an assistant were wearing white coats with a red cross on the lapel. As the singing and rattle shaking became more intense and Nzembela distributed dried tufts of an aromatic plant to inhale, several of the participants began waving their hands about. Nzembela was leading the rhythm, but it was her young assistant who first became fully entranced and provided the central mediumship role for the seance. This woman was a client of several months, about twenty years old. She had been married, but her husband had not paid her family the bride price, and he had left her with a young child. Her family was angry with her and the young man. She was under great stress. Nzembela had taken her in to work and counsel with her.

When the young assistant, following the singing, became possessed with Janet, she announced—in an altered voice—Janet's greeting. Thereafter, "Janet," in a painfully distorted voice, spoke about each case before her, in turn, interspersing her comments with addresses to "Mama" Nzembela, telling her what she was seeing in the cases. The case of another young woman's affliction, she said, resulted from her "witchcraft" of having lured her sister to Kinshasa. Her abandonment of her rural parents had generated conflict in the family. She would need to be cleansed and reconciled with her parents to be whole again.

The young medium, possessed with Janet, turned to me and asked about my marriage. When I assured her it was good, she wanted to know with what problem I had come. I decided on the spur of the moment to mention a work-related problem. "Janet" said, and this was confirmed by Nzembela, that there were indeed persons or spirits who were trying to hurt me, even though they had not succeeded in doing so. The medium gave me some *pemba* powder to put on my forehead and temples, and under my feet and under my pillow, to help me in dreams to see the truth about my situation. This would also return the evil intentions back upon their perpetrators.

series of other walled compounds

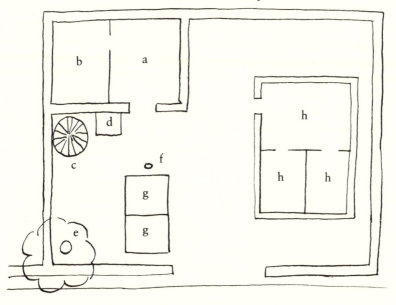

busy street: cars, pedestrians

Figure 1. Kishi Nzembela's compound in Kinshasa, Zaire: (a) Nzembela's therapeutic chapel decorated with paintings of Jesus and the angels, and daughter Janet; (b) storeroom; (c) patrilineal ancestors' shrine with wooden figures depicting particular persons; (d) matrilateral female ancestors' shrine; (e) tree shrine with base painted with white and red dots; (f) water tap; (g) latrines; (h) living quarters.

Another seance began with Nzembela, shaking the rattle, singing her hymnlike song about Jesus and God who had saved us and Janet who would bring solace. A young man was in deep prayer, as if trying to enter trance to see his problems. Nzembela picked up a second rattle to intensify the rhythm and to bring the young man into trance, but he did not come. Later she took up his case in a semiprivate counseling session and listened to his complaints and miseries. Presently the young woman assistant entered trance, "Janet" again greeted "Mama" and the others and then turned to the young man to divine his case. Through the assistant, "Janet" said she could not see his problem behind his dizziness and loss of memory. She then turned to her own child. "Janet" began thumping on the child, holding it between her legs, rolling around, while the child screamed. "Janet" said the child had a bad spirit of death in it. The child's mother (in trance) was evil, and the child was in terrible shape. I feared that this outburst of self-negation by the young woman would hurt or even kill her infant. However, this did not happen.

Further cases were more mundane. There was the woman who wanted to find out why her husband's Mercedes had crashed. He had seen bad spirits, said Nzembela. A woman whose husband was roaming around unfaithfully, "Janet" accused of wrong actions toward her husband.

The voice of "Janet" lapsed and Nzembela, as herself, began listening, occasionally offering advice, to the quiet young man who had been sitting in the corner throughout all this. She moved close to him, "in therapy" now, and spoke softly to him, prohibiting him from thinking of suicide. She encouraged him to pray, to take white powder, and to return next day for cleansing. The others present also received similar counsel and attention from Nzembela.

She also told of a case of a white man's family that had come to her for the presentation of their problem: his failing business and a marriage that was breaking up. During the divining and therapy session the family's daughter went into trance and revealed that her husband, a Latin or Italian, was from a people who had something against her own people, the Flemish. Her ancestors were against her marriage to him. After some confessions and the revelation of other problems, this family was helped to resolve their differences.

Apart from the young apprentice who had entered possession several times, it was unclear how many of these clients would eventually be drawn into a network of similar Bilumbu medium-healers. The session ended when all the clients had been dealt with for the morning.

URBAN CHANGES IN CULTS OF AFFLICTION

This brief account of two urban cults of affliction from the Western Bantu setting, both emphasizing lineage or family mediation, does not exhaust the range of types and regions represented in Kinshasa. It hints of some of the changes that cults of affliction undergo with urbanization.

Zebola, which originated in the upriver Equator region, manifests itself in physiological and psychological sicknesses of individual men and women. In its historic rural context, Zebola affliction is usually traced back to possession by nature spirits. A regimen of seclusion, counseling, and ritual therapy brings the clients, mostly female, back to health through therapeutic initiation in the Zebola order. In its urban setting, especially Kinshasa, Zebola possession is frequently diagnosed in cases of women who are pathologically affected by isolation from their peers or families in their urban households. Becoming a Zebola sufferer and neophyte puts the individual into permanent association with a peer group of fellow sufferers, and through therapeutic initiation, eventually gives the individual a leadership role in the wider Zebola community and network.

Ellen Corin's penetrating study of Zebola (1979), both in Equateur Province and in Kinshasa, demonstrates that the women and (a few) men who enter Zebola are increasingly from a variety of cultural backgrounds beyond the upriver Equator region. She notes that the therapeutic initiation, which lasts for months or years, brings the isolated individual into close bonding with others, and from obscurity to a recognizable ritual position in the society. Trancelike behavior inspired by Zebola spirits is less marked in the city than in the countryside.

Mpombo and Badju (Bazu) originate from the Mai-Ndombe region a few hundred kilometers upriver. Zairian psychologist Mabiala, who is studying these cults, notes that a variety of ill-defined signs and symptoms are the modes of affliction here, including dizziness, headache, lack of mental presence, skin rash, lack of appetite, difficulty in breathing, heartburn with anxiety, rapid or arhythmic heartbeat, fever with shivers, sexual impotence, dreams of struggles, or being followed by threatening animals; weight loss or excessive weight, especially if accompanied by spirit visitations; and a variety of gynecological and obstetrical difficulties. Therapeutic initiation also characterizes the entry into the cult of the afflicted.

Mizuka in Kinshasa is a cult of affliction brought to the city and represented largely in the Swahili-speaking community. Men and women are initiated following psychic crises, hallucinations, nervousness, weight loss, weakness, dizziness, and bad luck (Bibeau et al. 1979). Other cults of affliction in Kinshasa include Nzondo, Nkundo or Elima of northern pygmy influence, Mikanda-Mikanda, and Tembu.

Mabiala (1982) has summarized the recent trends in Kinshasa cults of affliction in both negative and positive terms. The high cost of living in the city has driven many people to become healers to earn an income. Many of these individuals are not well trained and have promoted widespread charlatanism. In the village, where most people knew one another and where authority was more intact, this was not so common.

Many people, seeking solutions to their problems, fall victim to the charlatans who hide their incompetence behind a mask of anonymity and fakery, claiming to be competent in whatever their clientele seems to need. This willingness to broaden the competence of the therapeutic focus for increased business, Mabiala and others call "excessive generalism." This, however, also reflects the continued adaptability of traditional medicine in the face of a changing variety of problems, including the broad and vague conditions that may lie behind specific organic symptoms. The importation of a therapeutic tradition into an urban setting far from where it has been learned or originated may lead, in certain circumstances, to a greater degree of abstraction of the principles involved in the selection and combination of medicines and techniques. If specific plants or materials called for in the recipe are not available in the city, substitutes may be selected based on the dictates of underlying principles. A final, negative development Mabiala sees is the trend of African healers to mimic Western medicine. They may modify their practice with technical items such as stethoscopes, microscopes, syringes, and of course the white coat and the "doctor" title.

On the positive side, Mabiala notes the progressive detribalization of therapeutic rites. Clients' willingness to consult healers of language and cultural traditions other than their own permits a greater adaptability to urban conditions and circumstances. The exchanges of therapeutic knowledge that result from healers themselves receiving treatment in cultural contexts other than their own, or being in "isolation" with another tradition's care, has the effect of spreading and enriching the knowledge base available for all. At the same time, there tends to be a rejection of those techniques that seem irrelevant or obsolete. A very positive development in African therapeutics is the addition, to this therapeutic base, of ideas of hygiene acquired by reading, from mass media, or through more focused programs by agencies promoting public health. The encouragement of healers' organizations by the government and the formation of a variety of such groups has also been a positive development, giving greater visibility to healers and bringing recognition by scientists and health-care agencies.

NGOMA ON THE SWAHILI COAST

One of the foremost common characteristics of the cults of affliction of Kinshasa and Dar es Salaam is that they are rituals imported by immigrants from all regions of the nation. In Tanzania these cults of affliction from the coast and the interior are differentiated around particular themes and issues; they are also ethnically diversified. In the urban setting, their practitioners continue the particular emphasis of the classic rite. But they also are sensitive to the changing expectations upon healers in the urban setting and may shift their emphasis to new issues.

Despite the diversity of cults from across Tanzania and the tendency for them to become generalized to the urban setting, there is a sense in which cults of affliction are more homogeneous in Dar es Salaam than in Kinshasa. The term *ngoma* is widely recognized as connoting performance, drumming, dancing, celebration, and ritual therapy. This understanding of ngoma means that the performances are independent of the healing functions, leading to a distinction between ngoma of entertainment and of healing (*ngoma za kutibu*).

The dominant community of ngoma therapies in Dar is that of the coastal Zaramo and Zigua peoples. An important work devoted to the subject by Finnish ethnographer Marja-Lisa Swantz (1979) identifies the major indigenous ngoma as Rungu, Madogoli, Killinge, and Ruhani. Many other distinctive ngoma rites have been identified among immigrants to Dar from coastal cities and the islands. A Kilwa healer practices ngoma Manianga and Mbungi. Another ngoma cell group of healers practices Msaghiro and N'anga. In addition to these ngoma of coastal societies, one also finds ngoma of inland groups in Dar. The BuCwezi cult of the lake region is found in the city, as are those of other Western Tanzanian societies such as the Nyamwezi, the Sukuma, and even some Nilotic groups such as the Maasai. The extensive writing on ngoma in Sukuma society near Lake Victoria may be summarized briefly for its excellent portrayal of a backdrop to some of the national activities that occur in ngoma today.

A CLASSIC PROFILE OF NGOMA IN
SUKUMALAND, WESTERN TANZANIA

The Sukuma people, studied extensively by Hans Cory earlier in this century, offer a rich and elaborate array of historic ngoma comparable to that described among the Ndembu by Victor Turner. Cory, an Austrian ethnologist who worked for the British colonial government, left both extensive published and unpublished archival notes, now housed in the African Studies Center Library of the University of Dar es Salaam. These documents illustrate varied approaches to classify and understand the ngoma associations.

According to Cory, some ngoma were devoted to ancestor worship and divination: Ufumu, on the paternal side; Umanga, on the maternal side; Ulungu and Luwambo specifically belonged to particular clans. These ngoma Cory called "non-sectarian churches," since individuals could belong to several at once, and they were never intolerant of one another. Mabasa was joined by parents of twins and was concerned with the ceremonial cleansing of twin children. Other ngoma Cory saw as guilds for the study and practice of particular arts and occupations. They formed strong, disciplined fraternities, involved in mutual assistance and the protection or perpetuation of professional and technical secrets and obligations. These included: Uyege, for bow-and-arrow hunters of elephants, which had evolved into a fraternity and dance society; Utandu, a type of guild for rifle hunters of elephants; Uyeye and Ugoyangi, for snake handling and treating of snake bites; Ununguli, for porcupine hunters; Ukonikoni, a guild of medicine men devoted to witch finding; and Usambo, a thieving or thief-catching society. Ugumha (or Ugaru) and Ugika were ngoma societies without discernible function other than performance in dance competitions. Salenge was a mutual aid and dance society into which only the leader was fully initiated. Uzwezi (or Bucwezi), which had come to the Sukuma from Usumbara, and Migabo, which had come from the Swahili coast, had, after being concerned with the ancestor worship of certain clans, evolved into generalized dance societies (Cory 1938).

Cory, the colonial ethnologist, thought that the ngoma orders among the Sukuma had a positive role because they did not meddle in politics. In the absence of other Sukuma initiations, they instructed the youth in respect for elders, provided social solidarity, and instilled fear of the consequences of neglected social obligations. Thus they contributed to social stability. They also offered outlets for artistic and histrionic expression. The dance competitions he saw as generally positive, although they took much time away from the peoples' work in the fields.

NGOMA OF THE LAND, NGOMA OF THE COAST

The particularism of naming in the Sukuma ngoma setting suggests that there is much innovation and adaptation in the overall idiom. In ngoma of the Dar es Salaam Swahili coast, the proliferation of orders arises at least as much from specific spirit classes as from particular functional specializations. Whereas the ngoma association names appear to offer a particularized view of ngoma, spirit classes diagnosed to possess afflicted individuals are generalized into two or three groups. Among the coastal Islamized peoples, spirits are called masheitani or majini, both Arabic-Swahili words. The distinction between the two is not as important, apparently, as that distinguishing spirits of the water from those of the land, with some occasionally identified with the beach or coast. Thus, Msaghiro is an ngoma for sufferers of chronic and severe headache caused by a combination of Maruhani, Subizani, and Mzuka spirits, all coastal or beach spirits. Each of these classes is subdivided. The Subizani, of whom there are ten, are beach or rock spirits; some are male, some female, who have to do with children, both making them ill and helping to raise them to health. N'anga ngoma is a manifestation of Warungu spirits of the land, hills, baobab trees, and mountains; their mode of affliction is chronic severe headaches. Frequently each spirit type will be "played" in an ngoma ritual by a particular type of instrument. Not surprisingly, it is the major inland spirits that are usually represented by the classic single membrane ngoma drums.

Emmanuel Mshiu and I. A. J. Semali of the Traditional Medicine Research Unit had arranged for me to see Botoli Laie, a healer they knew from their surveys, to work with ngoma. Botoli was a Mutumbe from coastal Kilwa who lived in the Manzese locality of southwest Dar es Salaam, not far from the main road but back in the villagelike area filled with houses surrounded by banana and palm trees and lush gardens. Botoli was home, with his two wives and children, and yes, he would gladly talk. And yes, he did work with ngoma: Manianga and Mbungi. His house was large for the area, with a raised courtyard suitable for ngoma performances and a *mazimu* ancestor shrine in one corner (see fig. 2).

Botoli had become an *mganga* (healer) in 1952 and had obtained the ngoma dimension of his work apparently without sickness having drawn him into it. I asked him whether he had suffered prior to his initiation. "No," he said, he hadn't been sick, but he was called to do ngoma Manianga and Mbungi after he was in practice. He resisted it, but then went ahead anyway.

Botoli was a vigorous man who talked in an authoritative voice. He willingly answered my questions, ready to show me the basic lines of his work with ngoma. He was a full-time healer, established with a well-built house, exuding a cohesive ambience. His children and two wives listened attentively to our conversation.

"Ngoma Manianga," he said, is used to deal with spirits of the interior of the country, that is, from Tabora and other regions across

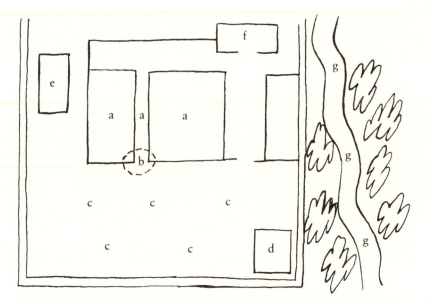

Figure 2. Compound of Botoli Laie in Dar es Salaam; (a) house; (b) ngoma
drums kept here; (c) ngoma performance area; (d) *mazimu* ancestral
shrine; (e) tomb; (f) consultation and medicine room; (g) stream lined with
banana trees.

Tanzania and East Africa. These masheitani are ten in number: Ma-
kogila, Ali Laka, Akiamu, Akolokoto, Akimbunga, Amiyaka, Akitenga,
Ananditi, Chipila, and Ndwebe. When people are affected with these
masheitani, they have bodily weakness, loss of weight, or general bodily
swelling; they get shaking of the body, headache, and loss of appetite.
They need then to be treated, to be taken through the course of treatment including specific materia medica from the *mkobe* (medicine basket), as well as dancing.

For his work with ngoma Manianga, Botoli uses a simple costume
consisting of a red blouse and matching skirt, with designs sewn on
the blouse (see plate 7). His paraphernalia include a small ngoma drum
(*musondo*, also used in puberty rites) sometimes a smaller double membrane drum, and about ten sets of gourd shakers. There were also sets
of cloths in red, black, and other colors, associated with various spirits.
The strings Botoli wore around his shoulders had red, white, and black
bags sewn onto them, which symbolically articulated cosmological oppositions such as the domestic versus the wild and land versus water.
Each of his ngoma included a medicine basket (*mkobe*), in which he

kept a collection of a dozen or so small jars and tins of medicines specific to the ngoma. (This set of ritual items is strongly reminiscent of the *nkobe* of western Kongo.)

Ngoma Mbungi has much the same paraphernalia: drums, shakers, and *mkobe*. The five ngoma drums of Mbungi represent five up-country masheitani: Mchola, Matimbuna, Mbongoloni, Chenjelu, and Kimbangalugomi, each of which is roused and manipulated by its own drum. The instrumentation also includes two wooden double gongs, which Botoli demonstrated. The resemblance between this ngoma kit and those of the Southern Savanna-to-Kongo region is striking and raises questions about their common history. Further research is needed to establish the approximate historical connection in the spread of these rituals across the mid-continent. Were they products of the coast (Kilwa)-Tabora-Kigoma trade route in the nineteenth century and earlier? Or were they the product of an even earlier common framework?

Botoli said he works with five to seven other *waganga* (healers) in the ngoma rites when the performance is at his house and he is the leader; elsewhere the host for that event is the leader. He noted that he has had many novices and was still in touch with them through ngoma events, although he could not give their precise number.

Although Botoli owns the instruments that are part of the paraphernalia of each ngoma of which he is healer, he is not the expert drummer in the rites. For major rites he hires drummers who are noted for their skill; they need not be novices or patients. The performers who do therapeutic ngoma are thus the same as those doing secular ngoma, or ngoma for circumcision, or any other festival or ceremony. It is the context and content of the songs, then, that identifies ngoma as therapeutic.

NGOMA DISPENSARIES, FEE-FOR-SERVICE RITUAL

Further insight into the organization of ngoma in Dar es Salaam was afforded by a visit in Temeke District of Dar es Salaam with the Hassan brothers, who are prominent in the Shirika la Madawa ya Kiasili, a coastal organization of healers. I was accompanied by E. K. Makala of the Ministry of Culture, whose music and dance section not only sponsors ngoma dance competitions around the country but also is conducting research on the song-dance aspects of therapeutic ngoma.

Mzee Omari Hassan's house is also his clinic. The main hall and several side rooms and the back court were loosely filled with sick people and Omari's family. In this family all three wives helped care for the sick, as well as the two sons. The wives were introduced at one point, then disappeared; the sons were allowed to participate in the talks and even asked questions later. Omari's brother Isa, who is also a healer, came by at one point to say hello.

This particular tradition had been transmitted from one generation to the next in the patriline for a long time, well before the time four generations ago when the family had converted to Islam. Omari and family are of the Wazigua tribe, of the Bagamoyo District. He had moved to Dar in the 1940s.

Omari Hassan spoke of the way he had learned the teachings of healing from his father. His father, like himself, had involved his children in the work. The children would go along with him to search for medicines in the forest, and he would explain details to them. Similarly, Omari involved his family; the children play the ngoma drums in the rites.

As in the case of Botoli, Omari's ngoma techniques had been picked up as part of his occupation, rather than in connection with an ordeal of sickness and possession. He specifically denied having been sick with the diseases that were treated through the ngoma he knew. All six had been learned from his father, and were very old: Msaghiro, for persons suffering chronic headache, if no other cure is forthcoming (small drums resembling tourist drums are used); Madogoli, for treating mental disturbances in persons with a high state of agitation; N'ganga (or N'anga) for incessant, severe, migrainelike headaches; Manianga, for persons with numb or paralyzed limbs, especially on one side of the body (shakers are the instrument here); Lichindika, for lower-back pains, when persistent; and Kinyamukera, for those suffering from an affliction whose signs include partial loss of eyesight and twisted mouth or face. When asked how many ngoma he had performed the previous week, Omari indicated that it had been about fifteen, that is, several per day. This occurred in the context of up to fifty patients per day frequenting his clinic.

This picture of ngoma differed from the one I had encountered earlier. Rather than a sufferer-novice being initiated to a cell or network, this style of treatment resembled a clinic with a doctor and many public clients. Was this the result of urban complex society, or of professionalization, in which the rituals are taken over by a specialist and dispensed to patients?

Omari treats a variety of cases with herbs and mineral medicines. When asked what his most frequent cases are, he mentioned cancer, diabetes, asthma, gonorrhea, hemorrhoids, headaches, backaches, mental disturbances—in other words, he tries his hand at about anything. Makala told of how Omari Hassan had treated a boy with a distended eyeball, after this child had been to the State Hospital at Muhimbili and they could not do anything for him. A picture taken by Dr. Emmanuel Mshiu had been in the newspaper with a write-up of traditional medicine as a resource. The eye had been put back, or had retreated back into its socket, following Omari's treatment. When asked what cases he would refer to hospitals, he said, "ordinary sickness" but not *sheitani* (spirit) sicknesses.

I tried to determine how Omari related his work as mganga ngoma to Islam. He had studied in Koranic school, as had some of his sons. When asked which order he belonged to, he said "Muhammadiyya," unwilling to commit himself on whether he was Sunni, Shi'ia, or Sufi. When asked about those Muslims who believe their Islamic belief will not permit them to practice ngoma rituals, he said that was an indication of their not being well trained. They do not know about ngoma. A competent Muslim doctor has to use ngoma, if one is confronted with *sheitani*-caused illnesses. Ngoma, he said, helps the patients to express their anxieties and to perceive treatment methods from the *sheitani* as they speak through the sufferers.

Omari's guidance for his therapeutic work came from another source, an Arabic text. He showed me a thick book, "from Egypt," without title or author (it had been rebound and started on page 15). He also kept notebooks in which he recorded some of his own techniques and interpreted them for his sons. He said that he had not added to the very old ngoma his father had taught him, but that he had improved on some of the methods. He also showed me notebooks (Swahili in Arabic script) in which he copied and interpreted medical practices from the book, as well as his findings about plants and ngoma techniques. This gave evidence of the active codification of African herbal and ritual therapy in interpretative writing, alongside whatever version of Islamic medicine this book offered.

Omari's involvement in the Organization of Traditional Medicine, Shirika la Madawa ya Kiasili, meant that he could practice in an authorized ngoma dispensary. The organization, with branches in Dar, Bagamoyo, and Morogoro, utilized these dispensaries for their meetings and their therapeutic sessions. Omari showed me a file of correspondence with the government, dealing with the Shirika's organization and with government authorization. One letter authorized him to practice on condition his place be checked annually by someone from the Ministry of Health.

During another visit I was witness to performances of ngoma Msaghiro and N'anga. We received the same welcome as before; little children came to meet us and took our bags from us for the last part of the walk. We again received Pepsis. Omari came in and welcomed us, although he dashed off again to make preparations for Msaghiro and N'anga. We sat for a time, and Makala of the music section of the Ministry of Culture chatted with an Msukuma fellow and with another man, dressed in a suit and dark glasses, who said he represented the political party in power. Another individual was a patient, and a second said he, too, was a patient, but he also turned out to be involved in a healers' organization with the Hassan brothers.

Presently we were ushered several houses away where about twenty-five to thirty men and women and many children were seated or stood around the open courtyard that led to the roofed and partially enclosed ngoma dispensary. One part of this area was a dance or performance area. Beyond this, accessible by a door from the performance area, was a medicine room on whose door was posted the doctor's hand-painted shingle (see fig. 3).

When Makala and I entered the courtyard we shook hands with nearly everyone, amidst much excited pushing and positioning. Then they began Msaghiro, an ngoma for sufferers of chronic and severe headache caused by a combination of Maruhani, Subiyani, and Mzika spirits, all coastal or beach *sheitani*. The Subiyani, of whom there are ten, are "beach" or "rock" spirits. They are male and female, and have to do with children, both with making them ill and helping to raise them to health. If a male spirit appears, the healer treats the right side of the body; if female, the left side.

The female patient of this session was told to sit on a small stool, before which were placed three small gourd medicine containers covered with strands of red, white, blue, and yellow beads. Omari's brother Isa took one of these and spread the medicine, with a form of swab or tube, atop her head, and at several symmetrical points on her face, and down her limbs, and on front and back, thus "outlining" her person. As the singing continued, with five small double membrane drums and a rattle, the men and women danced and sang in pulsating movement toward and away from the patient (see fig. 3). Then Isa brought out a

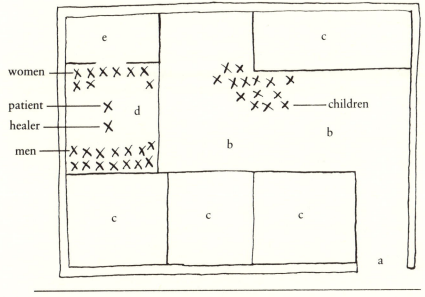

street

Figure 3. Ngoma dispensary in Dar es Salaam, as used by Isa and Omari
Hassan of the healers' organization Shirika la Madawa; (a) street entrance;
(b) open courtyard; (c) household rooms; (d) roofed ngoma performance
stage; (e) medicine room. Stage shows locations of performers in session
witnessed by author and described in text.

big antelope-horn container, and circled it around the patient several
times counterclockwise (looking down).

Following Msaghiro, they announced they would do a traditional
greeting of the visitor, first one of them being the subject of attention,
to show how it went, then it would be me. The greeting pattern, similar
to the therapeutic ritual, was that all adults present would dance-shuffle
toward me, first a row of men, then women, and thrust themselves close
to me, then back off in the same shuffle. After a number of these group
advances, each one in the row shook my hand three times. It made me
feel I had become the event's center, that they were affirming me. I felt
strengthened and focused by their attention. Surely there was iconic
power in the healing dances around a sufferer, although it was difficult
to analyze the components or even the source of this power.

Then came the N'ganga (pronounced "n'anga") dance, again for
chronic severe headache, a manifestation of Warungu *sheitani*, spirits

of the land, hills, baobab trees, and the mountains. The instrumentation was limited to shakers this time. Singing was led by Isa, in a call-and-response manner. The patient was the focus of the dance. The short "fee for service" dance was a highly eliptical version of ngoma compared to what I had seen in Southern Africa, or in the historic Western Equatorial African examples. It was closest in comparison to one ngoma unit I observed in the Western Cape (see chapter 4). The patient did not enter trance, although this had probably been done previously.

Evidently each of the ngoma sessions follows a divination that identifies the spirit utterance and that then leads into the therapeutic response. M. L. Swantz speaks of the healing rite in the coastal ngoma as "exorcism." This may well fit the situation in which there is no initiatory follow-through. This may be related to the very low rate of persons treated (exorcised) going on to be trained as waganga, which, according to Isa Hassan, is only three to four per hundred, a rate confirmed by Lloyd Swantz (1974). The implications of this pattern for professional control of the resource, as well as of the model of therapy, are taken up again in chapter 6.

NGOMA AND ISLAM

Not far away in Manzese-Kwadjongo lives mganga Mahamoud Kingiri-ngiri, a Sufi Muslim of the Matumbe people from Kilwa. Unlike mganga Botoli, described earlier in this chapter, Mahamoud works with *Kitabu* (the book), *magi* (water), and *nzizi* (roots), and with Ruhani and Majini spirits of the sea. Unlike mganga Omari Hassan, who is Muslim and uses ngoma, as does non-Muslim Botoli, Mahamoud does not use or relate to ngoma, on grounds of his adherence to Sufism. The matrices of Bantu-African and Muslim culture, and the use and nonuse of ngoma by waganga, are clearly illustrated by these three healers.

Mahamoud has a well-built house near a stream, with banana and palm trees surrounding it. The two-story house contains his study, where he has his books; it also features a consultation bench, a place of prayer, a purification-bathing room, and an outdoor treating area.

When I visited him with a guide from the Traditional Medicine Research Unit, several of his four wives were seated in the hallway, with children on their laps. Mahamoud has had fifteen children, twelve of whom survive. He impressed me as an ambitious, intelligent, religious man, who took his work seriously and cared for his family. When asked whether he had been to Mecca on a pilgrimage, he said no, he could not leave his wives and children that long, they needed him; anyway, he did not have the money.

With his several interrelated treatments, Mahamoud works with afflictions as diverse as polio (for which he has a compound of twenty-one medicines, to be taken with water over three days), excessive or irregular menstruation (I observed him treating one such patient; he read to her from a book), convulsive fevers, diarrhea and vomiting, and the preparation of aphrodisiacs for the impotent. He also works with Majini (of which seven are good and help treat, and five are bad and bring disease), and Maruhani (all seven of which are good and help treat). These spirits all stay in the ocean, but they come out or are found in other places; the Maruhani at clean places, the Majini at dirty places like latrines. When he treats, he begins with the name and other aspects of the life of the patient based on the birth date. Following a reading of his Arabic (geomancy?) texts, he goes to sacred places, starts to pray, and the spirits come forward, telling him what to do with the patient.

The Arabic text Mahamoud uses most is by the Egyptian Abdul Qattah of Macina. It tells of all types of diseases and treatments, including Maruhani and Majini. He also uses the Koran and has numerous other Arabic books in his study. He spoke Swahili and English. His father had insisted on sending his three sons to Koranic school, but he was the only one who had followed this line of work in the family tradition from his father and grandfather. One of his sons was being groomed to succeed him.

The family (patrilineal) therapeutic tradition began in the context of village protection during the Maji-Maji revolt earlier in this century against the German colonialists. Mahamoud's great-great grandfather had been head of a Matumbe village near Kilwa. In the thick of the Maji-Maji struggle, his grandfather was sent to the Arabs to learn of better medicine, for they felt inadequately protected. When his grandfather died, the work was passed on to Mahamoud's father, then to him.

When Mahamoud became mganga, he locked himself in a room and read books. Thus in isolation, the Maruhani came to him and asked, "What do you want?" "To be *mganga*," he replied. The Maruhani explained cleanliness and emphasized purification with water. His house, especially the areas for prayer and healing, was immaculately clean; a floor of white porcelain tile was visible beside the "bath tub."

I asked Mahamoud Kingiri-ngiri why he did not use ngoma, when some others—Zaramo, reported in Swantz, and Zigua such as Isa Hassan—did, especially with Ruhani spirits. He emphasized Islamic restrictions but also that ngoma was just "happiness," not real medicine. Perhaps a further answer lies in his being part of a Sufi brotherhood, which is in effect a ritual community that functionally substitutes for ngoma. This Sufi brotherhood did not have a saint, he said, but they had a tradition of sheikhs.

The three Tanzanian waganga profiled here represent a continuum from classical ngoma practitioners to degrees of Islamization. In the coastal association in which the Hassan brothers are instrumental, Islamic brotherhood structure and urban professionalism have changed the ngoma tradition. The symbolism and the rituals have been affected less. With Mahamoud Kingiri-ngiri, the etiology of ngoma is addressed from within an Islamic framework. Plant lore has been retained, but the legitimation has become that of folk Islam and mysticism. A similar continuum could be traced from classic ngoma to independent Christian churches in Tanzania, which, however, I could not pursue.

NGOMA OF HEALING, NGOMA OF ENTERTAINMENT

The distinction between "therapeutic" and "entertainment" ngoma is an important one in understanding the larger dynamics of religion and ritual in Dar es Salaam society. This distinction already seems to have existed in early twentieth-century Sukuma ngoma, as described by Cory. It was implicit in the observation of Botoli Laie that the ngoma drumming-dancing is distinct from the medicines and is done for the exorcistic or therapeutic initiatory seances by hired musicians. Here the definition of *ngoma* as "performance" comes into its own. The sacrality or secularity of ngoma depends not on the music or dance form as such, but on its function or use, its context. Ngoma performances in night clubs and folkloric events put on by the national dance troupe do not, thus, differ in their form from possession or exorcistic rituals conducted by waganga. However, the secular ngoma "for entertainment" possibly reflects an evolution of the particular ritual from its original context, focused on a sufferer in the midst of personal crisis, to a more generalized performance outside that focus and the timing of a crisis.

On a particular day during my stay in Dar es Salaam in 1983, the following ngoma, licensed by the Ministry of Culture, were performed. Mungano, its name derived from the Sukuma snake dance ngoma, was performed in a bar, and later in the week at the Village Museum; Tanita; Utamaduni, an ngoma group sponsored by the Tanzania Railway Corporation; DDC Kibisa; Zinj Dancing Troupe; and Kikundi Cha Sanaa, sponsored by the National Textile Corporation. At the urging of the staff at the Ministry of Culture, I attended a Sunday evening performance of the Baraguma ngoma group from Bagamoyo at the Almana Ilala nightclub (see plate 8). Over thirty such groups were registered in Dar es Salaam alone, in addition to dance bands and jazz groups (Martin 1982). This richness in entertainment music reflects not only the musicians' openness to new idioms such as jazz, but the diversity of musical offerings in the historical culture of East Africa.

E. K. Makala at the dance section of the Ministry of Culture, who concentrates on ngoma, noted that ngoma in the "traditional" setting is used for a range of occasions, including circumcisions, weddings, and mourning, not to mention healing and dance competitions. The songs are about the occasion, thus highly contextualized. Every performance features extensive improvisation. The size of the group depends on the wealth of the promoter or sponsor. Makala found it impossible to speak of a "typical" ngoma group. However, groups are distinguishable by criteria of song, dance step, distinct rhythm, and sometimes costume. In the village, he noted, one would hire a local group; in Dar one might be obliged to hire one from another ethnic background. All of the thirty ngoma groups in Dar derive from rural areas. In their hired events these groups might perform a song-dance (his term) that had been used for healing, such as Manianga, but this would be a "mistake," that is, a misapplication or change of the pure form of the rite from its original purpose. Makala feared that these kinds of changes meant the real meaning of the dance was getting lost in the city. He lamented the lack of good teachers and a loss of awareness of the dance's history. However, the standard of staging in the urban setting is better, he thought, with lights and amplifiers for live performances, performances on Radio Tanzania, and even promotion for overseas tours. In 1983 the ngoma groups rarely made recordings for resale.

Mungano, the name of a historic Sukuma and Nyamwezi ngoma for snake handling, had been adopted by Norbert Chenga of the Ministry of Culture as the name of the ngoma group he organized. He had studied with a Sukuma mganga for about six months but had not completed his apprenticeship. His Mungano troupe performed regularly at the national Village Museum in Dar es Salaam for an audience of Dar residents and a few tourists and foreigners. The troupe consisted of fifteen young men and fifteen young women, who donned a different costume for each dance, mainly arrangements of colorful African print cloths. They were accompanied by about twelve—mostly ngoma—drums and two xylophones. An amplifier was rigged so that the microphone could be shifted from one instrument to another. Prior to the performance, it was propped against a cassette recorder playing Congo jazz with Lingala lyrics.

The troupe began with ngoma Msewe, which originated in Zanzibar, and it used to be performed at Islamic festivals. The dress was appropriately Islamic, with white caps for the men and print aprons for the women. Men and women danced separately in two long lines. This was followed by Masewe, a dance originating in the Lindi region of southern Tanzania, performed on "happy occasions," for which the dancers whitened their faces.

Ukala, a "hunting" dance from Tanga, depicted a hunting expedition and glorified hunting as a reputable activity. It was preceded by a pantomime of two hunters stalking game, shooting, cutting up the meat, finding honey. Then they were joined by troupes of men and women with bows and arrows and baskets.

After an interlude of acrobatics, the group performed ngoma Sindimba from the Makonde region of coastal Tanzania and Mozambique. Sindimba is done when the youth return from initiation camps, having graduated into adulthood. It is a lively dance with sexually suggestive movement.

This was followed by Chitumbo, Lingwele, and Ngongoti masked stilt dancing. Then came Bugobogobo, a "social realism" ngoma in which the dancers used hoes and baskets, shields and guns, as props. It was a rigidly choreographed depiction of work with these tools that took the ngoma work-song idiom and applied it to national consciousness. Everyone must take up arms and be vigilant, just as farmers work together with hoes. The *ujamaa* cooperative spirit that has always been evident in productive work is pointedly applied in this dance. The big ngoma drum used here is an original instrument used as pacer in communal farming among the Sukuma, even today.

Finally, at the close, came the snake-handling dance, Mungano, after which the troupe had been named. It was preceded by skillful acrobatics by members of the Directorate of Culture. As the drums beat their special Mungano rhythm, a large chest was opened in the public circle. Two pythons were taken out by the dancers and released to slither around and frighten the crowd. Volunteers were sought to let themselves be bitten by the snakes. A man and a boy came forward, and when the lethargic python finally did strike the boy in the buttocks, the crowd roared. Chenga, the director, told me later that these snakes are very tame and have short teeth, and are not, of course, poisonous. The principle being demonstrated was, however, a very serious one. In western Tanzania, where there are poisonous vipers, this exercise is intended to educate the public about snakes, and to teach them not to fear snakes. Within Mungano, members of the ngoma have knowledge of antidotes and are themselves immunized with the venoms; they allow themselves to be bitten during the performances.

The "folklorization" of ngoma, as seen here, reflects the process of bringing together ethnically and regionally diverse dances that are performed in a rather different context than originally intended. This process is to some extent guided by the governmental units. Competitions are organized, just as in earlier times; song-dance is sometimes utilized, as in the Bugobogobo, for nationalistic emphasis. Some of these same dances were performed by Baraguma—actually the teaching staff of a secondary school—at the night club, where the audience had paid at the door to see the show. Therapeutic ngoma are thus, in Dar es Salaam, a small part of all ngoma, but a very central and formative part.

SANGOMA: DIVINING THE STRESSES OF RAPID INDUSTRIALIZATION IN NORTH NGUNI SOCIETY

Far to the south, the Drakensberg range divides the interior plateaus from the coastal flatlands, in what is now South Africa, Swaziland, and Lesotho. The mountains also separate two major cultural historical groupings: the Nguni-speakers of the wetter, more tropical setting; the Sotho-Tswana on the drier, highland interior. Major sociocultural distinctions separate these groupings in a way that influences our subject. The Nguni-speakers, through the eighteenth century, lived in decentralized small homestead settlements of cultivators who also kept livestock. Their social and political organization was lineage-based. The Sotho-Tswana, by contrast, had larger town settlements, with strong centralized chiefdoms. Their cattle remained at outposts in the arid regions to the west; their fields were arranged around the towns and cultivated seasonally. Social life and most public affairs were conducted in the towns, particularly in the chief's court, the *kgotla*.

At the beginning of the nineteenth century social and political upheavals—known as the Mfecane—among the Nguni gave rise to the centralized states of the Zulu, Swazi, Ndebele, and Pedi, and those of the diaspora groups to the north in Zimbabwe, Zambia, Malawi, and Tanzania. These states were not so deep-rooted as to offer the stable, courtlike context and type of public life that had evolved gradually among the Sotho-Tswana. Therefore, among the Nguni, ngoma as it is being studied in this book was the major way of dealing with adversity, misfortune, and sickness. It is largely among the Nguni-speaking societies of southern Africa that this story may be found.

However, the setting of ngoma in Southern Africa requires fuller contextualization than simply a contrasting of Nguni with Sotho-Tswana. The Mfecane was followed shortly by the incursion of Afrikaaner wagon trains into what is now the Orange Free State and the Transvaal. The societies that had newly formed as states were engaged in battle and defeated; their proud citizens were reduced to servants of the Afrikaaners on their own lands. This was followed, late in the nineteenth century, by the discovery of gold and diamonds and the emergence of the major labor migration pattern that engulfed the entire subcontinent. Africans, deprived of their land, needed to work in the mines and farms of the white man to make a living.

Thus the story of ngoma in Southern Africa also needs to be situated in the context of a divided society, of broken homes, of labor camps and mines, and in the twentieth century, of the urban settlements and the townships. For these reasons the two Nguni-related sites that came to be of particular interest in this survey were the Manzini-Mbabane corridor in Swaziland, an industrializing, urbanizing setting in an independent country, and the townships surrounding Cape Town, where the various cultural threads of South African society come together in the context of apartheid rule. These two settings allow for comparison between several contrasting situations, both across the middle of the continent and in the region of Southern Africa.

Ngoma in Southern Africa is far more unitary in its institutional organization than what we have seen in Kinshasa and Dar es Salaam. It is not organized into several dozen functionally specific ngoma orders as among the Ndembu or the Sukuma. Nor is it as frequently, nor as extensively, used for entertainment. The unitary structure of ngoma in Southern Africa combines both divination and therapeutic network building.

The Mbabane-Manzini and Cape Town comparison permits us to see contrasts between a setting outside South Africa and one inside South Africa—within the framework of a single cultural-linguistic grouping, the Nguni-speaking societies: Shangani, Thonga, Ndebele, Swazi, Zulu, Xhosa, and Pedi. One of the most startling contrasts in ngoma expression across this region is the shift, from south to north, of increasingly elaborate technique and demonstrative trance in divining-healing. Among the Xhosa, undramatic meditative and counseling techniques are used between healers and their clients. The spirits who are called on are usually ancestors, or vague evil or nature spirits. Among Zulu diviners, mechanistic bone-throwing techniques prevail. The Swazi, however, although the same holds true for a part of their work, have recourse regularly to far more demonstrative possession trance behavior as they are visited by a series of increasingly powerful and distant nature and alien spirits. The reasons for this marked contrast in ngoma within a single cultural-linguistic region will be addressed later in this chapter after the introduction of ethnographic material.

A SWAZI COLLEGE FOR DIVINER-HEALERS

My major exposure to ngoma activities and institutions in the North Nguni setting came through several extended visits to the ngoma training college and clinic of Ida Mabuza of Betani, midway between the industrial center of Manzini and the capital of Mbabane.

Ida Mabuza had trained in the Tshopo area of Mozambique. She enjoyed royal patronage from King Sobhuza II to follow through on her therapeutic initiation. When she experienced *kwetfwasa,* the call from the ancestors to enter a life of ngoma, she was ill for five years before beginning her training, suffering from back pains and difficulty in walking, as well as other serious problems that included vomiting blood. As her illness progressed, she became solitary, hostile, and withdrawn. She had many dreams of people with sangoma-type hairdos. Her condition worsened, leading eventually to daytime visions, so that others and she herself feared she would become totally mad. When her condition became unbearable, her husband took necessary steps for her to be healed. As she began to train, the spirit literally "came out" in her dancing; a song was given to her by the spirit. Her family and healer realized she was possessed by a Thonga spirit; indeed the spirit had announced itself. In due course she, a Swazi, became the channel of Thonga, Zulu, and Shangani spirits. These spirits drive you about, she said, they possess (*femba*) you, speak through you, particularly the Manzawe spirits. The Benguni spirits are the main ones behind the div-

ination with bones; they are mainly Zulu (victims of Swazi wars), although some are Thonga. Others give insight as well, including Thonga
and Shangani spirits.

The main points here seem to be that these shades that aid in divining
and healing are alien Nguni ancestors, and that they speak directly
through the medicines and diviners. This is in contrast to most Zulu
(and other) tangoma, who work with or in power of their own shades,
and seemingly the Xhosa, who work similarly. Harriet Sibisi, who was
with me and interpreted the interview, pointed out that Zulu tangoma
would try to get rid of an alien spirit and try to bring in a person's own
shade to inspire divination work. They would not work exclusively with
alien spirits.

The contrasts between Zulu tangoma and Mabuza's approach seemed
sufficiently pronounced that when I asked about the meanings of the
term *ngoma* she noted that, although they accept the appellation sangoma, technically they call themselves *takoza* mediums, distinguishable
by their red ochred and oiled dreadlocks, whereas tangoma wear their
hair black with beads woven in them. According to Mabuza, the takoza
have spirits speak directly through them, whereas the tangoma listen
to spirits (or sometimes their ancestors or deceased grandparents) and
use their own judgment. Thus the difference is in methodology. The
takoza's spirit sees right into the cause of illness; for example, one may
be limping today, but the cause is an ancient childhood injury. Tangoma are more skilled at reading the present, or they tend to restrict
their work to present-day issues. The takoza, because they are mediums,
get much more excited, said Mabuza, who sat there before us with great
composure, looking very professorial through her glasses. The takoza
combine mediumship (*ukufemba*) with bone-throwing, or inspire their
bone-throwing with mediumship from spirits directly. The tangoma
learn divination from other tangoma. The tangoma figure out the problem and refer more readily to other types of practitioners.

One of Mabuza's twenty apprentices explained her own training and
her introduction to the hierarchy of spirits. Novices learn many songs,
both those taught by their teacher Mabuza, as well as their own, which
they receive in visions and dreams from the *amadloti* (ancestor shades),
the Manzawe spirits, and the Benguni "victims" of wars, killed by one's
paternal forebears. These several spirit or shade categories were represented by the bead strings across the novices' shoulders (see fig. 4).
White beads represented the Benguni autochthonous victims; the red,
the Amanzawe (nature spirits); the mud-colored, the *amadloti* (lineal

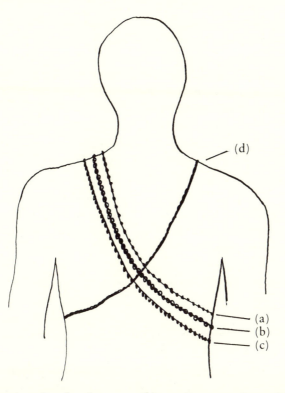

Figure 4. Body and neck strings as used in ngoma to represent categories of spirits. This example is from Swazi takoza mediums: (a) *amadloti* (lineal ancestor shades), mud-colored beads; (b) Amanzawe (nature spirits), red beads; (c) autochthonous Benguni victims of Swazi wars, white beads; (d) Tinzunzu victims of drowning, white beads.

ancestor shades); another white string, Tinzunzu (victims of drowning). She had other necklaces and beads that had been donned at points in her training. The fuller bead bracelets and anklets indicated her completion of training.

Teaching and practice in this tradition, which combined the sangoma and takoza, appeared to consist of the two standard components, divining and singing rituals. The former mainly consisted of "throwing bones" (*pengula*), the latter the singing-pronouncing of the affliction or announcement of spirits (*ukufemba*) in which drums were used. Ma Mabuza had twelve *tigomene* drums for these *ukufemba* sessions (see plate 6), although not all were used at any one time. The drums, made of cowhide membranes on oil barrels, were huge and sonorous, recalling the sacred royal drums of the north Sotho, Venda, and Luvedo, or the

Luvedo *tigomene* initiation drums. Ida Mabuza's own patron spirit was a male *iloti*, which was why whenever a request was made, the apprentice who was our guide had to go ask "him" (through Mama Mabuza) for permission.

Mabuza, when asked about the prevalence of types of cases brought to her, noted that daily she has about ten clients. Even though she does not keep records, she noted the following types of issues brought to her in order of frequency. There are both "African" and "non-African" problems. She has both African and white clients. The most common African problem is vague pains and anxieties, explained by *umbelelo* or *mego*, harm or sorcery resulting from interpersonal tensions. The next most prevalent illness is *amakubalo*, resulting from broken social or moral precepts, such as illicit sex with a protected married woman. The first type of problem brings both men and women, the second mostly men. Further, there are many young people who come to her wishing to learn of their fates, seeking good fortune in job applications, exams, and love.

Whites' main concern, she said, is fear of poverty—that is, their inability to hold on to their money and property. They also come for help in promotions and other work-related matters. They come with illnesses not properly diagnosed in the hospital or not effectively treated, such as especially high blood pressure, whose root cause frequently can be traced to tensions or conflicts with domestic workers or subordinates who, they fear, have retaliated against them.

Mabuza told us of a case she had recently done that illustrates her approach. A white woman came in, accompanying someone else. Mabuza divined for her that she was involved in a struggle with her family. The woman did not believe it. Two weeks later she returned, acknowledging that, indeed, in their purchase of a farm, payments had been embezzled by another family member, and they had been doubly charged.

One day as we arrived we saw another car parked below the compound. It belonged to a well-dressed Swazi couple who had just emerged from one of the divination rooms and a consultation with Mabuza or an apprentice. Later, as we were waiting on a mat outside the rooms, another car drove up with a grandmotherly Swazi woman at the wheel. She had come for a consultation, either for herself or another family member. She waited on a mat beside us while one of the staff prepared to see her. Clients who do not have their own vehicles, or who cannot walk or take public transportation, may call Betani by phone and be picked up in one of the center's vehicles. Since Betani is midway between the industrial center of Manzini and the capital, Mbabane, and not far from the royal Swazi capital, Mabuza's work is tied into the vibrant pulses at the center of Swazi society.

The narrow line between conventional clients and those who eventually become apprentices is articulated by the etiological category *kwetfwasa,* to be called by a spirit to enter the life of the sangoma. Although she commonly diagnoses cases to be of this type, it is an article of emphasis in ngoma circles that the master-novice relationship must be entered voluntarily. The diviner-healer who makes the diagnosis is not necessarily the one with whom you apprentice. Clients are quite free to go elsewhere, with whomever they feel comfortable. Those who do come to Mabuza stay in residence five to six years; for the first four they are counseled and participate in the sessions. Then they become involved in intensive training. During this time she delegates responsibility in pengula bone-throwing divination and in the *femba* mediumship. Anyone who is available gets an opportunity to learn through practice. If one's spirit cannot read a case, another helps out or takes over.

The novices must be sexually abstinent throughout their stay with her. They do not shake hands with others; they are ritually apart. Mabuza was surprised at the pictures of the Cape Town novices who held wage-labor jobs, wondering how apprentices could be part-time or intermittently in isolation.

The presence of clients who stay in residence overnight or for longer periods (in addition to whom there are up to twenty apprentice diviner-healers) suggests that Mabuza's establishment at Betani is very much an institution, with anywhere from thirty to fifty people "in residence" at a given time. The institutional dimension of ngoma at this place was apparent to us one day when, driving up the steep road to Betani, we came upon two young apprentices working to get the Datsun truck, heavily laden with groceries for the college, up the hill. They had to unload some of the flour sacks so the vehicle could drive up a particularly steep eroded passage. Later, I saw them unload thirty dozen eggs, a fifty kilogram bag of mealie flour, bags of wheat flour, cartons of canned condensed milk, sugar, and the like—food for twenty novices and their families, as well as the inpatients. Six times a month they send to town for such a load of groceries. It was reported that the tazoka novices, conspicuous in their red ochre and sand hair-dos and loin-cloths, are frequently seen in the bank in Mbabane drawing money from the Betani account for their shopping.

PENGULA: DIVINATION BY "THROWING THE BONES"

Throughout northern Nguni society and among Shona and Sotho-Tswana society, the most common method of divination is called "throwing the bones." The diviner sits opposite the client, with a mat between them (plate 9). In a small bag the diviner has a set of bones, usually vertebrae of an animal, which are thrown out upon the mat. The constellation of bones, their relationships and profiles, are "read" in a manner similar to divination methods of the Southern Savanna Ngombo basket ingredients, or the Ifa oracle's shells when cast. Constellations identify areas of social life, personal problems, and cultural emphases. Accordingly, in Betani, divination "bones," which include dominoes, dice, coins, shells, stones, as well as the standard ver-tebrae, are interpreted to include not only luck (good if dominoes turn dots up, bad if down) and various interpersonal relational profiles and bewitchment (vertebrae in various positions), but also the presence of tuberculosis, diabetes, and other conditions. One constellation of bones refers people to the hospital. Another constellation tells the diviner that the client has come in bad faith.

A third individual, in addition to the diviner and client, is often pres-ent in sessions of bone-throwing as a type of interpreter or mediator. This individual may be part of the divination staff, as was true in a number of cases at Betani, or may be a friend of the client or a family member. The mediator's role is to know the case, to have gotten ac-quainted with it, just as the expectation upon the diviner is that clair-voyance will be used to "see" the truth of the case with the help of the bones or the spirits. As the bones are thrown and the diviner begins to interpret, using a format like "twenty questions," the mediator re-sponds with "I agree" (si ya vuma) or "I disagree." Such sequences of questioning reveal whether the issue is in the paternal or maternal fam-ily, whether it is a family- or work-related issue, or whether it has to do with the client's own responsibility or with another's involvement. If the constellation does not seem appropriate, and the diviner reaches a dead-end in the incantation of questions, another throw may reveal a new constellation with another sequence of questions.

Clients who come to Betani for good fortune stay overnight to take emetics, which Ma Mabuza teaches them how to administer it themselves. Emetics and purification are important for people who have taken in contrary medicines (what Kongo call intoxification). The medicine "releases them"; the spirits allow them to change. Those who stay overnight receive free meals prepared by the apprentices or other staff. The overnight fee is fifteen *emlangeni* ($12, in 1982), whether the client is African or white. Pengula divination has grades of elaborateness, beginning with the simple bone throw for two emlangeni for a basic outline of the issue, which tells whether one can count on chance or has no chance (as in a court case). Sometimes lengthy counsel apart from the bone throw may increase the rate. The maximum fee for pengula, an overnight stay with a meal, and an extended *femba* possession session by the entire hierarchy of spirits is thirty-five emlangeni. A diviner as skilled as Ma Mabuza can earn a good living at these rates.

UKUFEMBA: DIVINATION BY MEDIUMSHIP

We had been told that in Mabuza's school, divination by mediumship (*ukufemba*) was held about every other day. The exact timing, however, depended on the spirits. One evening we arrived at Betani unannounced at about five o'clock. The resident novices were eating and drinking in front of Mabuza's house. One of them came to us and welcomed us and spoke with us, and another brought us a well-sifted container of beer. Another male novice came with a similar bucket of medicine (*ubulau*) to an area before the seance house, and the entire group of about twenty novices gathered around him and the ubulau. He raised the froth with his stirring stick, then knelt over to take some with his mouth, spitting it out in the four cardinal directions as if forming a cosmogram. The others did the same one by one as the leader sang. Then they knelt in a circle and prayed.

We continued speaking with the novice who had come to us earlier. She spoke about her health (her sore foot, bilharzia) and health education, about age (our graying hair, her impression of our youthfulness), about doctoral degrees, including her sister's. A child walked by carrying a shirt on its head. She observed that when a child holds something on its head in that way, "someone will soon come." We had no idea what she was talking about. Suddenly one of the young takoza bellowed out from the seance house in the now familiar sound of spirit trance.[2] "There you are," said our companion, "the *amadloti* [ancestors] have come." Others moved to the seance house and began drumming almost immediately. We were invited to sit down on a mat with them. Several of the male novices were grunting and spluttering and crying out, possessed, we were told, by the Benguni spirits of the victims of Swazi wars. Presently, to drumming-singing of six *tigomene,* four of the men who had donned white waist cloths and patterned loincloths over their other loincloths, began to rush in and out of the door. In the minutes that followed these Benguni-possessed men went through a threefold routine: (1) initial trance met by drum-song response; (2) suddenly rushing out and disappearing (to present themselves, we were told, to "him," i.e., Mabuza), then returning to greet those present. A definite call-and-response pattern was apparent here; the drumming-singing occurred only while the possessed entered the room.

When this was finished, four women followed suit in approximately the same way, also possessed with Benguni. Several other persons danced, including some very agile boys and girls, who apparently were not possessed. Each of the classes of spirits—the *amadloti,* Benguni, Manzawe, and Nzunzu—is said to have its distinctive dances and songs, although I could barely discern them. The drum rhythm was a heavy regular beat on six drums; the dance was a heavy pounding step a little like that of Cape Xhosa amagqira healers, only faster and more vibrant, interspersed with leaping jumps.

At the very close there entered a "senior" graduate sangoma-takoza, the woman who had done the pengula divinations. She was dressed in her full set of beads and carried her beaded baton and cow's tail whisk. She held a stick under one armpit and a knobkerrie under the other. Then the session was over and the group moved outside to go through a seance with Manzawe spirits. We left.

The next afternoon we drove to Mabuza's place again to seek a better understanding of the relationship between individualized pengula bone-throwing and the collective mediumistic *ukufemba* approach. The case we would see treated was that of a small child, several months old, who had been sickly and weak. Mother and grandmother were present with the child and all necessary diaper bags, aprons, clothing, even a bottle of diaper softener. They had taken the child to the hospital, as well as to an African independent Christian faith healer, but it was still sick and weak. They had come to determine what was causing its affliction, since hospital medicine in their eyes had failed.

Another case came to our attention after the femba session began. A young woman, a university student, offered to translate the proceedings for us. She had had a nervous breakdown shortly after the term began. The hospital doctors had diagnosed her persistent headache, nosebleeding, vomiting, and nausea as due to "nerves" and "heart failure," although a further consultation with another doctor had revealed "nothing wrong." She came to Mabuza feeling miserable. After divination and treatment in residence she began to feel much better, saying she was now fine, although she continued staying at the center.

The sick infant was the final case of the evening, after several cases that kept them busy until about eight o'clock. Then the floor was covered with matting and the drums were brought in from the courtyard where they had been tightening in the sunlight. Children came in and sat down along the wall opposite the door. A pressure lamp had been brought in to illuminate the room. While another *femba* session was continuing in the other house, the mother, infant, and grandmother entered with their baggage and sat down. A young male takoza from Mozambique brought in the straw basket of medicines with which he would *femba* the case (fig. 5). Although the book definition of *femba* is that of trance or possession to identify the spirit cause of an illness, the beginning process here seemed more like positive medicine to prepare the patient.

At first the infant was held on the grandmother's lap; the mother sat aside against the wall, looking on. The diviner-healer began by kneeling before the basket of medicines. While praying, he took off his body beads and donned another set of necklace beads; he donned a new cloth and over all this put on a waistband of six cowrie shells, as well as a headband of two rows of cowrie shells. Then he took several small medicine containers out of the basket. From one he took a grease or ointment and rubbed his face with it. Nearby he had a pottery shard with coals of fire through which he passed some of the medicine. Then he washed his face in a bowl of water. Throughout the next stages he regularly partook of a snufflike substance that may have been hallucinogenic.

The diviner-healer then went to stand before the grandmother, his back to the door. He gestured with his hands to the child, then at one point rubbed medicine on various parts of the child's body: soles of the feet, top of the head, temples, chest and back, wrists and ankles. He pulled the child's limbs out taut. He repeated some of this for the grandmother. Throughout this segment of the session a young female assistant brought him the ointment and helped him take the snuff substance. Then he seemed to go into a semitrance and gave the following expla-

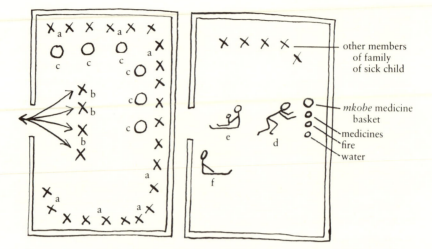

Figure 5. The arrangement of participants in the ukufemba divination session at Betani, described in text. Left diagram: (a) participants including novices, family, and guests; (b) active trance performers, who enter and leave as spirits; (c) *tigomene* (drums) in performance. Right diagram, in same space: (d) healer kneeling before medicines during case of sick child; (e) grandmother with grandchild; (f) mother of child.

nation of the causes of the illness, as translated to us by an English-speaking patient.

The first cause was put in the form of an exegesis of family history. The family cattle had strayed onto the fields of others, and those others had taken revenge on the child. Vengeful ancestors were working through living persons, who were trying to hurt the child and its mother. The falsetto voice in which the medium spoke, possessed by the spirit, was said to impersonate the one who was behind the injurious work. The clients would know from the sound of the voice who it was; the person could not be mentioned by name. A further cause was the vengeance of a war victim killed by a family member. Third, there was the matter of the unmarried mother and displeasure by spirits over this. The vengeful forces had already stolen the child's "soul," and unless the forces were neutralized the child would soon die. There followed the blessing of the child's effects, first piece by piece, then a whole bag full, and finally the bottle of diaper softener. The child was now moved to the mother's lap, and was given some emetic fluid to drink, as well as a bit of the snuff in its nose. At one point there was also a brief exorcism near the door, with the comment that the spirits were not all willing to leave but wanted to hide in the room. Then for a while there seemed to be a calm.

A Manzawe spirit struck in the back corner of the room with a powerful cry through another young medium, who rushed up to where the mother was seated with the child. Several other novices and observers took drums in hand and quickly provided rhythmic accompaniment to the spirit's song. This was a "white" Manzawe, evidenced by the possessed medium's controlled gesture of donning a white cloth from the wooden cross beam above him, where all the cloths were draped.

After dancing about for a while in his characteristic manner, this "spirit" went out and came in several times. Then he came before the mother of the sick child and harangued her for several minutes, in a heavy, intense voice, about her case: She had sought help in vain from other places, including the hospital and "church"; she was the victim of dissatisfied spirits because of the family affair and the cattle; there was a victim of the family's involvement in past wars. He appeared to repeat some of the earlier findings. Perspiration poured down his face and body; it was a most impressive effort, for which another two or five emlangeni note was produced. Then this white Manzawe spirit left the room and the medium returned, composed.

Several other male diviners took up the work, donning this time red cloths over their shoulders. These were again Manzawe spirits, more bizarre and strange than the earlier ones. They voiced very strange, incomprehensible, animallike grunts. Their "dance" was as odd as their appearance; they "stood" on all fours before the door, tossing their heads about wildly, their long red clay dreadlocks thrown this way and that. These spirits left as they had come, through the open door. Each time a spirit-medium would enter the door, the drumming would begin anew; each time it left, there would be silence. Someone said the drumming was needed to "bring out the spirit."

Finally, the two mediums who had performed the "red" and the "white" Manzawe moved on to host Nzunzu spirits of those who had drowned. This time they danced upright, but their voices were so strange that our interpreter said, "if you don't know the words of the spirits you can't understand this." After a time the drumming came to an end, and all present dispersed.

I found interesting the decreasing involvement of the mediums with the case at hand, as if the latter spirits made their appearance simply to articulate their niches in the spirit cosmology. It was a kind of "gloria" to the farthest-out spirit world. At an earlier point, the first Manzawe spirits had done battle with the lingering evil forces around the child. The final spirits proclaimed an uncontested victory over them.

MEDIUMISTIC TRANCE VERSUS MECHANISTIC TECHNIQUE

As noted at the beginning of this section on North Nguni, this exaltation of the spirits and the emphasis on a hierarchy of ancestral, alien, and nature spirits stands in sharp contrast to the absence of these features in South Nguni settings within South Africa, that is, Zulu, Xhosa, and Pondo. I will not develop this issue in any great depth here, but will explore several hypotheses that will be taken up again in subsequent chapters.

One of the external factors that may influence divination and healing bears on the contrast between South African and Swazi society, from the perspective of Africans. In the Republic of South Africa, laws are clear-cut, rigid, and oppressive. South African pass laws, work restrictions, and hardship have not succeeded in eroding the basic worldview of people in African society; it has rather hardened it, so to speak. In Swaziland, on the other hand, which has an intriguing mixture of sociopolitical organization combining an ancient kingdom with modern bureaucracy, and a per capita income that is near the highest in black Africa, there has been a middle-class revolution of rising expectations and realizations. The middle-class work force of both men and women is in an upwardly mobile current that has shaken family and religious values to their core. The boundaries or limits of society and worldview have been exploded open. Divination regarding work opportunities, social crises resulting from individual decisions, and marital or nonmarital arrangements all lead to an enormous clientele for the sangoma (or the takoza, as they call themselves). This is the setting in which ngoma roles and activities are associated almost exclusively with divining. Lydia Makhubu (1978), who has been a student of Swazi healing, emphasizes that several decades ago neither the sangoma nor the takoza used drums at all, and that there was no possession or trance in connection with divination. The progression from the pengula (bone-throwing), to the *femba* "smelling out" mediumistic exercise provides a hierarchy of resort from dealing with the known, controlled world of the lineage, to dealing with the unknown and unclear realms beyond the family.

The new divining did not, however, appear from nowhere. Oral reports and references from Tanzania, Mozambique, and Swaziland trace the takoza mediumistic divining, as well as the N'anga ngoma in Tanzania, to the Thonga in Mozambique, more specifically the Vandau, a group that was a part of the Ngoni diaspora following the early nineteenth-century Mfecane. Harriet Ngubane, a Zulu South African anthropologist who has lived and worked in Swazi society, suggests that the distinctions between the sangoma, who practice only pengula, and the takoza, who practice pengula and *ukufemba* (mediumship), are the signs of an ideological emphasis in Swazi divination rather than the result of distinctive structural characteristics in society and culture. Although mediumship is emphasized by the takoza, like all Nguni diviners their training period is extensive—five to six years. Clearly the bone-throwing and pengula questioning techniques are learned and require disciplined practice. According to Ngubane, this mediumistic divination and the emphasis on the spirit world reflects an ideological emphasis or predisposition in Swazi thought. Reliance on alien spirits in divination—alien Nguni spirits—is in character with Swazi reserve, with their pacific character, according to Ngubane. Just as they have historically accommodated strangers and are extremely charitable toward strangers, so in the spirit world there is a very considerate memory of those they killed in former wars (Benguni) and those who drowned or were not properly buried (Nzunzu). The spirits are the cutting edge of a sensitive worldview that includes collective guilt toward warfare's victims and care for strangers among them. This view contrasts to that of the Zulu, who have a history of much more bloodshed but who in their spirit worldview try to replace alien spirits with their own, and in divination rely on their own spirits.

Further evidence of an ideological emphasis in the Swazi takoza approach to divining lies in the point Mabuza made about her own patron spirit. When she began her training, and her teacher began to hide things for her to find, the spirit-shade who took over for her was that of an *inyanga* diviner, very much a particular ancestor. Mediumship is thus for her an added element of her training as a general healer and diviner, not the primary core of her practice.

Thus, although direct mediumship is emphasized in current Swazi divination, there is plenty of evidence of structural comparability with Zulu and Xhosa divining-healing. This structural comparability bridges the apparent distinction between spirit possession, on the one hand, and the learned skills of an apprenticeship, on the other hand. Mabuza and

other takoza of Swaziland are equally adept in discourse on exotic
spirits and on types of cases, case load, methods of analysis, and other
empirical issues. One has the impression, in visiting ngoma in Swaziland, of an ancient institution in the course of constant evolution, very
much tied into national life and in tune with the stresses and strains of
individuals.

THE AMAGQIRA: SURVIVING THE
TOWNSHIPS OF SOUTH AFRICA

In the townships of Cape Town—Guguleto, Langa, Nyanga, Crossroads—are the scene of much civil disorder and police and army repres-
sion in recent years. The work of the amagqira-sangoma is to a far greater
extent than in the other urban settings that of providing solace and encouragement and social network support to the many who come to
them. African society of the townships has very little genuine authority.
A survey taken in Guguleto found one in four households was involved
in one way or another with an ngoma network: as sufferer-novice,
mid-course-novice, or graduated and practicing healer-diviner (igqira-
sangoma). In addition to the churches, trade unions, legal or illegal
political groups, and the mistrusted township committees, the ngoma
structure is one of the most pervasive dimensions of the social fabric.

As already noted, the institutional structure of ngoma in Cape Town
is unitary, that is, without disparate, named ngoma orders, as in Kinshasa or Dar es Salaam, despite the varied ethnic backgrounds of the
Xhosa, Zulu, Sotho, or Tswana participants, and without the hierarchy
of modes of divining and possession, as in Swaziland. Divination is
done without any discernible paraphernalia, more as a Western social
worker interviews clients. The third party who "agrees" or "disagrees"
with the divination is, however, on hand.

The participants of ngoma in Cape Town, when interviewed about
their own histories, reveal the usual accounts of headaches, weakness,
disorientation, and other afflictions; of dreams of ancestors or of healer-
dancers with furred and beaded costumes. There are many novices, but
not all make it through the therapeutic initiation to become builders of
personal networks. Yet those who do make it through the initiation,
the "course through the white," far from fitting the classic image of the
psychotic healer, strike one as very strong individuals who have overcome psychological and social contradictions to act out their calling and
to be pillars of society.

The following case illustrates some of the characteristic stresses of life for blacks in the Western Cape, where there is chronic anxiety related to jobs, in view of the pass laws and a 42 percent illegal worker presence. There is extensive tuberculosis in the black population; frequently an outbreak of TB accompanies joblessness and malnutrition. The incidence of broken or fragmented families is very high, as is the rate of single mothers and working women living alone.

A CASE STUDY IN INITIATION TO NGOMA

This was Ntete's second initiation-therapy undertaken after a two-year lapse and much suffering since the first attempt to come to terms with his *twasa* (call) and affliction. He had gone to the north Sotho homeland Qwaqwa to "accept his illness" (*invuma kufa*) and to take over his grandmother's beads (i.e., the family line as healer). He had done the initial steps, the goat sacrifice, but he continued feeling bad; it had not worked out. So he had returned to Cape Town, to his wife and children, and his job with a stainless-steel pots-and-pans company, and—accordingly—a house permit. But sickness had followed him; he could not continue the instructions and therapies. Headaches, nosebleeding, and most recently what he had feared was a heart attack had brought him into the hospital.

Yet he continued dreaming of a particular woman with beads. After two years of this, he decided to take up his case anew. He had gone to Elsie, an igqira (healer), whose judgment was that the figure in his dreams was really igqira Adelheid Ndika. So he came to her, and a week later they were holding the goat sacrifice and the *nthlombe* celebration that inaugurated his novitiate with her.

Adelheid, his sponsoring igqira, was accompanied by several other fully qualified healers. In characteristic Western Cape manner, they represented a cross section of Southern African societies. Of the seven fully qualified healers present, four were Zulu, three Xhosa. Their training had been with Swazi, Sotho, Xhosa, and Zulu healers. Ntete was Sotho. Present also were the dozen or so novices of the head healer of this event; they would participate in ngoma therapy sessions and in the welcoming of Ntete to their cell group. This event, like most ngoma activity in South Africa, had to be fitted into the work schedules of the participants. Whereas custom called for those entering their apprenticeship to be in continuous seclusion, this was not possible in urban South Africa. Thus the fragmentation of life extended to this area as well. Ritual mat-

ters had to be dealt with on weekends when others could get free from
their jobs and when the principal figures themselves had the time to deal
with their personal conditions. Of the women present, some were domestic workers in whites' homes, nurses, and teachers. The men were
factory workers, drivers, or in one case, the owner of a fleet of vehicles.

This initiation *nthlombe* was held in one of those standard South
African government houses for blacks with four cramped rooms and
a small backyard (see fig. 6). This rectangular space was transformed,
according to some informants, into ritual space corresponding to the
Nguni homestead: the street became the courtyard, the front room the
rondevaal house, and the backyard the cattle kraal. The ritual spaces
also corresponded to Central and Southern African categories dividing the human or domestic from the ancestral spaces. Throughout the
weekend event, next-door neighbors ignored the nthlombe, attended at
times by up to 150 people.

The first stage of the event on Saturday morning, calling on the ancestors and preparing the novice for "entering the white," was held in
the "living room" with the presiding igqira and two colleagues. Several
signs of whiteness were prepared. Ntete was dressed in a white toga
over his white undershirt. His face was smeared with white kaolin.
Medicine (*ubulau*) in a bucket, made from several plants, was stirred
into a froth and smeared on his face and body. This was done during
a series of songs that invited the ancestors to come and be with the initiate (plate 16).

Now thoroughly "white," the novice, led by his sponsoring igqira
and his father, and followed by the amagqira and others present, pro-
ceeded to the backyard to construct the ceremonial kraal out of old
boards and some twigs, both substitute materials, since the appropriate
plants were not at hand. The goat was brought into the kraal beside
the kneeling novice. The pails of medicine and beer were placed before
the goat. It was made to kneel and also drink from the liquids. The
animal about to be sacrificed was taking the same substance, taking the
sufferer's old person upon itself, to die vicariously. As the goat was held
down it bellowed loudly, and the singing increased in volume and
tempo. The goat's bellow was a good sign, indicating its consent to die
for the novice's life and health. The goat's jugular vein was cut and the
blood spilled out onto the ground. When the goat was still, the drumming and singing stopped, and the skinning of the carcass began. A fire
was lit nearby within the enclosure. A strip of meat was cut from the

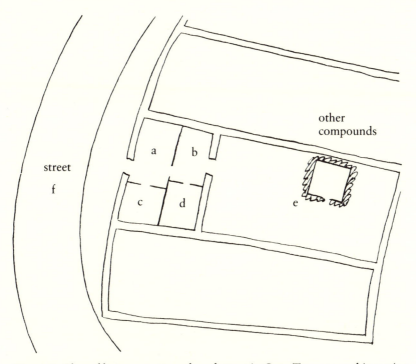

Figure 6. Plan of house, compound, and street in Cape Town township setting
   where Ntete's therapeutic initiation was held, as described in text: (a) living
   room and intermediate ritual space where all ngoma sessions are held, as
   well as "calling down ancestors"; (b) kitchen; (c) bedroom; (d) storage
   room; (e) backyard and transformed "cattle kraal" for most sacred site
   where sacrifice is performed; (f) secular public space where "coming out"
   is held and where darkness of pollution is "thrown away."

right side of the animal and roasted, representing the *umshwamu*, the
last place to twitch near the heart, indicating the life of the goat. Ntete
ate bits of this meat in a solemn communion with the sacrificed life.

I had to leave shortly after this because dusk was falling and it was
illegal for me, a white person, to remain in a black township overnight.
My hosts did not want an incident and urged me to drive to my home
without stopping or opening my car window or door in the township.

Later the other novices would begin to "do ngoma" together, the
short presentations followed by singing in rapid sequences (discussed
at greater length in chapter 4). When I returned late morning of the following day, it was apparent that they had gone on most of the night,
for there were novices asleep in chairs. One was slumped back with feet

on the drum and head against the wall. In the kitchen three pots of goat meat and potatoes and cabbage were cooking over a gas fire, preparing the sacrifice of yesterday for today's feast.

At noon the presentation of novices and the dancing continued for a time, as others came: family of the novice, some neighbors, other diviner-healers and their novices. Novice Ntete's family spoke in gratitude and encouragement for the session. Again, the medicine and beer pails were put before the novice, who was still dressed in a white blanket with white face, hands, and feet. The entire group moved in procession to the "kraal" for the first donning of the novice's beads and bits of the goat's hair. He would also now receive his new ngoma name.

The first string of white beads went around his head. The goat's gallbladder was attached to the string at the front of the forehead. Just as the gall is bitter, so this bladder would ward off danger. A second string of beads around the head would "hold his head," for that is where his sickness was. A string of beads and goat hair around his neck represented his acceptance of his "called" (ntwasa) condition. Other strings with goat hair were put on his wrists and ankles. These were the beginnings of his igqira costume, which would grow and become elaborate over time as he dreamed and developed his own identity. His stark, plain white robe and beads contrasted markedly with the colorful beadwork of the full amagqira and their elaborate wild animal skin dresses.

Mid-afternoon, Sunday, the entire group moved through the house onto the street to present the new novice to the public. The crowd of onlookers grew around the assembled full amagqira and novices, and the family and friends of Ntete. In a speaking and song-dance pattern reminiscent of that used in earlier sessions by the novices, here the full amagqira and sangoma took their turns exhorting Ntete, then breaking into song-dance, which was joined by everyone around (plate 17). After thirty minutes for this presentation, novices gathered inside and continued with self-presentation and song-dancing. For the first time Ntete joined them, one of a dozen white-clad amakwetha (novices) under Adelheid's supervision.

This event, typical of the ngoma networking in the townships of the Western Cape, combined several key features of the ngoma institution: the entry of a troubled individual into a cell under the supervision of a senior healer; participation in what we might call an ngoma working session in which novices present their thoughts, dreams, and anxieties and join the other novices with singing; commemorating critical passages in this career of an ngoma participant with a sacrifice and a communal meal. Moments in these careers, and constellations in the networks, bring together fully qualified healers and their novices to listen, counsel, console, share, sing, dance, and commune.

The Western Cape extension of this widespread African institution offers both some apparently basic features of the historic institution, as well as some unprecedented changes having to do with the uniqueness of the South African urban setting. Many of the ngoma participants are "illegals"; others are legal residents and can host events such as this. The migratory labor situation requires working residents in the townships to collapse their ritual status into weekend moments in order to meet the expectations of their jobs. The strains of pass laws and residence restrictions in South Africa make the dominant distresses those of families breaking up, of being paid meager wages for difficult work, of chronic diseases such as tuberculosis, and of being told by whites and by the system that they are worthless. Against this, the sodalities of ngoma and the longings for family ancestors are a haven and a coping resource.

CONCLUSION

The foregoing cases and resumes of problems typify those brought to ngoma diviners and therapists. Most cases of this kind are dealt with on an individual or family basis and are referred to a range of other therapists as well. Only a few of the cases are diagnosed as appropriate for full therapeutic initiation by ngoma dance and song. In both Nguni and Sotho-Tswana societies the diagnosis *ukutwasa* characterizes these latter, meaning they have been singled out by the spirits or ancestors, and afflicted. As in the Central African examples cited above, so the Southern African "twasa" cases demonstrate very little symptom-sign specificity. The question of who is singled out or called in this manner needs to be answered in connection with a more general study of contextual issues. It is not appropriate to assume that the twasa diagnosis, or call, corresponds to Western psychoanalytic or therapeutic labels. In fact, there may be better reason to suspect that this diagnosis singles out individuals for recruitment to ritual leadership roles on the basis of characteristics of greater sensitivity, ego strength, and cultural receptivity in a time or situation of stress.

2
Identifying Ngoma

Historical and Comparative Perspectives

The contemporary settings of ngoma-type cults of affliction in Central and Southern Africa, as seen in the previous chapter, may now be joined by historical and comparative perspectives of the entire region within which these cults appear. Evidence for ngoma's origin, spread, and distribution can be gleaned from a range of types of sources: linguistic evidence from a comparison of Bantu language cognates; evidence for the distribution of material culture artifacts of ngoma, mainly musical instruments utilized in healing rituals; evidence of political variables in the presence of distinctive alternative forms taken by ngoma. This historical evidence, joined with the contemporary profile, permits us to sketch the basis of a unique institutional profile for ngoma, one that has often been misrepresented by scholars.

Readers acquainted with African culture history will recognize the "ngoma" region as approximately that of the distribution of the Bantu languages, that is, with the distribution of the cognate *ntu* which gave the Bantu language family its name. By itself, the term *ngoma* and its distribution do not tell us much about the common, and varying, features of the institution. However, when this verbal cognate is associated with the cluster of other terms and features that commonly accompany it over a wider region, we begin to see the larger picture that relates linguistic evidence to religious, social, and therapeutic, or health-related, cultural phenomena. This approach, to which is sometimes added archaeological research, has found increasing application in Sub-

Saharan African historical research of the history and nature of domains such as livestock husbandry, agriculture, iron working, political systems, and titles.

Such an approach to scholarship raises questions about the formal relationship of language to other domains of culture and society. Do phonetic units, the cognates, consistently carry common referents to conceptual thought, symbols, and emotions? How consistent are linguistic referents to behavior, techniques, and material culture? How consistent are rates of change in the relationship between "words" and "things"? These are practical research issues that may require specialized methodologies in particular domains. They are also theoretical issues bearing on the claim that language does (or does not) convey meaning, does (or does not) carry structures homologous with institutional or behavioral patterns, or is (or is not) patterned by physiological determinants.

After presenting core therapeutic-related cognates in Bantu languages, and some of the issues pertaining to the basic research on Central African linguistic history, this chapter will consider similar evidence about the constellation of musical instruments utilized in the rituals of therapy, in an attempt to clarify, in a formal sense, the relationship of the instrument type named *ngoma* to the other aspects of the ritual and the wider institution. The chapter closes with an exclamation of social and cultural variables that have shaped the institution, and considers how, as a distinctive institution, it has been represented, or misrepresented, in social research.

THE BANTU CONUNDRUM

Societies across the middle of the continent, from Luanda and Libreville in the west to Dar es Salaam in the east, and from Cameroon to the Drakensberg range and the Cape in the south, share many words and grammatical features that have come to be called the Bantu family of languages. Designation of these languages as "Bantu" is to some extent arbitrary, the result of nineteenth-century European linguistic research, which recognized large regions in Southern and Central Africa whose languages shared cognates. The cognate *ntu*, meaning "person," (plural, *bantu*, people) was but one of hundreds that could have been utilized to describe the entire set. In twentieth-century linguistic and archaeological research, the extent of commonality and variation in this common linguistic base has become much clearer.

In the twentieth century the notion "Bantu" has also taken on a range of connotations, positive in one setting, negative in another, and both in other settings, depending on whose perspective is entertained. It has come to stand for a mode of thought, or ethnophilosophy, presumably based on indigenous ideas, an approach to the study of African thought that is roundly criticized by some. It has become a rubric of major historical research, especially in Equatorial Africa, where the Centre International des Civilisations Bantoues of Libreville, Gabon, conducts cross-disciplinary work and publishes the journal *Muntu*. In Southern Africa, however, the notion "Bantu" has taken on a negative connotation because of the South African government's reification of a stultified tribal and imposed interpretation of African culture, particularly as carried out in education for blacks. The simultaneous positive search for civilizational heritage that one sees in Equatorial Africa under the rubric of "Bantu," and the negative tribal connotation of "Bantu Education" in South Africa, contribute to the Bantu conundrum.

For present purposes it suffices to summarize the central findings of some of this historical research. A body of current scholarship (Bastin 1983; Bastin, Coupez, and de Halleux 1981; Meeussen 1967, 1980; DeMaret 1984; Heine 1984; Phillipson 1985; Vansina 1984; Hyman and Voorhoeve 1980; Ehret and Posnansky 1982; and Van Noten 1981) establishes the origin of Bantu languages in the eastern Nigerian and western Cameroonian area, in the early first, possibly the late second, millennium B.C. Linguistic classifications, based on methods of "least common" and "most common" (or shared) lexical and grammatical features, determine that these languages are genetically related to West African languages.[1] "Bantu" is thus defined as a narrow language group—though spread across a vast subcontinent—in a wider set of interrelated language families that are sometimes referred to as "Bantoid" (Heine 1984) in the much more extensive "Niger-Congo" group (Greenberg 1955).

The same methodology—that is, genetic classification of least common and most common cognates or features in sets of languages within the family—establishes further that the Bantu languages had, by the first millennium B.C., begun to spread southward through the forest zones and the Atlantic coast of Equatorial Africa, and eastward along the northern edge of the forest-savanna border into the Interlacustrine region (see fig. 7).

Thereafter, additional "nuclear zones" are posited, from which further dispersion occurred eastward and southward. One of these was the

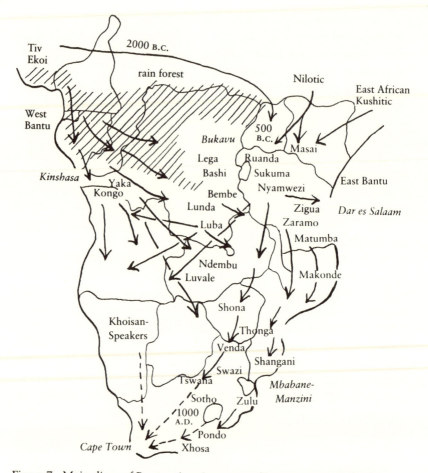

Figure 7. Major lines of Bantu migrations, according to recent scholarship,
and four sites of field research for this book: Kinshasa, representing
Western Bantu; Dar es Salaam, on the Indian Ocean coast, representing
both inland East African and Swahili coastal influences; Swaziland, the
northern Nguni-speaking setting; Cape Town, a cosmopolitan South
African setting.

"Congo nucleus" in the forest regions of Cameroon, Gabon, Congo,
and Zaire (Heine, Hoff, Vossen 1977), also spoken of as "Western
Bantu" (Vansina 1984, 1990). Another was "East Highland," from the
lake regions (Heine, Hoff, Vossen 1977), also called "Eastern Bantu."
Later, in the first millennium A.D., the expansions continued into East
Africa and to Southern Africa, and, with a mixture of Eastern and West-

ern, across the Southern Savanna to the southwest, in Zaire, Angola, and Namibia.

This demonstrated expansion of the Bantu languages raises a number of questions about the relationship of language to other facets of culture that are germane to our interest in therapeutics, particularly ngoma. What was the technological basis of these societies that permitted their expansion into territories occupied by the hunting-and-gathering populations preexistent in the continent? Was this Bantu expansion more on the order of a gradual technological and cultural transfer, community by community, or was it more like a migration? Were Bantu languages tied to a more intensive agriculture? If so, at what point did iron working become the basis of this agrarian technology? Further, what types of food crops were used? Given the contrasting environments into which the speakers of Bantu languages moved—from savanna into rain forest and back to savannas—what were the adaptive advantages that gave the Bantu speakers the resilience to replace other ways of life and other languages? Were the speakers of Bantu languages organized in any particular social structures? What were their beliefs? What were their assumptions and values about health and society, and their approaches to healing? Are these reflected consistently in the common cognates across the region? How did they utilize the varied environments and natural products to improve health? Were the ngoma rituals of any particular importance in the process of expansion? Finally, if we assume a common source for ngoma, which features have remained continuous and which have changed? Are these reflected in the common and varying cognates across the region?

It is now argued, on the basis of recent archaeological research in Cameroon and Gabon (Van Noten 1981; Vansina 1984, 1990) that the Western Bantu expansion along the Atlantic coast and into the rain forest was a gradual expansion of stone-tool utilizing cultivators of West African forest-related cultigens, that is, trees such as the oil palm and root crops such as yams. The Eastern Bantu cultigens, which presumably brought the West African grassland crops to the Southern Savanna, and later to Southern Africa, included millet, sorghum, and cowpeas.

The appearance of iron working in this technological-cultural setting is now believed to have occurred about 750 to 500 B.C., the date of early iron-working finds in Nigeria. Related iron-working sites, or evidence of iron, have been found recently in Gabon and Cameroon. The expansion of the eastern lake Bantu may have occurred as early as 750 to 500 B.C. with the use of iron smelting and smithing. This accelerated the ability of Bantu speakers to dominate the landscape, to grow crops, to hunt, and in general to improve their adaptive advantage. It is thought also to have contributed later to the ability to form centralized states. The earlier hypotheses that Bantu expansion might have been due to iron and selected introductions of crops from Asia (Murdock 1959) have not been borne out in recent archaeological and linguistic research. For one thing, the archaeological finds of iron are simply too late to support such a hypothesis. Also, the language cognates that pertain to iron working are too disparate to lend credence to a hypothesis of dispersion from a common point.

The role of cattle and other livestock in the Bantu expansion has been studied at some length because of the absence of livestock in the Western forest region (due to tsetse fly infestation) and the extensive use of livestock in East African and Southern African Bantu-speaking societies. Ehret, studying the character of language cognates associated with livestock, demonstrates that this part of an Eastern Bantu complex was introduced from Central Sudanic peoples to the lake region by 500 B.C. (Ehret 1973–74), from where it spread southward.

The Bantu expansion must not be construed to have been a migratory spread of a biological or "racial" group, except in selected dimensions. Genetic markers of the northeast Bantu region north of the lakes resemble markers of populations in the origin area in the Cameroon and eastern Nigerian region (Hiernaux 1968). Otherwise, genetic studies have revealed diverse populations, in many instances reflecting "pre-Bantu," but speaking homogeneous Bantu languages.

Many of the recent specialized linguistic studies in the Bantu zone have had their basis in the massive lifetime work of Malcolm Guthrie, published in the four-volume work *Comparative Bantu* (1967–71), which maps the distribution of several thousand cognates. Guthrie's compilations are not exhaustive. The lexica are built around key word sets determined by linguists to represent basic cultural domains; they are then expanded into more culturally particular domains. Further, Guthrie's lexical reconstructions are of necessity limited to those Bantu languages for which dictionaries and vocabularies were available in the 1950s and 1960s when he did his work. Guthrie interpreted the evidence, based on degrees of common lexical stock, to argue for a Western and an Eastern Bantu divergence from a central point on the Southern Savanna. Although this hypothesis has been discredited by subsequent research, his compendium, and subsequent work to build up the basic project,[2] provides a growing foundation for new studies that test additional hypotheses. It is Guthrie's lexicon, with a few supplemental sources, that permits us to demonstrate the character of a proto-Bantu level of therapeutic-oriented verbal cognates and derivative secondary, Western and Eastern, subsets of cognates, concepts, and practices, and the place of ngoma in this set.

THE LEXICON OF A CLASSICAL
SUB-SAHARAN THERAPEUTICS

The terms that pertain to health and healing in Guthrie's lexicon, and which occur in the entire region of Bantu languages, are assumed to have been part of the earliest—thus, proto—level of the Bantu-speaking societies several thousand years ago. Other cognates that appear only in Western or Eastern Bantu respectively, are either derived from the earlier terms as variants, were independently created, or were introduced from the outside. The following set of cognate terms reveals symptoms, etiologies, healer roles, medicines, and ritual activities with the end-goal of health (asterisks and numbers indicate Guthrie's "Comparative Series" (c.s.) of cognate reconstructions based on a comparison of modern semantic variations; see appendices A and B for the approximate distribution):

Proto-Bantu:
wound, boil, sore (1608 *-pútá-, 1609 *-púté)
to become ill, illness, to suffer (677 *-dúád-, 678 *-dúádì-, 679 *-dúáídé-)
to bewitch, curse, witchcraft, power of words (644 *-dòg-, 645 *-dògá-, 646 *-dògí, 647 *-dògò)
medicine man, medicine (786 *-gàngà, ngàngà, 787 *-ganga)
medicine, tree (1730 *-ti-)
medicine, consecrated charm (1534 *-píngú-); curse (1557 *-píng-, 1558 *-píngö-)
drum, drumming, dance (844 *-gòmà-, 1401 *-gòmà-)
to become cold, cool down, become cured, well (1564 *-pód-, 1565 *-pód-)
interdiction, prohibition, to abstain (826 *-gìdò-, 822 *-gìd-, *-gìdú-, gìda) (also Huygens 1987:59–70; Obenga 1985:209–211)

Western Bantu:
disease (*okon*) (Obenga 1985:196)
ghost (50 *-bàndà-*); healer, medicine man (51 *-mbàndà-*)
to cure (195 *-búk-*); to divine or cure by divining (196 *-búk-*)
white clay, kaolin (1474 *-pémbà-*, 1477 *-pémbé-*)
consecrated medicine, charm, fetish (1072 *-kítì-*); spirit (1073
   -kítì, kícì)
to protect with medicine (990 *-kàg-*); leaf (1021 *-káyí*)
to bleed by cupping horn (439 *-cumik-*)

Eastern Bantu:
sore (656 *-donda-*)
witch, witchcraft (240 *-cábi-*); ordeal, poison (1884 *-yábi-*)
to practice medicine, divine (471 *-dagud-*)
spirit, spirit of dead (619 *-dímu-*)
consecrated medicine, fetish, charm (293 *-càngó-*)
cupping horn (412 *-cúkù-*, 440 *-cúmo-*); to bleed by cupping (700
   -dumik-)

Recognition of sickness is signaled very widely by the cognate term
dúád, or *dúádì,* whose verb form *luala* in KiKongo, *halwa* in KiNdembu
(Turner 1967), or *umkhuhlane* in SiSwati (Makhubu 1978:61), expresses the existential quality of suffering, injury, or misfortune. Across
the entire region this is differentiated from physical injury or sore, for
which *pútá* or *púté* is used. In northwestern Bantu, *okon* expresses this
(Obenga 1985:196), or in Eastern Bantu, the term *donda.*
   Health is identified by numerous metaphors, including "balance"
(*lunga,* in both Zulu and Kongo), "purity" (*veedila* in Kongo), and
"coolness," whose most widespread cognate is *pód,* "to become cool,
or cool down" or "to become well, healthy," in contrast to the heat of
disease or witchcraft. This is related in some Western Bantu languages
such as Kongo to the action of the cupping horn (*mpodi*), one of the
most widespread therapeutic and religious features of Bantu-speaking
African societies, which "sucks out" through the cupping horn (*hola
mpoka*) the impurity. Regional terms for the cupping horn are *cúkù*
(Eastern Bantu), *cúmo* (Western Bantu); the action of bleeding by cupping, with scarification or scratching the skin followed by sucking, is
cumik (Western) and *dumik* (Eastern).
   In a recent thesis by Huygens (1987), as well as the work by Obenga

(1985), the concept of interdiction, prohibition, or abstinence has also been related to the Bantu-African sense of health and illness. The cognate *gìdò, gìda, gìdú* (in its nominative form, e.g., *ngili* in Teke, *cijila* in Luba) or *gìd* (the verbal form) emerges in the context of ritual activities, initiations, or naming, but also with practical circumstances having to do with abstinence from specified foods in connection with an affliction or ailment (Huygens 1987:59–70; Obenga 1985:210–211). Not only are sickness and misfortune held to be the result of transgression of the prohibition; health can be maintained or controlled by keeping the interdiction.

The widespread dichotomy that distinguishes misfortunes or afflictions stemming from "natural" or God-given causes from those stemming from human involvement is recognizable throughout the region, although there is no proto-Bantu term for God, suggesting that terms for God emerged later. In the Western region the most widespread term for God is *Nzambi* or *Nyambi* (925 *jambé,* 1917 *yambé* or *nyambé*). In Eastern Bantu *Mulungu* (715 *dungu*) is common, and in the Southern region *Mukulu* or *Umkhulane* (Zulu), utilizing the very widespread term *kulu* for aged one, or *kula* for growing up. Everywhere these High God terms are associated with misfortunes that are "in the order of things," thus "of God."

By contrast, unnatural or inauspicious misfortunes are said to be caused by "people": in Kongo, [*kimbevo*] *kia muntu*; in Zulu, [*ukufa*] *kwa bantu*. The cognate stem used here—*ntu*—is of course that from which the name *bantu* was drawn by nineteenth-century linguists. The association of the basic term for human being with a major cause of affliction touches on a fundamental feature of etiological and therapeutic concepts couched in Bantu cognates.

The most common and widespread action terms that spell out human-caused misfortunes are the cognate stem verbs *dòg, dògá,* and nouns *dògí* or *dògò*. These terms describe the use of powerful words and the intentions behind them—whether good or evil. In Kongo in the west *loka* is the use of powerful words in oath and curse, and *kindoki* their imputed use, which is believed to cause sickness and misfortune. In a review of *lok* in Central African life, Luc de Heusch (1971) identifies the ways in which "good" and "bad" uses of spells or powerful words are used to reinforce particular dimensions of social structure. In Zulu, in the south, *thak,* the verb, and *ubuthakathi,* refer to the process or state of sorcery and witchcraft used by many scholars who have encountered some derivation of the cognate *dòg* across Central and Southern Africa have masked the originality of the verbal concept, and the recognition that words, anger, and all other expressions of the social setting can affect health and illness. As words and their associated thoughts can afflict, so words and the thoughts of kin and affliction-peers can heal. Theophile Obenga, in his discussion of Bantu-African therapeutic practices among the Duala of Cameroon and the Mbochi of North Congo, stresses that the pronunciations made in the *esa* rite of the Duala and the *ndoo* rite of the Mbochi become a therapeutic force in their own right, simultaneously effective at the mental and the physical level (1985:204).[3] In any event, the reality of kin and extra-kin communities in ngoma demonstrates the dynamic of the cognate *dòg* at work.

Other notions reflect further dimensions of human causation of disease and misfortune. Such a notion is reflected in the term *cábi* (or *tsawi*), found in Ekoi and Tiv, as well as in Eastern Bantu languages, meaning the substance of witchcraft power in a person, and *yábi*, in Eastern Bantu, for the poison ordeal that identifies this power. Similar to this is the notion *kundu* in Western Bantu to denote the congealed power of witchcraft in the body of the perpetrator.

Ancestors represent an extension of the human community as a major cause of misfortune and cure in African society. Very widely, definitely in Eastern Bantu, ancestors or spirits of the dead are referred to by the common term, *dimu*, which is probably proto-Bantu. In Western Bantu, the generic term *kulu*, elder (in Zulu, *unkulunkulu*), is also used to refer to ancestor or shade, and as with *dimu*, to the power that may cause both life, if channeled properly, and misfortune, if the community is not duly cognizant of the ancestral shades. A major dimension of ngoma is, of course, coming to terms with these "living dead" in relation to the fortune and misfortune of the sufferer and his or her community.

Moving from the etiological and worldview terms to those defining therapy, we may note that *tí*—tree, stick, or medicinal plant—is found through the entire region and may therefore be assumed to be proto-Bantu. In some settings, for example among the Hemba of Eastern Zaire, *buti* carries further connotations of consecrated medicine and of sorcery and witchcraft (Blakely and Blakely 1986). *Kàg* or *káyí*, herb, a Western Bantu variant, is the generic term for leaf, or for medicinal plants, as well as tobacco, an American import.

The well-known color triad of white, red, and black is represented

everywhere in the therapeutics of Bantu-speaking Africa and can probably be classed with a proto-Bantu ritual scheme, although none of the
terms for color are pervasive throughout the region. One example of a
widespread ceremonial color term is the Western Bantu *pémbà,* or
pémbé, white clay or river chalk, denotative of "clarity" or "purity,"
an attribute of the ancestors. White clay, red ochre, and black charcoal,
or other referents of these properties, are commonly used as basic ingredients of health care. Whiteness defines the status of the novice who,
from the time of initial entry until graduation, is "in the white." This
ritual symbolism is extended to the arena of the sick role, as ngoma
well illustrates.

The notions of *tí, káyí,* and, *pémbà* are usually not, per se, charged
with overtones of power. When combined with other substances into
compounds and given the "interpretation" of a spoken phrase, they
become so. Such compounds, especially when spoken or sung over, become powerful medicines invoking the attributes of ancestors and
spirits. Guthrie believes that *pengo* is the proto-Bantu term for this
function. *Píngö* and *phungu* in the West, and *càngó* in the east and
south of the Bantu-speaking realm, are its derivative regional variants.
The power of medicine at the level of the compound, spoken or sung
over, is evident in its ambivalence. Thus *píng* or *píngö* refer not just to
medicines but also to cursing in Western Bantu. Similarly, the Western
Bantu notion of *kítì* or *kící* refers both to the possessing spirit of an
affliction, as well as to the medicine used to deal with the affliction.
In the easternmost appearance of this cognate among the Lubaized
Nsengo of Tanzania (Waite 1987), it refers only to spirits. In the Western region, as in Kongo, it carries mainly the connotation of the consecrated packaged medicine compound. Local variations represent both
or a range of variants between the two extremes here. Ngoma in the
kící zone is often situated within this context as the therapeutic performance of the medicine. A more localized term among the Western
Lunda peoples of the Southern Savanna (e.g., Yaka, Suku, Tshokwe,
and Pende) for the category of medicine as spirit-induced compound or
shrine is *hamba.* In East Africa, the Arabic-derived term *dawa* carries
this same connotation.

In the same way as the formulation and identification of the sickness
or its agent may generate the treatment mode, through control of that
agent, so often the therapeutic technique and the specialist are described
by the same term. Thus, very widely in the Bantu-speaking area tonal
or contextual emphases separate the cognate stem *ganga,* medicine,

from *gàngà,* doctor, according to Guthrie. Whereas the former emphasis is sporadic, the latter is nearly universal in the region, ranging from *ngàngà* in Western Kongo, to *mganga* in East Africa, and *inyanga* among the Zulu. Regional terms for specialized types of practitioner include, in Western Bantu, *buki,* combining curing and divination/diagnosis; *banda* and *mbanda* in Western Bantu, the first meaning spirit of affliction, the second healer; *dagud* in the northeast, meaning to practice medicine or to divine; and *lumbu* or *bilumbu* in the central Southern Savanna region and *igqira* in the south. These general terms for doctor or healer are given more specificity through combination with another term. Thus, the Kongo *nganga nkisi* deals with consecrated medicines (*minkisi*); *nganga lunga* is the orthopedist; *nganga mpodi* the cupping horn expert, *nkisi mpodi,* the cupping horn, and so on.

Divination is a nearly universal technique in these societies, although the particular character of the technique varies immensely. The basic diagnostic question for which an answer is sought is that of whether a misfortune or affliction is due to natural—God-ordained—causes or to human forces, or is related to the misuse of medicines or inadequate control of spirit forces. Because of its integral place in the interpretation of human experience in societies of the area, divination methods have shifted frequently to respond to the forces of social change. Unlike the pervasiveness of the term that expresses the hypothesis of human-derived misfortune (*dòg*), there seems to be no common or even regional term for the interpretation of misfortune in particular cases (unless it is the cognate *gàngà*). In recent decades there has been a widespread trend for mechanistic techniques such as the Ngombo basket of the Southern Savanna and west coast, and pengula bone-throwing in the southern region, to be replaced by inspirational diviners who may be possessed by a range of spirits: nature, ancestral, Christian, Islamic. The urgency to respond to the basic metaphysical and social questions about the causes of misfortune has maintained the diagnostic and therapeutic system of Central and Southern Africa amid major changes in the past century. The ideational superstructure, more than particular techniques, has remained highly resilient.

Ngòmà is a final central cognate of the medicine of Bantu-speaking Africa which arises from and draws on all the foregoing features. So far this work has translated it as "cult of affliction," or "drum of affliction," since in many regions *ngòmà* refers to drum, the instrument. However, this connection between the term and the wider phenomenon is far from being a neat single-stranded relationship. At the core of the "Bantu conundrum" is the fact that although there are some wide-spread referents of the terms we have seen here, few if any are present everywhere as a fully consistent complex of different elements. The musical instruments that accompany ngoma and other healing rites offer intriguing clues from a nonverbal domain which will support preliminary hypotheses to the questions we seek to answer.

INSTRUMENTS OF RITUAL HEALING
AS A NONVERBAL COGNATE SET

We may think of the issues to be addressed here as a puzzle with several interlocking pieces. If the verbal cognate *ngoma* is nearly pervasive in Bantu languages (with the exception of zones B and C, and in the Khoisan south; see maps, appendix B), how do we account for the limited distribution, within that cultural and linguistic space, of ritual therapeutic institutions named *ngoma*? Related to this, how do we account for the even less widely distributed occurrence of the drum type ngoma within that space? The distribution of the set made up of word, behavior, and object will offer clues as to the origin and character of the institution.

There is more to the puzzle. Although the type of music that accompanies therapeutic activities in Central and Southern Africa varies a great deal, well beyond the core area in which ngoma drums are used, the association of musical instrument types with healing is not random. Instrument types seem to be defined by regional sets or traditions, but in such a way as to dissuade any zealous reductionist of an inherent relationship between the ngoma drum type and the therapeutic rituals.

A first step beyond the lexicon, for the purpose of testing the extent to which behavioral or nonverbal culture may align with verbal cognates having to do with healing, takes us into the realm of the material culture of ritual therapy, namely the musical instruments, their names, and the constellations in which they are combined in ritual performance with singers. This evidence, added to the lexical evidence offered above, strengthens the inferences that may be drawn about the origin, history, and character of the institution. As we progress in this analysis of a complex institution, we will examine the relationship of these instruments to voice, song text, rhythm, trance-possession, and the social makeup of therapeutic communication within a sociopolitical context. (appendix C offers a distillation of findings on the formal composition of instruments, singers, and the overall makeup of the ngoma-type groups, from a range of sources based on observation and the literature.) The research to date is of mixed quality. In addition to my own observations, and the recordings and publications of specialized scholars on particular peoples—for example, John Blacking (1973, 1985) on the Venda, Paul Berliner (1981) among the Shona—a major systematic compendium of great usefulness is the survey of music in Zairian healing rites by researchers Arnaut, Biolo, Esole, Gansemans, Kishilo, Malutshi, and Querson of the National Museum of Zaire in the 1970s and early 1980s (see appendix C). This work is backed up by another, earlier, set of data found in the work of Olga Boone, whose 1951 classic *Les tambours du Congo belge et du Ruanda-Urundi* identified drum types and their names across Central Africa.

In the belt across the middle of the continent, from Kongo to Swahili, where Guthrie finds the greatest convergence of common Bantu terms, *ngoma* refers primarily to the elongated wooden drum with a single membrane attached at one end with pegs. Boone noted that this major drum type was distributed along an east-west line roughly at the Southern Savanna/forest border. North of this line was a region of "mixed" drum types, with the pegged ngoma type interspersed with a type that uses cords to fasten the membrane to the body of the drum. Drums whose membranes were attached with cord or string were rarely called *ngoma*.

In the region of ngoma rituals, ngoma the instrument usually is also identified as a dance drum and a sacred medicine drum. It may also be a drum of state. In societies where trance-possession and therapeutic cults are present, ngoma more than any other drum is used in this therapeutic setting, to the accompaniment of shakers and singing. To the north of the region where this set of practices prevails, stringed and wind instruments are more common in healing rites; ngoma drums are absent.

Therapeutic rituals in the rain forest of Equateur Province of northern Zaire generally demonstrate the typical call-and-response pattern of musical interaction found elsewhere: a sufferer and healer, and a "choir" made up of sets of additional individuals on either or both sides, with the accompaniment of hand clapping, rasps, rattles, whistles, bells, stringed zithers or harps, horns, gongs, and kettle or slit-gong drums, as well as occasionally the xylophone (see appendix C). Spirits that are invoked in these rites are often ancestors ("Elima," "Balimo,"

"Malimu," consonant with the cognate *dímu*) or nature or wild spirits ("Wetshi," "Nzondo").

All of the Equateur examples in the Zaire survey are taken from north of the line, established in Boone's *Tambours* (1951) study, beyond which no lanced-skin drums are said to have been made and used. In other words, the northern forest picture of therapeutics from the Zaire survey demonstrates that healing rituals in Central Africa occur widely without the characteristic ngoma drum. Although Guthrie includes these regions in his Bantu language area, they are conspicuous for the absence of *ngoma* as a verbal cognate, a pattern that is also true of the eastern Zaire Warega rite "Butii."

By contrast, the Southern Savanna, East African, Southeast, and Southern African examples of therapeutic rituals demonstrate the near pervasive presence of the ngoma-type lanced-skin drum in the performance of the ngoma rite. As one moves south and east, ngoma drums are the rule until one reaches the North Nguni beyond the Zambezi river. They are present in Venda *ngoma dza vadzimu* rites, in Swazi and Shangan rituals, and in some area royal settings. But among the southern Nguni peoples (Zulu, Xhosa) they are absent from both royal and cult settings. Here, ngoma refers neither to the drums used (cowhide stretched over sticks or oil drums), nor to the dancing, but exclusively to the singing, divining, and the designation of those who do these things. Thus, the Zulu *isangoma* diviner is literally "one who does ngoma"—that is, sings the songs. Among Xhosa, much influenced linguistically by Khoisan, the role term for the ngoma-singer becomes *igqira*; divination is handled not with bones but through contemplation. Group and network support plays a more important place than individualized divining in the work of ngoma. There is thus a host of regional and societal variations around which the notion "cult of affliction" or "drum of affliction" must be analyzed.

Exceptions to this pattern are coastal Swahili, the Shona setting of Zimbabwe, and the western Kongo setting. Generally, in the examples we have from the vast region mentioned, sufferer(s) and healer(s) either constitute or are joined by a choir and other instruments, such as shakers or rattles, gongs, and hand clapping.

In the Shona region the drum is replaced by another instrument, the large gourd-resonating hand piano, *mbira,* usually played in an orchestra of a dozen or so members, in performances called *bira.* The Kongo region reveals a mixed picture, insofar as musical instrumentation of healing rites is concerned, consonant with Boone's determination (1951) that western Zaire was a region of "mixed" drum types. Kongo therapeutic rites utilize a mixture of horns, single and double gongs, whistles, rattles, and a range of drums (including ngoma to drum up major *nkisi*, "ritual medicine" see appendix C). The Swahili coast features the "pure" ngoma types of healing rites, invariably from the interior, although the Islamic-influenced rites utilize small double-membrane drums and shakers.

This instrument survey, suggestive of type clusters around the widespread ngoma region, belies the impressive musical consistency across the subcontinent in terms of a few features I shall take up later in more detail, but which need to be pointed out here. Throughout the rites cited, the musical scores offer a pervasive use of call and response between the single "soloist"—the sufferer, novice—and the "choir"—the local cell or a group of "significant others."

The patterning of the instruments in therapeutic rites, against this backdrop of the call and response and song-dance, suggests that there are regionally, or culturally, specific constellations of instruments. We may think of these in terms of the common-sense designations of instrument types—harp, zither, whistle, horn, drum—or in terms of the formal designations of musicologists (Marcuse, in Merriam 1977:250): the *idiophone*, an "instrument that yields a sound by its own substance, being stiff and elastic enough to vibrate without requiring a stretched membrane or string" (e.g., xylophone, mbira, sansa, likembe, rattles, bells, gongs, slit drums); *membrophone*, "any instrument in which sound is produced by vibration of a stretched membrane, brought about by striking, friction, or sound waves" (e.g., drums); *aerophone*, "any music instrument in which tone is generated by means of air set in vibration" (1977:252) (e.g., horns, flutes, panpipes, and ocarinas); and *chordophone*, "any instrument having strings as tone-producing elements, the pitch of the instrument being dependent on the strings" (e.g., harp, zither).

The chordophones—the stringed instruments—although they are present throughout, are used in healing rites only in the northern forest region. Most common in healing rites throughout the Central and Southern African region, is the idiophone, that is, the shaker, gong, xylophone, slit-gong drum, and the thumb or hand piano. Second most common in healing rites of the entire region is the membrophone, the single or double membrane drum. The areophone seems to be more common in the northern forest region than in the Southern Savanna and other southern regions.

In terms of the hypothesis announced earlier concerning the relationship of instrument type to the therapeutic rite, great variation is apparent. Nevertheless, the variation is patterned. It is not merely a reflection of the general stock of musical instruments used in the regional culture. Stringed instruments and horns are widespread but are not frequently used in therapeutic rites outside the forest region. Drums, readily available in forest societies, are not frequently used for healing there. On the Southern Savanna, drums are the primary instrument of healing. The pervasive African hand-piano—*nsanza, mbira*—is used in major healing rites only among the Shona group of Zimbabwe.

A second conclusion, announced earlier, follows from this finding on the pattern of distribution of musical instruments utilized in therapeutic rites. Thus we must be suspicious of claims that explain a specific pattern of therapy, or possession ritual, in terms of the effects of a particular type of instrument, such as the drum. This is particularly the case given the background of common musical style features such as call and response and polyrhythm, and of the choral nature of African therapeutic song-dance.

One final piece of the puzzle, of those with which we began this section, remains to be put in place. What, then, explains the distribution of the ngoma-style drum and the use of this name for the therapeutic and celebrative song-dance? As we have seen, this distribution is roughly outlined on the north by an arc running southward of the Congo/Zaire River, then northeastward from Lake Victoria across southern Kenya. It extends from the Atlantic to the Indian oceans, and southward to the boundary of Nguni-speakers and the Shona. Plotted on Guthrie's language map, this corresponds approximately to the F, H, K, L, M, N, P, and parts of the S zones (see appendix B). It is absent from the C and most of D zones in the north, present only along the coast of A, and sparse in the R zone; absent in the large Khoisan zone, as well as in part of the S zone, the south Nguni.

A tentative interpretation of this distribution of the associated drum type and therapeutic rite would point to its presence, as a cognate, in early or proto-Bantu, with some kind of amplification in the Eastern Bantu migrations from the lake region, westward across the savanna to the Atlantic coast, southward across the Zambezi and the Limpopo, and eastward to the Indian Ocean coast. The early Western Bantu pattern of ngoma drums is not clear at this point; the identification of both the drum type and the ritual is extremely diverse and needs further study. It is clear, however, that over much of the western Congo basin, as in Kongo society, there is an overlay or melding of presumably Eastern and Western Bantu elements. It is probable that ngoma techniques and material culture—the ngoma drum—complemented or incorporated the eastward spread of distinctly Western Bantu cultural elements such as the *nkisi* (known from the Kongo coast to the Luba-ized Nsenga in Malawi and far western Tanzania). The coastal Atlantic rites in Gabon and Cameroon, where the pegged-membrane drum is present, are suggestive of Central African rites. Whether these are due to proto-Bantu or more recent Eastern Bantu impulses is unclear. Our Eastern Bantu origins hypothesis for ngoma must remain suggestive for the present.

SOCIAL AND POLITICAL VARIABLES OF A COMPLEX INSTITUTION

Formal one-dimensional cultural historical indices such as verbal cognates and the distribution of material culture have set the broad historic boundaries of ngoma. We must now look within the region and its societies to further identify the subject at hand and to establish the hallmarks for its presence within this broad context. The next two chapters on "core features" and "doing ngoma" will further identify behavioral and normative correlates of ngoma, as used in its broader meaning as has emerged in the foregoing pages, and as the set we have been describing as a "cult of affliction." However, first we can identify some of the broad-stroke social and political corollaries of those settings in which ngoma is present and in which it is absent. Second, within the region and societies where this set occurs, we can begin to look for the reasons for the rise and decline of particular manifestations of ngoma the institution, and why it is segmented into many specialized groups in one setting and homogeneous or unitary in other settings. Third, given that ngoma combines features that are normally differentiated in Western institutions and in Western scholarship, what is an appropriate understanding of the cult of affliction and its functions as an institution?

CULTS OF AFFLICTION IN CENTRALIZED AND SEGMENTARY SOCIETIES

Many of the societies of the subcontinent have been lineage-based agrarian communities, practicing some hunting, and in regions where the sleeping sickness–carrying tsetse fly is absent, livestock tending.

Especially in coastal regions, commercial cities have emerged, linking the continent to overseas mercantile centers. The region includes Southern Savanna matrilineal societies such as the Kongo, Lunda, Cokwe, Kimbundu, and Bemba of Zaire, Angola, Zambia, and Malawi; patrilineal societies such as the Luba, Lozi, Nyamwezi, and others of the central region, and in the southern region, the Nguni-speaking societies of the Zulu, Swazi, and Xhosa; and nearby, the Shona, Sotho, and Tswana, to name a few. The region has seen the emergence of numerous precolonial states and empires, including the cluster of Luba, Lunda, Kimbundu, and Cokwe states; on the western coast, the Kongo, Loango, Kakongo, and Ngoyo states; the states of the eastern lakes, Busoga and Buganda, and eastward, Nyamwezi; in the Zimbabwe region, the historic state of Monamotapa; more recently, in the early nineteenth century, the Zulu empire and the Tswana chiefdoms, and the Sotho kingdom in the Southern Africa area, associated with the great disturbances known as Mfecane.

Ngoma-type cults of affliction have related dynamically to these states. They have either been brought under the tutelage of government and served the purposes of, and the legitimation for, sovereign power, or they have preserved and perpetuated segments of society not directly related to the state. In the absence of the state, they have provided a format for the perpetuation of social segments, particularly those marginalized or afflicted, such as women, the handicapped, those struck with misfortune in economy-related tasks such as hunting, women's reproductive capacity, or commerce. In some settings, the model of the cult has provided the basis for normative social authority, defining and organizing economic activity, social organization, and more esoteric religious and artistic activities.

In colonial and postcolonial Africa, the logic of the use of affliction and adversity for the organization of social reproduction has contributed to the perpetuation, even the proliferation, of cults of affliction, often in a way that has baffled governmental authorities and outside observers. Cults have arisen in connection with epidemics, migration and trade routes, shifts in modes of production, and in response to changes in social organization and the deterioration of juridical institutions. Colonialism itself undoubtedly generated many of the cults of affliction that appeared in the twentieth century. Postindependence conditions have continued to provide grist for the mill of cult formation.

The picture of cults of affliction within, or in relation to, centralized historic states contrasts markedly with that in the decentralized societies. Under the shadow of the state they are less influential, or entirely absent, or transformed into the rituals of statecraft. Instructive is their apparent absence in the Tswana chiefdoms, where strong historic chiefship has provided social continuity, a format for the juridical process, and some means of material support to marginalized and needy people. By contrast, in neighboring Nguni societies, they have thrived alongside or under the tutelage of chiefs and kings.

In other contexts cults are known to have provided the impetus for the emergence of centralized polities, as in the case of the Bunzi shrine of coastal Kongo. Elsewhere, cults have emerged in the wake of historic states, picking up the aura of royal authority, the trappings of sovereignty, and transforming them into a continuing source of mystical power. A prime example is the cult of Ryangombe and the BuCwezi of the lakes region of eastern Central Africa, whose spirits are said to be the royal dynasties of the ancient Cwezi kingdom (Berger 1981). BuCwezi is today found in Tanzania's major cities. The same model has been reported in Mayotte, off the coast of East Africa, where possession spirits are the Saklava kings of Madagascar (Lambek 1981:152).

The dynamic relationship of cults to centralized polities has been accompanied by changes in the way spirits and shades are focused in consciousness and ritual. As the scale and function of a cult expands, narrowly defined ancestor shades may give way to nature, alien, or hero spirits. In a few instances, centralized shrine cults have persisted over centuries, defining primary values and social patterns for generations of adepts. The Bunzi shrine of coastal Kongo, Mbona of Malawi, and Korekore and Chikunda in Zimbabwe are well-studied examples that continue into the present. Some authors have made a distinction between these centralized "regional" cults and topically focused cults of affliction (Werbner 1977). But the orders, taken in their entirety, suggest more of a continuum along several axes: centralized to segmentary, inclusive to specialized, controlled by state sovereignty to independent (or even opposed to state sovereignty). Cults have crystallized opposition to states, both in precolonial, colonial, and to a lesser degree, postcolonial settings. Thus, the Cwezi cult channeled opposition to hierarchized structures in the Interlacustrine state of Rwanda (Berger 1981). Cult leaders organized opposition to Rhodesian labor recruitment practices in the early twentieth century and inspired early strikes in the mines (Van Onselen 1976). In the Zimbabwean war of independence, mediums played a role of legitimating the claims to land by the elders, and the aspirations of the guerrilla fighters, although the particulars have only begun to be studied carefully (Fry 1976; Ranger 1985:187–216). The role of ngoma networks in popular resistance in South Africa's townships is not yet known to scholars, but it may be substantial.

In the twentieth century, cults of affliction have tended to be short-term movements of panacea (DeCraemer, Vansina, and Fox 1976), often born in desperation. They have provided expression to the pains and social problems of wide segments of the populace. There has been a great deal of interpenetration between the cults and independent Christian churches, and with Islamic orders. New permanent cults have arisen around characteristic ills such as the isolated nuclear household in the urban setting; epidemic diseases such as tuberculosis, and getting by with the chronic problems related to it; the divination of social problems such as unemployment in a proletarian setting; how to succeed in business and how to retain a job; how to protect wealth once it is acquired. Many cults focus on the alienation and entrapment so common in the African urban setting.

In the urban centers of Zaire, Tanzania, Swaziland, and South Africa the historic cults as well as new adaptations are represented by part-time and full-time healers and priests and their adepts. In most instances the ethnic communities of the rural hinterlands have brought their religious institutions with them to the city, where they have undergone shifts of function and signification.

UNITARY AND DIVERSE MANIFESTATIONS

A further issue in considering independent variables surrounding the origin, persistence, and change in ngoma has to do with its alternative unitary and diverse manifestation across the region where it is found. This contrast is most marked in comparing the central region of the continent with the southern region. Across the mid-continent, from the Congo coast, across the Southern savanna, to the Tanzanian highlands and the coastal region, ngoma-type institutions are usually represented in multiples. Turner's work (1968) among the Ndembu, a society incorporated on the periphery of the Lunda empire, counted twenty-three ngoma orders; Cory's writing on the Sukuma of the Lake Victoria shores in western Tanganyika enumerated about twenty-five ngoma orders. Some of these pertained to women's reproductive disorders or child rearing. Others had to do with men's problems, either in productive work or in social roles. Several had to do with societal dangers, either from the natural world (e.g., poisonous snakes) or from spiritual threats (witches) or alien spirits. Others could be seen as ceremonial leadership organizations that consolidated responsibilities such as witch finding or the sponsorship of periodic rituals. In the southern region, particularly in Nguni-speaking societies of Mozambique, Zimbabwe, South Africa, Swaziland, and Lesotho, ngoma is mainly presented as a homogeneous type of institution, devoted to the recognition of ancestors and addressing general human problems.

It is difficult to interpret this contrasting configuration in terms of an independent variable, either in the past or in the present. It is tempting to look at this contrast in terms of a kind of Durkheimian or Spencerian social structural proliferation or specialization that occurs in most societies with advancing time. The older societies in the Bantu expansion, notably of the central area, would have shown greater institutional diversity because of their greater historical depth in that setting. Whereas the Nguni in the south, exemplifying the end result of migrations and frontier-type settings, would have retained a less differentiated type of society. This perspective might then reveal something about the original role of ngoma in the "Bantu frontier," perhaps in the need to consolidate authority and to come to terms with threats and contradictions of various kinds. However, there is no way to test such a theory or hypothesis, much less determine which are the independent and dependent variables, until far better historical understanding is available.

There are indications in specific settings of trends in cults of affliction toward greater proliferation, or toward greater homogeneity, which may offer a less grandiose approach to the issue. The salient independent variable here seems to be political and social consolidation. In the seventeenth- to nineteenth-century coastal Congo setting, in which the Lemba cult emerged, there was a proliferation of *nkisi* medicines, charms, and ngoma-type orders, especially along the coast as the coastal trade eroded political states such as Loango, Kakongo, and Ngoyo, as well as the Kongo kingdom, and undermined the juridical functions that these states were able to fulfill. The decline of the states may be correlated directly with the increase of charms, medicines, and cults, including Lemba. However, within Lemba—the major regional ngoma-cult organization, which reflected trade, alliance building, and healing—there emerged a consolidation of some of the diverse sub-charms and functions. For example, the coastal midwifery order Pfemba, the prevalent way of dealing with women's reproductive issues, was co-opted by Lemba (Janzen 1982:56). Its representation in the Lemba order and *nkobe* basket of medicines came to be known as "Pfemba-Lemba" (Janzen 1982:253–254). In other regions Lemba appears to have incorporated, or aligned with, other distinctive ritual functions and medicines. We may project this procedure to its logical extension and imagine that multiple ritual functions might be similarly absorbed within a single institution, leading to greater functional homogeneity. At the extreme, this might have led to complete integration of ritual functions within the state or some other absolutistic type of institution. Or, it could, as in the case of coastal Kongo, indicate that where the centralized state had collapsed, ngoma-type orders took up some of the functions of state, such as conflict resolution, social control of threat, and the channeling of useful knowledge as applied to problem solving.

Another example of movement toward ritual consolidation from the contemporary ngoma picture comes from Tanzania. There, a modern state-sanctioned organization of ngoma healers, the Shirika la Madawa described in the previous chapter, controls the resource of ngoma recruitment. Indeed, this control of accesss to the role of ngoma healer and membership in the association is sufficiently restrictive that one of the major legitimating criteria of admission, namely certified possession by a *sheitani* spirit, occurs in only four out of a hundred individuals treated by the ngoma group. But the Shirika's ability to control diversity is offset by competition from the many other ngoma orders in Dar es Salaam.

It is difficult to formulate a strict calculus of the myriad range of transformations ngoma may undergo across the region where it has been reported. A few generalizations are possible. Ngoma appears to fade away where there is a strong central authority with a highly developed judicial tradition (e.g., Tswana). It seems to proliferate on the social and geographical margins of large empires (e.g., Ndembu in the Lunda empire; BaCwezi in Ryangombe) or as a mechanism for the consolidation of authority in the interstices of society where misfortune lurks (e.g., Bilumbu in Luba society). It proliferates where misfortune is rampant and where social chaos prevails (e.g., early colonial resistance, postwar Zimbabwe, South African urban townships). In the wake of the demise of centralized states, it may take on the functions of the state (e.g., Lemba in coastal Kongo).

Do the constant features through all these transformations represent an institution? If so, how can that be characterized?

SCHOLARLY BLINDERS AND THE
ONTOLOGY OF A UNIQUE INSTITUTION

Scholars, administrators, policymakers, and therapists have predictably come up with varying opinions on how to characterize the ngoma-type cult of affliction. As a final task in this chapter on identifying ngoma, I wish to argue for the proposition that it is a unique institution.

Definitions of institution abound, but they reflect a common understanding of how society is put together and functions. Durkheim suggested (in Parsons 1949:407) that "[a] body of rules governing action in pursuit of immediate ends insofar as they exercise moral authority derivable from a common value system may be called social institutions." A falsifiable proof of this definition held, said Durkheim, that "the means to these ends may vary, but the rules reflect the common values. If they are lost sight of, the result is a breakdown of control, and anomie." In another tradition, M. G. Smith noted (1974:212) that "whether culture is restrictively defined as the symbols, norms, values, and ideational systems of a given population, or more inclusively as their standardized and transmitted patterns of thought and action, all institutional organization has a cultural coefficient, since each institution involves collective norms, ideas, and symbols as well as standardized modes of procedure."

These general theoretical comments about the broad basis of institutions—norms, common beliefs, ends met by a range of means—would certainly be appropriate to describe what ngoma does in Central and Southern African society. The problem, of course, is that by Western institutional and scholarly standards some of the examples of ngoma are strange indeed. They have heretofore been put into rubrics of either Western institutions or have been allowed to languish in ethnographies as local culture, for example, Ndembu religion, Zulu diviners, and Kongo fertility magic.

The interpretation of African cults of affliction is analogous to the study of some other domains in anthropological research in that scholars have been faced with the need to bridge the indigenous concept with the analytical notion. Sometimes scholarship has come down on the side of the former, as in totemism, taboo, or shamanism; other times it has come down on the latter, which is frequently a reflection of a Western institutional category.

The debate about kinship in Western anthropology is instructive here. David Schneider's *Critique of the Study of Kinship* took issue with the pervasive assumption by generations of anthropologists since Morgan of the universality of the family and kinship. This he explained, not so much by faulting Louis Henry Morgan for finding the family and kinship among the Iroquois, but by faulting anthropology at large for adopting Western notions of basic institutions and imposing them upon societies of the world. The "big four" institutions of Western society are, for Schneider: kinship (the family), the economy (business), politics (the state), and religion (the church).

Western social science, including anthropology, has extended this quartet as analytical categories onto other societies, much to the detriment of insights to be gained. Societies in which these institutions or attributes seem to be combined differently, or are only partially represented, are held to be "undifferentiated," and therefore "more primitive," or somehow disorganized or muddled.

One of the major challenges, then, in presenting ngoma has been to transcend Western institutional categorization. The difficulty of Westerners, and of Western-trained Africans, in accepting ngoma or the cult of affliction as a valid institution in its own right, has been instructive in this regard. In many African settings the colonial legacy of Western institutional structures clashes markedly with the African institution.

Ngoma in Tanzania, where there has been a commitment to build on African foundations, illustrates the point. Officially, African medicine and its institutions are recognized. Research units devoted to the subject have been sponsored. However, the research effort and the statement of the reality of therapeutic ngoma are initiated from the specialized basis of Western institutional categories. Thus, the Traditional Medicine Research Unit at the National Hospital is charged with examining the botanical and chemical character of medicines used in ngoma and other types of indigenous medicine and with creating a program for primary health within the framework of indigenous healing. The Music section of the Ministry of Culture is charged with researching the dance and song basis of ngoma, as well as sponsoring dance competitions of current ngoma groups and licensing entertainment ngoma. The Ministry also sponsors the national dance troupe and allied ngoma groups. The political party of Tanzania has de facto liaisons to ngoma and large healer's associations. Tanzanian bureaucracy thus sections ngoma into distinctive categories consonant with Western rules of social order.

In my earlier work on Lemba (Janzen 1982) I observed the struggle of publishers and reviewers to come to terms with this dilemma of the integrity of the institution versus the categories of Western scholarship. The publisher, in filling out the Library of Congress Catalogue Data page, described Lemba as a "cult," thus a subset of religion. Several reviewers tried to escape the straitjacket of Western institutional typologies but succeeded only partially in doing so, coming up with hyphenated categorical types. One reviewer, after a page of discussion, noted that "to define it simply [Lemba was] a cult and a social institution that controlled trade, markets, and processes of exchange" (Mudimbe 1986). Another, picking up on my vocabulary, called Lemba a "therapeutic-alliance-trading institution" (Feldman 1988).

These reviewers appreciated the unique institutional profile better than another who spoke of the book's having offered "a new framework for thinking about a little understood region of Africa and for analyzing the relations between the political, kinship, religions, and economic aspects of social structure" (Riesman 1985), thereby virtually sectioning the subject through the Western institutional categories.

Another reviewer (Stuart 1986), whose summary of the work is a model of succinct interpretation, offered this explanation of Lemba's mix of trade, alliances, and therapy: "The *ngoma,* or the 'drum of affliction' became the cultural symbol of a therapeutic society . . . which evolved to deal with the social stress and cultural change created by Europe's growing commercial influence." He concluded with this insight: "[T]herapeutics may be the metaphor serving to facilitate consolidation of substantial resources, material and human, and to aid long-term reordering of institutions of redress, economic redistribution, and ideological change."

We are thus confronted in Lemba, as in many other variants of the ngoma profile across Central and Southern Africa, with a constellation of practices and perspectives that are unique and yield to understanding only with some critical analysis. This realization highlights the centrality of the need to deal carefully with the homology between language, behavior, and institutions, which is closely related to the first activity of divining, science, religion, and a host of other human enterprises, to wit, naming the phenomenon.

To understand this better, it is instructive to look at reviews of the Lemba book, particularly one that discussed the question of naming ngoma. This reviewer (Stevens 1984:29–31) thought the study had been done a disservice by allowing "the term 'drum of affliction' to stand in the subtitle." It was not that "drum of affliction"—derived from ngoma—might be an erroneous label for Lemba but that only a handful

of specialists like Victor Turner know the term refers to Ndembu rituals. It has little recognition value as a more widespread type of phenomenon, he argued. Yet if none of the Western institutional labels are
appropriate, and an expert's English term for the indigenous term in
one African society is not appropriate, then by which term do we describe, or understand, the phenomenon if we wish to avoid having
it locked into one or more versions of, or a hyphenated version of,
the Western institutional grid? Beginning with Turner's local Ndembu
work, Stevens reasons out an approximation of ngoma in the broader
sense, freed of its Western institutional categorical boxes.

> [Turner's] use of the alternate Ndembu meaning, "drum," is significant to
> an anthropological investigation of symbol and meaning in African cultures,
> and it will serve students and collectors of African art well to consider for
> a moment the possibility that a drum, as an object, may be meaningful only
> as a construction of materials, barely even as a musical instrument; its cul-
> tural meaning is revealed only through the total socio-religious context of
> its use. In such a context, then, "drum" is symbol: it is drumming, and it is
> collective sentiment, catharsis, transcendence—indeed, the whole of the
> ritual process. The ritual process is social effort.

Finally Stevens comes to his "discovery point":

> In this sense, then, the phrase "drum of affliction" is justified as referring
> to a type of ritual; and we can understand why Bantu-speakers may use the
> term *ngoma* to refer even to a ritual in which drums are not used. "Drum
> of affliction" is a ritual with a therapeutic aim, the exorcising of some malign
> agency, but as both Turner and Janzen make clear, "drum" (*ngoma*) means
> the aims, activities, actors, and institutions, and the network of symbols by
> which they are linked and united, that constitute the ritual process. (Stevens
> 1984:29–30)

Stevens is correct that *ngoma,* however we wish to gloss this term
in English or another analytical language, refers over a wide area of
Central and Southern Africa to a cluster of recurring processes and
perspectives having to do with the interpretation of misfortune, usually
manifested by disease or disease symptoms that are imputed to spirits
or ancestors, and the rites to bring the thus "afflicted" into a supportive
network with others similarly afflicted and to treat them by empower-
ing them to deal effectively with the adversity. The particular source of
the adversity, whether it is the impact of foreign trade, twinning, snake-
bite, or lineage segmentation, is secondary to the fact of its definition
as the phenomenon of adversity.

CONCLUSION

Ngoma, then, is a composite, historically unique institution wide-spread throughout Central and Southern Africa, with many local and regional variations. Its identity as an institution and as a behavioral process, often with name recognition, should satisfy scholarship. That it has taken so long for scholarship to catch up with indigenous usage is tribute to the tendency of scholarship, and administration, to categorize in its own, often local, terms the phenomenon before it.

This chapter's goal of "identifying ngoma" has been external and formal, based on examining comparative and historical distributions of "words, acts, and things" and how they vary in relation to one another. Its apparent central purpose as an institution is to respond to the need for order, meaning, and control in the face of misfortune and affliction as defined by a core proto-Bantu cognate, *dòg*: that just as words and intentions by others can afflict, so they can heal.

3
Core Features
in Ngoma Therapy

A straightforward formulation of the subject of this work, based on material presented thus far, would be something like the following: Just as persons or social forces around the sufferer are involved in the cause of affliction (as understood in the proto-Bantu cognate *dòg*), so others may help in the diagnosis, decision making of health seeking, and continuing support of the sufferer to achieve well-being. As we have seen, these as well as other notions are embedded in the vocabulary of Central and Southern African languages and constitute a classic institutional form of the quest for therapy and wholeness.

And yet, this formulation does not cover all aspects of ritual healing in Central and Southern Africa. There are dimensions that are not so readily captured in the cultural vocabulary, or that are missing from that vocabulary. For example, I am not aware of a consistent vocabulary for the choreography or spatial layout of healing rituals, although they share a striking consistency of pattern across the ngoma area.

The social sciences, since their inception, have grappled with the relationship of the verbalized self-conscious model of a culture to the analytical account of behavioral and structural features and historical patterns observed by the scholar. On the one hand, there is the phenomenologist's insistence on studying only that which is consciously and verbally identified. On the other, there is the challenge to bring together analytical theories and interpretations to provide a convincing basis for those unnamed structures, contradictions, and historical changes that identify and clarify a body of disparate information. As Clifford Geertz notes, the ethnologist's task includes a good deal of persuasion in depicting a situation so that the reader finds it uniquely realistic (Geertz 1988:4–5).

Twenty years ago I asked what were the most characteristic features of Central African healing (Janzen 1969). Then I was not concerned with verbal categories, and I did not perceive the widespread existence of historical patterns. Part of the answer to the question of characteristic features has been provided in establishing the widespread use of the process I later called the "quest for therapy," which was spelled out in a book by that title. In Kongo society it appeared that the process of being afflicted and seeking relief for that affliction was driven by a compelling worldview issue, namely, the question of whether or not the affliction is merely matter of fact, or whether "there is something else going on," that is, other persons, spirits, ancestors, or the social setting itself, in the causation of the case. As soon as this determination was made, in cases I studied, significant others around the sufferer became involved in the search for an appropriate solution. These "therapy managers began the process [of] individuals around the sufferer assisting in offering support and diagnostic affirmation as the case came before numerous types of care, be it herbalists, biomedical hospitals and clinics, diviners, and assorted social therapies" (Janzen 1978a). Seven years later Marc Augé identified a similar process as "therapeutic itinerary" (1985). Many other scholars have reported comparable findings in their work around the continent.

This picture of Central African therapy seeking is still valid, although it is a limited one. Also, the exercise of creating a generalized, synthesized model of a culturally specific institution has its perils. One of these perils is that of using too limited an empirical or ethnographic basis of information, which might lead to a dull, stereotyped, and possibly erroneous depiction of the institution. Another danger is to abstract the core features based on a misunderstanding of the dynamics of the institution. A synthetic picture of an institution is correct not because it reflects the statistical averages of all practices but because it explains the underlying logic. And this may not correspond to any particular local tradition.

This chapter and the next present such a synthetic model of ngoma as a ritual therapeutic institution in terms of core features that include: (1) sickness and therapeutic initiation as a phased rite of passage; (2) identifying the causes of misfortune; (3) associating nosology with "spirit fields"; (4) the "course through the white," of sickness and transition; (5) a sacrifice that sets in motion a circuit of exchanges; (6) the power of the wounded healer, together with fellow sufferers, that is, transforming sufferer into healer. All of these come together in a final feature presented in the next chapter, the core ritual, "doing ngoma."

SICKNESS AND THERAPEUTIC INITIATION
AS A PHASED RITE OF PASSAGE

The first of the core features of the cult of affliction is the choreography of events over time. Throughout the region where ngoma affliction institutions are found, the process of sickness, labeling, healing, searching for answers, becoming well, and emerging as a healer is framed by rites that define the entry into, and exit from, the position of the ngoma sufferer-novice. These formal features and the spatial-temporal structure that results from them are distinguished here from the qualitative transformation of the individual (or group) as identified in another core feature, "the course through the white."

In the historic Lemba cult of the Congo coast and inland along the trade routes, this temporal framing was evident in all regional variants (Janzen 1982). To cite a specific example, after an nganga's initial identification of the sufferers' (in this case, a couple) condition as being Lemba-related, they were put in touch with a senior Lemba healer and, in the first event, purified and given the initial medicine. They were now Lemba novices under the supervision of their priest-healer. After sometimes years of counseling, of dream analysis, of song preparation, and collection of the funds for their final event, they were featured in a "graduation" event, after which they were fully qualified Lemba officiants.

In reading, and later in a comparative fieldwork project, I found that this same structure for the framing of ritual events was widely represented in ngoma settings. The events that open, close, and punctuate the therapeutic initiation are usually of a day-night-day sequence and duration. This was true in Kongo society, in Turner's accounts of Ndembu rites of affliction, in igqira initiations in the Western Cape, in coastal Cameroon rites (in contrast to the Grassfield area in the interior), and in Haitian voodoo, which carries a strong Central African institutional pattern. This pattern is commonly aligned with the preparation for meeting ancestors or spirits and bringing the novice into communication with them. Frequently the sequence of events also spatially reflects this with a move in the ritual choreography from a profane to a sacred or auspicious place, moves that are announced with transition songs to move the sufferer-novice through an intermediary space (see fig. 8).

These opening, closing, and punctuating events of the ngoma initiation are marked as well by the preparation of medicines, the utilization of color-coded stages and ointments spread on the novice, and by the sacrifice of an animal that is ritually identified with the novice and is then slaughtered, cooked, and eaten as a common meal.

Despite the pervasive presence of the foregoing pattern that structures the ngoma rites, there does not seem to be a set of common verbal cognates that relate to this structure. The events that open, close, and punctuate the process are variously called *nkembo* (celebration), or *mpandulu* (initiation to or composition of an *nkisi*) in Kongo; *nthlombe* (celebration, feast) in Nguni languages; *ngoma* in East Africa. These terms are all used fairly generally to speak of ceremonies, initiations, or rites of all kinds.

As in other widespread cultural patterns, these elements of Central and Southern African therapeutic initiation have been explained by authors utilizing several ethnological principles that go beyond the culturally particular and descriptive. Two major approaches that may be outlined here are those of the "rite of passage" and the "shamanic career." As with all ethnological explanations that are more general than descriptive, these have some value but they also remain problematic.

The elements of initiation in ngoma-type cults of affliction in Ndembu society were explained by Victor Turner as examples of Van Gennepian "rites of passage." They were opened by a rite of separation of the novice-sufferer from a prior social state. This was followed by an intermediary "liminal" or transitional state. The process culminated with a rite of reincorporation by the novice into society, as a full-fledged healer and member of the cult. Later, Max Gluckman argued for a more analytical approach to these rituals, especially in societies moving toward greater complexity and differentiation of roles (1962:1–52). Turner himself came to see the cults-of-affliction rites as more sophisticated and varied examples of ritualization in human society. However, it is useful to understand the African cult of affliction as a culturally specific case of the human rite of passage, on a level similar to that which sees the sick role and the encounter with the medical professional in the West as a "rite of passage." As in any therapeutic course, the outcome is not necessarily assured. Many are those who begin ngoma,

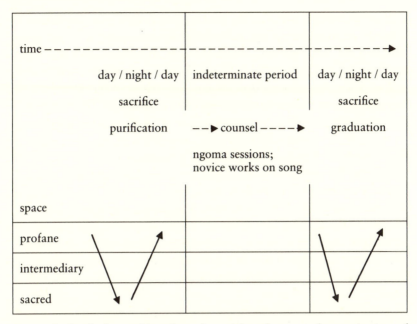

Figure 8. Synthetic configuration of spatial and temporal organization of
events in ngoma-type rites. This chart is to be read as a musical score. The
"time" line moves from left to right. The "space" score also moves from
left to right, but indicates the spaces in which activity is situated through
the rites.

or who participate in it, but who never complete it. For this reason it
may not be like a strict rite of passage. The progression through the
ritual grid is subject to the inner progress of the novice-sufferer.

Others have identified aspects of African cults of affliction with the
"shamanic career" (De Heusch 1971), although this has been held to
be problematic and inappropriate by most authors (I. Lewis 1986:78–
93), for reasons that will be developed at greater length in chapter 5.
In Lewis's analysis of the "career" of spirit possession, a series of stages
moves the relationship of the novice to the spirit from a point where it
is uncontrolled and involuntary to a point where it reflects greater control, indeed, voluntary interaction with the spirit through mediumship.
This "career" is also defined by the subject moving from being a patient
or sufferer to mastery over the source of affliction, and becoming a
healer of that condition, although, as noted above, the process may
stall. Some aspects of the shamanic journey may be seen in the choreographed move from profane to sacred space in every rite (see fig. 8).

And some novices do speak of having journeyed to the bottom of the river, or into the woods or wild bush to rescue a soul, or to commune with a spirit. Thus some of the elements said to universally define shamanism are also in keeping with ngoma ritual. However, rarely is the ngoma graduate or healer involved in classic shamanic journeys following the completion of the therapeutic initiation. Some, such as Botoli Laie in Dar es Salaam, admit freely to having been introduced to ngoma practice as an apprentice.

It thus seems clear that caution must be exercised in applying universalistic ethnological explanations to a phenomenon I have argued is historically and culturally particular, with its own distinctive vocabulary and significant variation within the region where it is found: for example, the day/night/day scheduling of the events; the use of white symbolism as the lengthy inner or middle passage; the role of percussion in setting the stage for passage; the spatial choreography that moves from profane space to sacred space and back.

THE DIAGNOSIS OF MISFORTUNE

The student of Central and Southern African collective therapies of the ngoma type is presented in many localities, including the urban centers under particular scrutiny in the present work, with a broad array of afflictions deemed appropriate for treatment. The array is in fact so broad that one can question whether the distinct diagnosis of signs, symptoms, or syndromes is at all a characterizing feature of the ngoma therapeutic mode. And yet, it is analytically important to differentiate problems brought into ngoma-type cults of affliction from other types of problems taken elsewhere.

One way to look for the distinctive arena of problems taken into ngoma healing is to note that, with some exceptions, many of the ngoma orders exist, as it were, beyond kinship. Even those such as Nkita in western Zaire and Angola, although about the reproduction of the matrilineage, are construed as being about how the lineage might transcend the internal dilemmas of factionalism, leadership problems, and ill will that are thought to occasion the sickness and death of infants and the sterility of the mothers. The proto-Bantu cognate verb *dòg* connotes all the sources of affliction—sorcery, witchcraft, backbiting—that result from relations within the closely knit human community. Ngoma interventions and appeals are made to get beyond the entrapment of *dòg* (see appendix B, section B.3). Frequently the ancestral shades and the spirits beyond are believed to call individuals out of their self-consuming destructive tendencies. Ngoma afflictions are thus not noticeably different from non-ngoma afflictions on the surface level of signs and symptoms. The diagnostic interpretation becomes important as a way of reaching beyond the mundane for a way out of an impasse.

An important dimension of all cults of affliction is the analytical and diagnostic function of evaluating sickness and misfortune. A distinction is often drawn, in this connection, between divination, the analysis of a situation, and healing, the attempt to intervene in the situation to change it. This distinction was the basis for Turner's book title *Revelation and Divination,* that is, the relationship between the cult of affliction and the diagnosis of the problems it addresses. The distinction accounts for some of the diversity of affliction cult types, for where social change is intense, the need increases for cognitive clarity. Thus, in eighteenth-century coastal Kongo, during the decline of the kingdoms with the increase of the trade, including the slave trade, divination cults were in great profusion, particularly those relating to adjudication and conflict resolution. In Southern Africa today, the term *ngoma* is associated mainly with divination. Closer examination, however, shows that the functions of divination and network-building are complementary.

Divination, or diagnosis, thus always accompanies cults of affliction, either independently of the healing role, or as a part of the specialized techniques and paraphernalia of a particular cult. Divination must be thought of as a continuing query into the "whys," "whos," and "wherefores" begun in the family-therapy management setting but carried through by specialists with expert judgment and training, who may have had their own profound individual dilemmas, who have been recruited to a particular mode of ritual life, and who have been initiated to the spirit world. As a technique, divination may be based on a mechanistic system of signs and interpretations, such as the Southern Savanna Ngombo basket filled with symbolic objects signifying human life, the pengula bone-throwing technique of Southern African Nguni society, or recitation from the Bible or the Koran. Alternatively, and according to some observers increasingly, divination is done by direct recourse to trance, in which the diviner, as medium, speaks the words of the ancestral shade or spirit in answer to a query. Some diviners use a combination of both techniques, or a selection of hierarchically arranged types. In Swaziland, master diviners today train novices in the arts of mechanistic bone-throwing divination as well as the mastery of trance-divination. In any case, these divined diagnoses, representing a type of analysis or interpretation of daily life, offer the basis for the more synthetic, ritualized follow-through of the cults of affliction. However, there is a contradiction or tension between the specificity and concreteness of the problems channeled into divination and treatment, and the overall hypothesis of spirit causation that brings an individual into a cult of affliction.

The work of Zairian researchers Mabiala (1982) and Byamungu (1982) illustrates this issue. Signs and symptoms (illnesses) accompanying recruitment to Mpombo and Badju are said to include dizziness with hallucinations; throbbing headaches; lack of mental presence (asthenie); skin rashes (algie); lack of appetite; difficulty in breathing; heartburn with anxiety; rapid or arrhythmic heartbeat; fever with chills; sexual impotence; dreams of struggles or of being followed by threatening animals; weight loss or excessive weight, especially if accompanied by spirit visitations; and a variety of gynecological and obstetrical difficulties. These "modes of affliction" are characteristic of most of the other collective therapeutic rites—*les grands rites*—in Kinshasa.

Byamungu, working in Bukavu, in the mountainous Kivu region of eastern Zaire, is more explicit about the generalized or random character of signs, symptoms, and syndromes in the mode of affliction associated with the five therapeutic rites of this trading and administrative city of about seventy-five thousand people. In the Kakozi rite, of Bashi and Balega ethnic origin, early stages of sickness are manifested by all types of behavioral and physiological problems, reflecting something of the diversity of Kakozi spirits behind these problems. In the Enaama or Mana rites of Bashi origin (a Nilotic, Rwandais group), the characteristic afflictions include behavioral troubles, alienation, and physical sickness such as weight loss. Here again the distinguishing feature of recruitment is not a particular symptom or sign, but affliction by the Enaama nature spirits of Bashi or Rwandais origin. In the Mitumba rite, of Bembe and Balega origin, behavioral and physical troubles of whatever sort may indicate this mode of affliction. The distinguishing feature is, however, evidence in dreams or hallucinations of the presence of "white" or "European" spirits. The same type of symptom-sign randomness exists in the Mulangoyi rite of Lega, Zimba, and Songe origin, in which the major spirits are nature- or river-related, and in the Nyamulemule rite, in which the spirits are of Luba origin, appearing among the Batembo and Bashi peoples. Byamungu emphasizes that al-

though signs and symptoms accompanying those afflicted may be identified and even treated with biomedical methods and medicines, the
salient point that brings these sufferers to diagnostic entry into the ritual
therapies is not so much the sickness but the identification of the spirit
force behind the sickness.

Our analytical approach would seem, however, to call for close study
of symptoms and signs of affliction or behavioral change in relation to
the circumstances of the personal life of the afflicted, on the one hand,
and the cultural logic that steers the course of therapy in the direction
of identifying the spirits, on the other. It may, of course, be very difficult to correlate the explicit and implicit conditions of distress with the
diagnoses and therapies in the Central African setting, where the initial
diagnostic work is done apart from therapeutic initiation to a group
setting. In Central African cities such as Kinshasa and Bukavu the collective rites are varied by regional and ethnic origin more than by a
specialized division of labor. The diagnostic work is often done by kin
groups and diviners working separately from the healers. Thus the novices are already identified as being in touch with the appropriate spirits
by the time they make their appearance in the ritual communities.

In the Southern African context, that is, in Nguni-speaking societies,
the relationship between diagnosis and therapy and the course from
diagnosis to therapy may be easier to follow. This is so because here
there appears to be a greater concentration of ngoma therapies within
a single institutional context, and thus a fusion of divination-diagnosis
and therapeutics. In the Nguni context it is easier to see the type of affliction or problem singled out for divination from among the wide
array of common afflictions in a populace, as well as those cases further
singled out for therapeutic initiation into the ngoma order. Illustrations
from Swaziland and the Western Cape, given in chapter 1, demonstrate
this process in an ethnically diverse and urban clientele.

The cases seen by Ida Mabuza of Swaziland are said to be both
"African" and "non-African"; she has both African and non-African
clients, the latter mostly Afrikaaners from South Africa. For Africans,
she says, the most common problem presents in vague pains and anxieties and is explained by harm or sorcery (*umbelelo ro meqo*) resulting
from interpersonal tension. This affects both men and women. Next
most prevalent is *amakubalo,* affecting mostly men, in the form of harm
or illness resulting from violated social or moral precepts resulting from
illicit sex with a protected married woman. Many young people come
wishing to divine their fates, desirous of good fortune in job seeking,

examinations, or love. She diagnoses their problems and offers advice accordingly.

Whites also come for these types of problems. Their main concern, however, is fear of poverty. They also come for help in seeking promotions and other job-related matters. Finally, they come with illnesses improperly diagnosed in the hospital or not effectively treated. Stress is a common complaint whose root cause can often be traced, she noted, to tensions or conflicts with domestic workers or subordinates who have retaliated.

The cases that are divined with the more powerful—and expensive—*femba* (possession) mediumistic method do not vary from those already presented, except perhaps that they are more chronic and less specific, and Western medicine has been unable to produce a perceptible improvement in health.

The foregoing problems typify those brought to ngoma diviners and therapists. Perhaps the most striking feature in this material is the random, vague, and ambiguous character of the connection of sign/symptom/syndrome to the therapy, both in terms of physiopathologies and psychopathologies. This seems to be the case especially in contemporary urban settings. Nevertheless, in these urban settings there occur quite precise diagnostic readings of life situations that lead to therapy or entry into one or another ngoma therapeutic group. It is not the particular sign, symptom, or syndrome that predicts the therapeutic course. Rather, it is the diagnostic and divinatory judgment that sends the case beyond the confines of a strictly relational interpretation—as found in the concept *dòg*—to the interpretation that the subject is called by spirits aligned with the ngoma orders.

NOSOLOGY AND SPIRIT FIELDS

Who or what exactly are these spirits? The worldview that inspires cults of affliction includes, as an axiom, the idea that ancestral shades and spirits, ultimately expressions of the power of God, may influence or intervene in human affairs. They are held responsible for visiting their sentiments and forces upon humans through sickness and misfortune. Who they are, why they come, and what to do about them is what cults of affliction are all about.

Scholarship has gone well beyond merely describing accounts of African spirits, to studying their configurations and relationships in society, in geographical space, and over time (Werbner 1977). Our aim here is to identify some of the common features in spirit constellations across the ngoma region and to grasp the meaning of some of the variations. The spirits or shades may be either direct, identifiable lineal ancestors, or more generic shades. They may include more distant nature spirits, hero spirits, or alien spirits that affect human events in many ways. They may be benign or malign; very generalized or particular; male or female; African or foreign. The lineal ancestors, who are generally beneficent, although sometimes stern, are contrasted to wild malefic spirits or enemy hosts with sinister and strange characteristics. There is a spirit "geography" or "ecology" that widely contrasts spirits of the land from those of the water. The well-known African color triad—red, white, black—often is invoked to characterize the spirits as well. The strings of colored beads or cloth worn around the shoulder and waist designate spirits with which the novice or practitioner has a working relationship. Old as well as new knowledge tends to be related to the shade and spirit forces, as events are interpreted and adversities dealt with. Sometimes the proto-Bantu term *zimu* or *dímu* is used to name ngoma spirits, as in the Venda *ngoma dza vadzimu,* but a range of other names or terms is used as well (see appendix B, section B.16).

We begin this review somewhat arbitrarily with an Nguni group in southern Mozambique, the Kalanga, studied by David Webster (1982). For them the "Ndau," "Ngudi," "Chikwembe," and "Majuta" are the four main groups of spirits. The Ndau, or Vandau, are considered the original ancestors of the Kalanga (a South Shona or Thonga group) and the most powerful spirit group, with a direct interest in the affairs of the living. Because of Henri Junod's work on the Thonga in the '30s, the Vandau have entered the anthropological literature as one of the major examples of "true shamanism" in Africa (De Heusch 1971:273–276). They are mentioned popularly in Tanzania as having inspired the N'anga cult, thus reflecting a thread of Nguni, or Ngoni, influence of early nineteenth-century conquest fame (Zaretsky and Shambaugh 1978). The Ngudi, associated with local affairs, are spirits inflicting traumatic disease who need to be placated to avert human disaster when they become involved. The Chikwembe are the ancestors of *isangoma* diviners. The Majuta are Arab spirits.

The distinction between lineal and alien spirits seen here is widespread. In nearby Swaziland the Emenlozi (literally, those one dreams about) are the personal ancestors and are often associated with white symbolism such as clay, white beads, white cloth, or with "mud," that is, the boundaries of water and earth. The Emenzawe and Benguni spirits are those whom Swazi warriors killed in previous wars. The Emenzawe prefer the red beads, the Benguni the white. The Emenzawe, Benguni, and Dinzunzu possess diviners. The Dinzunzu or Tinzunzu are those spirits of the water who died of drowning; they also are associated with white beads. These fields articulate Swazi culture and consciousness.

In the Xhosa region of South Africa, and in the urban extensions of Xhosa culture, spirits are commonly identified as being those pertaining to the family or clan, those of the water, and those of the land or of the forest. Clan ancestors are important to keep in touch with, but they do not inflict illness. The ngoma practitioners, the amagqira, are called (twasa) by the forest and water spirits, and are represented in igqira costumes by animal skins and colored beads, in medicines by plants and mineral ingredients, and in ngoma songs by mediatory imagery such as the crab, the horse, or birds.

In coastal Tanzania the distinctions of spirit geography always hinge on the land/water dichotomy. Like the Southern African spirit cosmologies, this one, too, identifies spirits of the trees and shrubs, that is, the forest, with the land. In the urban Dar es Salaam setting immigrant waganga (healers) from the interior, predictably, are specialized in "interior" spirits, and in the corresponding ngoma such as Manianga, N'anga, and Mbungi, whereas waganga from coastal areas relate to coastal or water spirits. The vocabulary of the Swahili coast has adopted Arabic terms *masheitani* and *majini* to speak of spirits. The spirits of the interior carry African names such as Mchela, Matimbuna, Mbongoloni, Chenjelu, and Kimbangalugomi (related to Ngoma Mbungi), whereas those of the beach or the water carry such names as Maruhani, Subiyani, and Mzuka (related to Ngoma Msaghiro). The colors red, white, and black also occur on beads worn over the shoulder of the mganga (healer), and in costumes.

The notion of "spirit fields" has been used by a number of authors to describe the organization of African spirits. It is an analogy of the concept "social field" used by Bateson and Turner long ago. Although some hermeneutic scholars such as Lambek (1981) insist that the spirits have little to do with social categories and forces, many other scholars prefer a Durkheimian correspondence theory between religion and society, economy, historical change, and psychological states. This permits scholars at least an opening hypothesis with which to assess such phenomena as the apparent shift in emphasis from lineal ancestors to more distant and alien spirits in recent decades. Thus the decline of certain local rites and the ascendance of others, or the rise and decline in many historic examples of spirit-possession rituals and cults, may be explained in terms of historical social forces and the changes that have occurred. For example, the breakdown of specific rituals in the late nineteenth and early twentieth centuries has been explained by the opening up of social relations and the expansion of the scale of known spheres of influence (Werbner 1977). Similarly, worldview as reflected in the understanding and treating of affliction reflects, in turn, changing social forces. It explains, for example, the generalization of symptom/sign and etiology relations in the context of the Lemba rite in western Congo over the period from the seventeenth century to the early twentieth century in the corridor of the great trade between coastal port towns of Cabinda, Loango, and Malemba, and the great market at Mpumbu near today's Kinshasa. Lemba's sufferers are said to have had a random variety of afflictions. Even the spirits behind the afflicting and therapeutic rites varied from region to region, indicative, I think, of the tremendous upheavals of the hour.

A brief review of the manner in which spirit or ancestor forces are aligned with social contextual disorders in contemporary urban settings suggests a trend toward greater reliance upon more broadly based, generalized in theme, symbolic figures, and a waning of local or lineage ancestors. Byamungu's overview of therapeutic rites in Bukavu, in eastern Zaire, shows the association of signs and symptoms to spirit nosology. In the Kakozi rite, present among Bashi (Rwandaise) and Lega inhabitants, all sorts of behavioral and physiological afflictions are attributed to "red" ancestral spirits or shades; red is also the color of the hair and clothing of the adepts. In the Enaama (also Mana) rite, found exclusively among the Bashi, a more open range of symptoms—for example, behavioral disorders, severe alienation, loss of appetite, and physical illness—is attributed to the Enaama nature spirits who frequently drive the afflicted to prolonged periods of wandering in solitude in the bush. In the Mitumba rite, among the Bemba and Lega, a similar wide variety of symptoms and signs is attributed to spirits of Europeans, that is, aliens, originally revealed or manifested in dreams and visions, and whose visitations are accompanied by loss of consciousness during possession; adepts of Mitumba spirits speak Swahili and smoke cigarettes. In the Mulangoyi rite, among the Lega, Zinga, and Songe residents of Bukavu, a variety of symptoms and signs is attributed to nature or water spirits, who in the possessed mediums present themselves in the Kisonge language, painted "white," eating earthworms,

toads, and so on. Finally, in the Nyamulemule rite, among the Batembo and Bashi of the city, Swahili-speaking spirits of Baluba ancestral
figures—whose songs are also sung in Lega and Tembo—afflict individuals who are recruited to therapeutic seances.

The Bukavu setting shows an opening up of the "spirit field" to a
wide variety of nature, ancestral, and alien spirits in a setting of ethnic
pluralism and an expanded scale of social relations characteristic of this
eastern Zaire and wider Eastern African setting.

However, the presence of spirits who represent the influences of
nature (particularly rivers) and aliens (Baluba, Europeans, Swahili-
speakers) in connection with behavioral troubles, alienation, and, in
the case of Mitumba, loss of consciousness in visions of Europeans,
introduces into the "spirit field" an attempt to deal with behavioral
pathology and its contextual causes. Although one may still invoke a
Durkheimian correspondence analysis between expanding scale of relations and behavioral pathologies resulting from strained role expectations and fulfillments, the more interesting issue is the possible correspondence between particular types of spirits and an indigenous
analysis of psychopathology and the appropriate therapeutic response.
Harriet Sibisi's work is suggestive in this regard.

Sibisi (1976) notes that Zulu sangoma, legitimated by a "call" from
their direct lineal ancestors, tend to analyze possession by nature spirits
and alien spirits as evidence of abnormalities. In their therapeutic interventions in these cases they strive to replace these "spirits of chaos"
with a more normative spirit patronage by ancestors, to fill a role in
ritual leadership. The sangoma therapist must thus identify the rehabilitative or reintegrative potential of a client before turning that client
in the direction of an initiation to the healer role. Indeed, the distinction
between pathological possession and ancestral call is made clear in
Nguni nosology: *mfufunyani* possession by chaotic spirits is a sign of
madness, whereas *ukutwasa* is a possession or call that leads to personal
strength and leadership in the sangoma or igqira. In the Southern African setting the symbolism of *ukutwasa* may also frequently be channeled into Christian fulfillment in Zionist prophet-healing churches, or
even in mainstream church roles, whereas *mfufunyani* cases may be
taken to a range of Western psychotherapists and African healers for
treatment.

Despite the logical elegance of Sibisi's interpretation of Zulu diagnostic categories, and its clear "fit" with the South African ethnographic data from Natal, the Western Cape, and probably other areas

in between, it adheres a little too closely to a sociological correspondence theory to account for all the ethnographic evidence of the entire area across which ngoma-type therapies are found. In particular, it does not seem to explain the cases in which, as in several of the Bukavu rites (Enaama and Mitumba), alien spirits are the principal symbols of therapeutic rehabilitative orders; or, closer to the basis of Sibisi's work, in Swazi ngoma, in which numerous types of alien spirits are used to inspire divination and healing. The Swazi instance is particularly challenging, since Swazi sangoma are considered part of the Nguni-speaking group and share most of the features of the religious and therapeutic tradition with the Zulu and Xhosa.

In addition to patronage by their lineal ancestor shades, the *amadloti,* Swazi sangoma feature patronage by the Benguni "white" spirits, who are the victims of Swazi wars with Zulu, Tsonga, and Shangani and who inspire divination with bones; the Amanzawe "red" nature spirits who inspire mediumistic divination; and both "red" and "white" Tinzunzu spirits of those who have drowned in rivers. Mediumistic work with Benguni victim spirits seems to be a recent development in Swaziland. Zulu-type sangoma diviner-healers have been in many regions replaced by "red" takoza mediums. In their more powerful forms of divining they put aside their bones and their attentive ear for very dramatic trance-possession dances of Amanzawe and Tinzunzu nature, and Benguni alien spirits.

To take Sibisi's analysis strictly, these Swazi takoza diviner-healers, as well as some of the Bukavu therapists, would be indulging in dissonant, and according to her, "charlatanistic," practice. And yet the appearance of nonancestral spirits and their mediums has become very widespread. Alternatively, to assume that therapists ignore the social forces of alienation and dislocation when they continue to attribute sickness to ancestral calls (particularly those that are considered amenable to integrative leadership roles), is to underestimate the skill of these talented individuals working often in extremely strained social settings such as in the Western Cape.

The anthropological analysis of the relationship of a "spirit field" to the social context of affliction needs one further analytical parameter beyond those of social scale (i.e., localized vs. regional or cosmopolitan) and of normalcy (i.e., role normalcy vs. situations precipitating abnormal response to role expectations) to explain the relevant variables of recourse to spirit nosology. I have in mind the place in affliction diagnosis hinging on the degree of ambiguity versus clarity in the overall perception of a social situation or a view of reality (Bernstein in Douglas 1970).

Bernstein's major point, taken over by Douglas, is that in the absence of a clear understanding of a phenomenon, in this instance the cause of affliction, one tends to formulate names, configurations, or stereotypes to compensate for the fuzziness. Following this line of thought, an escalation toward alien or chaotic spirit forces would be used in divination or therapy to come to grips with strange and new issues in a social situation. This hypothesis applies directly to the contrasting types of ngoma spirit manifestation in Southern Africa, notably the Western Cape and Swaziland.

In the Western Cape the challenge facing ngoma diviners and therapists is not an analysis of the situation before them; that is clear enough. Families are divided, and there is general anxiety regarding gainful employment. The major challenge is that of building up a cohesive social fabric out of the fragments of families and interpersonal relations. Accordingly, diviner-therapists forge a network of links within their ranks that bring fragmented individual lives and family segments into some more coherent and supportive arrangement. In Swaziland, there is generally greater economic security and much less anxiety about residence, freedom of movement, and one's personal welfare. Swaziland has one of the highest per capita incomes in black Africa—$800 per person in 1982, near that of Gabon and Cameroon. And yet, this very sense of economic development contains the ingredients to dissolve the normative order. Wage labor, urbanization, and education have had a significant impact upon Swazi society, creating enormous opportunities for upward mobility and prestigious jobs, especially for young adults. It has become common for young women to eschew marriage for professional work and to have a child or two out of wedlock along the way. Furthermore, the economic opportunities of Swaziland have inundated the country with outsiders, such as development experts, tourists, teachers, and traders. Thus, although there is not the material insecurity of the Western Cape and the threat to one's domestic living arrangement, economic development has unleashed other threats to the established cognitive order. This may account for the more aggressive spirit field in Swaziland, in which the spirits of bone-throwing divination (the *amadloti* and Benguni ancestors) have been partially supplanted by the spirits of trance and possession divination (the Emanzawe and Tinzunzu).

It is evident, then, that "spirit fields" provide a set of parameters having to do with worldview, order and chaos, legitimacy, and cultural categories against which to align, and begin to deal with, personal problems.

THE COURSE THROUGH THE WHITE

Therapeutic attention to affliction, through ngoma, often entails elements of initiation of the afflicted into membership, resulting in the elevation of the afflicted to the status of priest or healer in the group. Whether or not this actually happens (there are many dropouts) depends on the novice's progress through early states of therapy and counseling, on the novice's or kin's means, and the extent to which the cult is controlled by an elite that restricts access to its basic resources.

Across the ngoma region, whiteness defines the special transitional status of the sufferer-novice in the course toward health. It is expressed by the use of clay or chalk, cloth, beads, rafia, and other material indicators. In Western Bantu this concept is identified by derivations of the proto-Bantu cognate *pémbà* (see appendix B, section B.13). In Nguni-speaking Southern Africa the term *ikota* is used for white, but it is not clear how widespread this term is. In any event, whiteness is the color and dominant symbol of the transitional stage that denotes purity, separateness, isolation, the liminal zone between sickness and health, the condition of being sick. Some ngoma-type therapeutic settings become involved with red and black symbolism, often denoting exposure to alien or less familiar nature spirits.

Stages that articulate phases in the "white" may vary from two to as many as eight, each of which may endure from a few days to many years. In the Western Cape, for example, the stages of this progression begin with (1) being diagnosed as twasa, possessed or called by a spirit; (2) becoming a novice (*nkwetha*) following the initiation, and joining a sodality under the counseling of a senior diviner-healer; (3) moving through the "course," becoming a senior, a "five-to" (i.e., "five to midnight," almost completed), and being entrusted with aspects of ritual; (4) fully qualified, completing the course, graduating as a sangoma or in Xhosa, igqira.

Clothing and bodily paint indicate the progression through the white. Initially, the novice is fully smeared in white chalk or wears a white cloth. Gradually, over the course of time, colors replace whiteness; the costume of a fully qualified igqira/sangoma provides a medium for the self-definition and articulation of the new person.

Initially, face and body are smeared in white during the events of initiation. Two single strands of white beads, and the bladder of a goat, are worn around the head; bead strands are also put on each wrist. In time, more strands of white beads are added. The groups of amakwetha (novices) of a diviner-healer may be seen as a uniformed group, together, dancing, singing, in counsel, in isolation. However, as their therapeutic initiation moves to its final stages and they become more self-confident, they may paint only their cheeks and eyes. When fully qualified, only the eyes remain encircled with "white." Colorful beads and other headdress and costume elements, dreamed or creatively thought out, now replace the white. At this later phase, the fur of wild animals such as puma, cheetah, leopard, lion, beaver, and others re-places the strands of goat hair. Colorful blankets replace the white sheets.

The early novitiate phase is also signaled by the ownership of a forked stirring stick, used initially to bring the *ubulau* (medicine) to a frothy white whenever the ancestors or spirits are called in and the novice is smeared. This stick, which is also used as a dance wand, is replaced after graduation with a colorful, beaded dance wand compa-rable to the widespread Nguni knobkerrie.

This progression of exterior process of clothing, body paint, and arti-fact parallels the inner process that the novice has gone through and of social changes that significant others have created around the novice. The course through the white is the framework of the sick role. Initially, there is a marked withdrawal of self and individuality from the social setting, although often the family that assumes responsibility for the pa-tronage of a diviner-healer shows the support and care they have for the individual sufferer. During this phase the sufferer must acquiesce to ancestors and social others. The death of the sacrificial goat sym-bolizes the death of the sufferer's self, in exchange for a new life and identity. In the early counseling and therapies the sufferer-novice is passive, receiving songs from others. Then, as he or she develops skills in dreaming and handling spirits—that is, channeling the chaotic visions and dreams of the twasa (call) experience—the costume begins to show bits of color, of identity. Accompanying this outward manifestation of dreaming, of messages about the self, is the emergence of the novice's own songs, composed also from dream impulses. The initial passivity is replaced by a statement of ego strength as the novice composes, sings, and teaches others his or her song.

At the close, as the novice becomes a "five-to," ready for graduation, she or he should have a strong self-projection, capability in leading others in therapeutic dance and song, as well as a firmer control over his or her own life than before. The final graduation feast, marked by the sacrifice of a cow or bull and the making of a colorful dance wand, indicates the culmination of the course through the white. The next chapter will study the role of the ngoma song in this process.

The efficacy of the therapy, regardless of its specific techniques, is partially assured because all in the community feel shared affliction and support the sufferer, even though not all the community is kin. In most instances of prolonged sickness in African society, diagnosis and decision relating to the course of healing—"the quest for therapy"—are in the hands of a lay kin therapy managing group. In the cases that come into the orbit of cults of affliction, the support community broadens to become that of the cult members. The quality of support shifts from ad hoc kin aid to that of permanent involvement with such a network in the initiate-novice's life, corresponding to the long-term involvement of the individual with the affliction, as a healer-priest.

Some cults of affliction, such as Nkita among the Kongo peoples of western Zaire, are situated within lineages. Nkita responds to the unique circumstances and symptoms of children's sicknesses and barren women amid the stresses and fears of lineage segmentation. The imputation of a cluster of Nkita afflicted within a lineage segment provides the rationale and the setting for the regeneration of lineage organization; members are reaffiliated with the ancestral source of their collective authority.

Most cults of affliction, however, occur outside the kin setting, functioning as an addition to kin relations, and give the individual lifelong ties with others along the lines of the new affliction or occupation-specific community. The various Southern Savanna reproduction-enhancing ngoma—such as Mbombo (Goblet-Vanormelingen 1988); Isoma, Wubwangu, and Kula (Turner 1968); and unnamed *mahamba* among the Luvale (Spring 1978)—which isolate women with reproductive problems or during pregnancy and childbirth, radicalize the separation of novices from their kin. The rationale for this separation has to do with the danger of the stresses of daily life and family relations upon the fetus. The white symbolism of clothing and the *mpemba* chalk applied to the face and other places in the seclusion compound suggest the liminal special quality of this role. It is liminal, also, because the normal conjugal life of the novice has been interrupted to achieve an end that will enhance that conjugal life.

The social dimension of "the white" may vary in its particulars from occurring within lineage and family to removal from it. The common core beneath this is, however, that it usually represents a contrast from the prior state and brings the individual into touch with ritual experts who rebuild the individual's identity around a solution to the problem or affliction.

SACRIFICE AND EXCHANGE

Sacrifice of mammals and birds is widely present in the ngoma process of personal transformation. Particular illustrations of this are found in Lemba, where the chickens and pigs are killed at appropriate junctures of the novice's course. This sacrifice seems to occur most often at the initial entry into the course through the white and at graduation. It occurs at the close of the day/night/day event. It also occurs in the Southern African setting, as witnessed by the instances in Cape Town described in chapter 1: a goat at the time of an entry, a goat or a sheep at the time of a healer's or novice's purification, and a cow at the time of a graduation.

Why is sacrifice so important in the commemoration of ritual transition, in the moment of sickness? Victor Turner, in explaining the importance of sacrifice in ngoma rituals among the Ndembu, begins with the repetitive, or cyclical, nature of life in the society. Some of these features are due to the agrarian context of the Ndembu, who yearly plant their crops and harvest them. However, most of the drums of affliction are focused on the human life course, in which moments such as birth, adolescence, the varied conflicts and afflictions of adulthood, and death, need to be addressed. Ndembu society is involved in change, but the core of society, its values and patterns and ideals, are thought of as if they should remain constant. The rituals of affliction seek to return to that constancy, by subsuming misfortune to the permanence of the invisible spirit world. Misfortune that results from conflict creates victims. The sacrificial victim, in the abstract sense of a substitutionary victim, lets the conflict, the anger, so to speak "have its blood." To offer a sacrificial animal also purifies the universe in that it restores or regenerates the human community to its ideals. "At the moment when the wheel has come a full circle, [sacrifice] sets the cycle going again" (Turner 1968:276).

This is basically an "atonement" view of sacrifice, in which the violence in human society can be overcome through its symbolic manifestation in the victim. This is not far from the Judeo-Christian sacrificial tradition in which lambs, or first sons, are offered for the expiation of human sins.

Although the atonement notion of sacrifice is present in ngoma sacrifice, as the account of the case study of initiation in Cape Town related in chapter 1 suggests, there is another dimension to ngoma sacrifices that justifies an exchange concept of sacrifice. Having attended a few sacrifices in Africa, including that described in chapter 1, I can attest that there is a significant ritual economic dimension at work. The "horizontal" dimension of the distribution of food and the common meal that includes the consumption of the sacrificial animal represent as much a "communion" as a religious atonement. Together they bring out a social dimension that Turner does not specifically mention, namely, the beginning or the renewal of exchange relationships between individuals and social units that are at the basis of ongoing social relations. The nature of these networks that are created and celebrated in connection with the sacrifices will be explored more fully in chapter 6. Also, in the sacrifices of sheep, goats, and cattle, the red meat protein is significant in the diet of those attending.

A communal meal following an all-night communal dance applies tremendous energies to the reconstitution of the social whole that is assembled. This leads directly to the final core feature, the belief that misfortune, adversity, and affliction may be transformed into power and wholeness. There is a strong insistence in ngoma theorizing that singing, sacrifice, and communing turn life around and literally bring life out of death.

THE SUFFERER BECOMES THE HEALER

The lyrics of ngoma songs echo this core feature, as in this song from ancient Lemba on the Kongo coast: "That which was the sickness, has become the path to the priesthood." From the Western Cape: "Let darkness turn to light." The single most characteristic feature of ngoma is this transformation of the negative, disintegrative affliction into positive, integrative wholeness. There are, of course, other religious and therapeutic traditions in which this occurs. One thinks of the Western self-help orders, even psychiatry, in which the student receives psycho-analysis before being able to practice.

In the several local traditions of ngoma which have been used re-peatedly to illustrate the genre in this book, we have seen a variety of applications of this theme of transformation. Barrenness and threatened miscarriages give way to techniques for fertility and child care in the Southern Savanna and Western Bantu settings. In the Kinshasa urban setting, the trapped-wife syndrome is replaced by membership in the Zebola network of the formerly isolated. In western Tanzania, snake-bite is turned into knowledge of the use of venom for immuniza-tion. In Southern Africa, the chaos of rapid industrialization feeds the enhancement of divination techniques; the fragmentation of the family household leads to the amplification of networks linking fragile households.

The energy that comes to the afflicted from joining those who have "been there" and who have survived or recovered, or at least learned to cope with the affliction, often is represented in so-called "medicines" of office such as the *kici* of Western Bantu, or the *kobe* of Central Af-rica. Acquiring these medicines, or charms, or techniques, is part of the end stage of "the white," either generated by the novice during the long course of therapeutic training, or assembled at the time of his or her "graduation." Many times these medicines are outright magical or metaphorical mementos of the affliction, mementos that through as-sociation with material objects from cosmological, vegetal, animal, or human domains become statements about the condition of the novice. I come back to this process in chapter 5 and interpret it further under the rubric of "metaphors of difficult experience."

Much of the empowerment of ngoma is, however, in the newly ac-quired ability of the afflicted to meet specific or general problems with resolve. This often entails the adoption of a healer-prescribed prohibi-tion or rule, illustrating the proto-Bantu concept *gìdò*. As we will see, the personal song, developed through dream study, and through sharing ngoma with one's fellows, also plays an important part. Subsequent chapters will explore this further.

CONCLUSION

The core features of ngoma presented in this chapter are relatively static features. On their own they are merely aspects of the wider gen-eral culture or set of behaviors. Therefore we must stress that they are not to be taken too literally as *the* attributes of ngoma everywhere or that where they are identified, they have to do with ngoma. Together they reveal significant characteristics with which to understand how ngoma-type affliction and healing is organized.

The features discussed in this chapter are usually not identified by descriptive indigenous terms, although I have been able in some cases to relate them to proto-Bantu cognates. On balance, much of the most characteristic behavior in ngoma does not correlate strictly with a given vocabulary. It can be described, discussed, and interpreted, but it is not locked into a technical fixed vocabulary. This would suggest that the phenomenologist's constraint of studying only that which is consciously and verbally identified would be ill-advised, and that a culture's reality, while it may be described and shaped by language, is certainly not limited to verbal cognates.

Verbal cognates and these core features come together in a poignant action-term, "doing ngoma," to which we turn next.

4

Doing Ngoma

The Texture of Personal Transformation

Kuphilwa ngamutu. "We survive because of each other."
Xhosa proverb applied to ngoma

Mpimpa yoyo bana kina nkununu yanene nate ye bwisi bu kiedi. "This same night all dance a big Nkununu dance that ends at the break of day."
Kwamba Elie, Kongo ethnographer,
describing a Lemba gathering in 1912

"Doing ngoma" is the central event in ngoma. It is the "dominant trope," the "symbol that stands for itself" (Wagner 1986:29–30) and defines the institution. "Doing ngoma" opens with a declarative statement, prayer, or utterance, then moves on to song begun by the one who makes the statement; as the call and song is developed, the surrounding people respond with clapping and soon singing begins en masse, and then the instruments enter in. This basic set of features, with many variations, may be found throughout the larger Central and Southern African setting. The Ndembu call it *kwimba ng'oma,* "to sing an ngoma" (Turner 1975:63). The Venda of the northern Transvaal also use the same verb to speak of *nyimbo dza dzingoma,* singing an ngoma, "drum" (Blacking 1985:41). The Kongo of Western Bantu "drum up" (*sika ngoma*) a major medicine with a song, *nkunga.* In the Nguni-speaking setting in Southern Africa, the *isangoma,* diviner-healer, is one who (*i-*) does (*sa*) ngoma. All of these references identify ngoma with patterned rhythm of words, the use of performance dance, and the invocations or the songs that articulate the affliction and the therapeutic rite.

Many song-dance performances punctuate the sufferer-novice's course through the white. Even after becoming a fully qualified healer, the practitioner participates continuously in ngoma sessions. This chapter presents a single important example of "doing ngoma." In both content and structure, this ngoma performance reveals that here, in the consciously formulated exchange of song-dance, and in the movement of the individual from sufferer-novice to accomplished, singing, self-projecting healer, lies the heart of the institution. I believe it is a classic—that is, ancient and formative—institution in Central and Southern African healing.

Unfortunately, it has been least well studied of all the aspects of African medicine. Many scholars have missed the mark, in a sense, emphasizing only a limited aspect of it. Some have singled out only the healer-patient relationship for attention; others, the symbols; yet others, the plants. Many have followed trance behavior and assumed it is the central point of the ritual, without putting it sufficiently into institutional context. Very few scholars of African medicine and religion have bothered to look at the music. Scholars of African music, for their part, have ignored the therapeutic qualities, and intentions, of this kind of music.

TEXT AND TEXTURE IN AFRICAN HEALING

Amandina Lihamba, in a recent article, "Health and the African Theatre," has described the relationship between health and performances of all kinds in Africa. "Health and disease are social phenomena with implications beyond the individual, the physical, and the present. Performances are often concerned with the maintenance of community and individual health, the prevention of ill health, and the restoration of health and with instilling survival knowledge" (1986:35). Examples include W. Soyinka writing about the cleansing of society, cosmic equilibrium, and society as sufferer; Muhando on the madness of social and economic success, and society causing sickness; and Hussein describing the evil of corruption, exploitation, oppression, and class divisions and aspirations as devils (*Mashetani*) who have infiltrated society and need to be exorcised for health to be restored. Ngoma provides the fabric of personal transformation; it helps sort through personal or societal experience with prevalent metaphors and other types of knowledge.

There may be no close analogue in Western civilization to these combined features of ngoma. Lihamba and others' reference to theater and performance are accurate. However, for illustrative purposes I shall for the moment argue that an approximation of such an analogue exists in the conjunction of Latin and Old French roots *textus, textere,* and *con-textus* or *contextere.* These terms provide a picture of a fabric of meanings pulled out of a context and put into words. *Textere* refers doubly to "weaving a fabric" in the technical sense of putting together the warp and weft of cloth, as well as to the original written or printed words of a literary work, a single text. The *con*-text is where the separate threads are brought together into one fabric.

Ngoma brings together the disparate elements of an individual's life threads and weaves them into a meaningful fabric. It does this, particularly, through devices of mutual "call and response" sharing of experience, of self-presentation, of articulation of common affliction, and of consensus over the nature of the problem and the course of action to take. The ngoma text is created over the course of many months and years and finally is presented formally at the time of the sufferer-novice's emergence as a fully ready healer. In another sense the text of self-presentation is never completed, for as long as the ngoma participant lives, there will be moments and times of self renewal, in the context of others.

"DOING NGOMA": THE CORE RITUAL UNIT

The song-dance of ngoma may last all night, as in the Kongo example at the head of the chapter. Such a session is made up of many shorter units of song: the self-presented and the response. In the Cape Town setting, which will be featured here, it may be repeated by the same person (usually with a different song), or someone else "takes up ngoma" and "does his or her ngoma"—*sa ngoma.* The sequence of such units may go on for hours. It may occur within the context of events heralded as purification celebrations for established healers or as celebrative points in the initiatory course of novices. The familiar group ngoma song presentations may be seen at a wide variety of events within the local ngoma network. An important variant of the sufferer-singer presenting his or her invocation and song is for another singer to present the "case" of the sufferer. This may occur in the instance of a very sick individual, someone who has not developed her or his song or who cannot perform, or a senior healer who has suffered the death of a close kinsman and is being ministered to.

The case that will be illustrated is from a "washing of the beads" of a senior igqira/sangoma in the Western Cape following the period of mourning of the death of her mother. Her sister and host of the event sang the leads, reiterating the death of their mother. The spoken openings to each unit narrated the days leading up to the death, details surrounding the death. It was thus in effect a requiem ngoma and a coming out of mourning of the descendant. Death is impure, but mourning and commemoration allow the ngoma practitioners to cleanse themselves and to "throw out the darkness" and to "wash the beads" with medicines—in Nguni pollution terminology, to replace darkness with light.

At the site of throwing out the darkness, outside, the same format is again repeated. For the spoken prayer parts, the novices (amakwetha) sit down for the declaration, then rise for the dancing and singing (fig. 9).

In the following pages I present a sequence of self-presentations (*ukunqula*) and song-dances (ngoma) performed at the above event, first among senior sangoma and amagqira of the Western Cape, followed by a session by their novices.[1]

1. *Ukunqula* [by the senior healer whose mother had died, and who was being cleansed]: *Sukube ndilthandenza ke xa kdisitsho kumama.* In so saying I'm praying to mother. We'll leave having washed each other [repeated many times]. *Kuphilwa ngamutu.* We survive [or live] because of each other. While we say we came to "heal" here.

   Ngoma: Bambulele umama . . . They killed mama.

2. *Ukunqula*: You would have thought that the night "war" would have calmed down this [igqira spirituality]. But no, it doesn't. I'm in it, always facing a white person [at work], and maybe that's why I'm "on edge."

   Ngoma: Balele phezu kweentaba zuLundi. The [ancestors] are sleeping at the top of the mountains of Ulundi.

3. *Ukunqula*: Let's *camagusha* now! Let darkness be replaced by light. Nizala [a relative], I want you to say for me to these amagqira and these visitors what we're here for, they're welcome.

   Ngoma [in Afrikaans]: *Wat makeer vandag, wat makeer?* What's happening today?

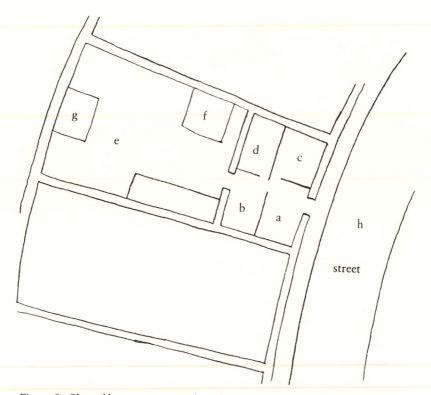

Figure 9. Plan of house, compound, and street in Cape Town township setting
where "doing ngoma" was performed, in the context of "washing of the
beads" of senior healer Adelheid Ndika following her mother's death:
(a) living room and intermediate ritual space where all ngoma sessions are
held, as well as "calling down ancestors"; (b) kitchen; (c) bedroom;
(d) storage room; (e) backyard; (f) subrenter shelter; (g) water tap, toilet;
(h) profane public space where "coming out" is held and where darkness
of pollution is "thrown away."

4. *Ukunqula*: *Hulle wil meet wat makeer vandag? Kaffirdans.* You
want to know what's happening here today? It's a Kaffir dance!
Let darkness be replaced by light.

   Ngoma: *Ndiyamthenda u Jesu; waklulula umoy a wam.* I love
   Jesus, he set free my soul.

5. *Ukunqula*: Let darkness be replaced by light. *Camagusha.* I thank
being welcome in this home, *camagu.* I was coronated in this home,
and the *isidlokolo* bushy hat was given to me here.

1. Young women and mothers of the lineage in procession, during Nkita rite in Kongo-Ntandu society, western Zaire. Photo archive, Institut des Musées Nationaux du Zaire.

2. Diversity of ngoma drums from the Congo Basin, Zaire: (a) with face of Mbuolo healing spirit, Yaka, Southwestern Zaire, Institut des Musees National du Zaire (IMNZ) 71.138.1 (59 cm. tall, 28 cm. wide); (b) Tshokwe-Lunda, Kasai, IMNZ 71.22.13 (53 cm. tall); from the collections of the Royal Museum of Central Africa, Tervuren (RMCA) and published in Olga Boone, *Les tambours du Congo belge et du Ruanda-Urundi,* 1951; (c) RMCA 38828, Luluwa, Kasai, 52 × 35 cm., collected 1939 (Boone plate VIII/34, "ngoma"); (d) RMCA 31696, Tabwa, Southeast Zaire, 28 × 27 cm., prior to 1882–1885 (Boone VI/12, "ngoma"); (e) RMCA 8977, Kusu, Maniema, 65 × 36 cm., before 1902 (Boone VI/2 "ngoma"); (f) RMCA 48.20.107, Hungana, Southwestern Zaire, 98 × 33 cm., before 1948 (Boone XIII/10); (g) RMCA 27729, Lele, Kasai, 98 × 28 cm., before 1924 (Boone XXXVIII/5); (h) RMCA 37955, Hutu, Rutshuru, Kivu, 83 × 41 cm. (Boone XXVII/7, "ingoma" or "impuruzu"), the thong-tied drum beaten with stick shown here, typical of northern forest and West African region, but with form and name of "ngoma" area. The faced drums articulate visually the idea of the spirit-rhythm in ngoma. Photographs c–h courtesy Section of Ethnography, Royal Museum of Central Africa, 3080 TERVUREN, Belgium.

a.

f.

e.

b.

c.

d.

g.

h.

3. Kishi Nzembela, of Kinshasa, Zaire, before painting of her late daughter Janet, for whom she is a medium in Bilumbu, a ritual of Luba origin. Photo by J. M. Janzen, 1982.

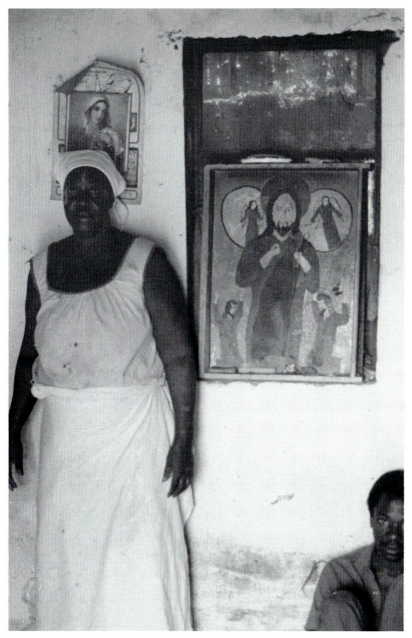

4. Kishi Nzembela, a Catholic, stands before this painting of Jesus in her healing chapel in her home compound in Kinshasa. Photo by J. M. Janzen, 1982.

5.   Pregnant woman "in seclusion" as part of reproduction enhancing ngoma among the Chokwe of Zaire, Southern Savanna. This is comparable to ngoma Mpombo in the South Kasai. Photo by J. M. Janzen, 1959.

6.   At Betani, the diviners' college, eight *tigomene* drums of cowhide over segments of oil drums lie in the sun to tighten the hide for the next performance. They will be used in mediumistic takoza divination ceremonies to reveal the causes of distress for clients. Photo by J. M. Janzen, 1982.

7. Tanzanian mganga Botoli Laie of Dar es Salaam demonstrates and displays paraphernalia for ngoma Mbungi: five ngoma drums, two wooden double gongs, and medicine
basket. Photo by J. M. Janzen, 1983.

8. An example of ngoma as secularized entertainment, performed by the Baraguma ngoma troupe of Bagamoyo, here doing the Sindimba dance at the Almana nightclub in Dar es Salaam, Tanzania. Instruments include ngoma, other drums, and xylophone. Photo by J. M. Janzen, 1983.

9. Senior novice in Ida Mabuza's college in Betani, Swaziland, performs pengula bone-throwing divination, widespread in Southern Africa, before a client (right) and a colleague (left) who indicates agreement or disagreement with each declaration by the diviner. Photo by J. M. Janzen, 1982.

10. A group of novices (*amakwetha*) in white performing an ngoma on the street in Guguleto township, South Africa, at the time of a "washing of the beads" purification for igqira Adelheid Ndika. Photo by J. M. Janzen, 1982.

11. Cowhide over oil drum is here used in an ngoma session in Guguleto, Cape Town, South Africa. It is drummed by a novice (*nkwetha*) who has her head bound with two strands of white beads to indicate that she is "in the white." She is accompanied by a hand-clapping noninitiate. Photo by J. M. Janzen, 1982.

12. Two novices (*amakwetha*) participate in ngoma session in Guguleto, Cape Town. They are part of a close circle of novices who are "presenting themselves" in call-and-response performance. The script of this event is given in chapter 5. Photo by J. M. Janzen, 1982.

13.   Ngoma session presented in chapter 5 was led by this woman, a just-graduated igqira (healer) whose manner of leading the others out, of dancing, and of bringing the participants together was as striking as is her composure in the picture. The beadwork is the beginning of her igqira costume, which began with a few strands of white beads when she was a novice and will flower into a colorful full costume. Photo by J. M. Janzen, 1982.

14. A "white" novice serenely watches others in ngoma performance after having presented herself to others in evocation, prayer, song, and dance. Photo by J. M. Janzen, 1982.

15. Preparing to "throw out the darkness," the pollution of death of a novice's kinsman. Igqira Golden Majola distributes tobacco to his novices, which they will throw into the waters of the Indian Ocean near Cape Town to the accompaniment of a singing and drumming ngoma. Photo by J. M. Janzen, 1982.

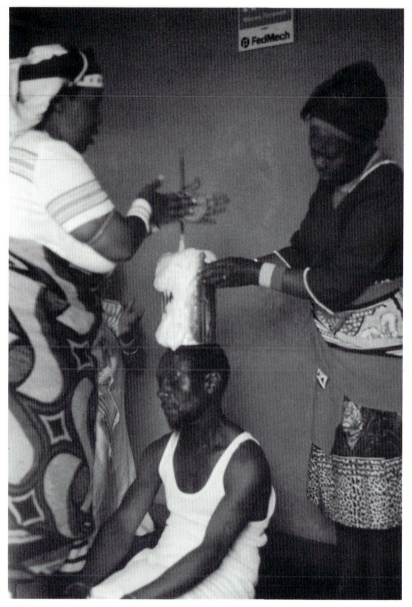

16.   Amagqira Adelheid Ndika (left) and helper (right) stir the *ubulau* medicine of entry into "the white" at the outset of the sufferer's novitiate. Photo by J. M. Janzen, 1982.

17.   Later, after the goat sacrifice and the all-night ngoma, the opening phase of ngoma initiation is concluded with ngoma sessions on the street of Guguleto, a black township near Cape Town. The "white" novice is seated in the foreground while fully qualified amagqira take turns encouraging him with song-dance ngoma. Photo by J. M. Janzen, 1982.

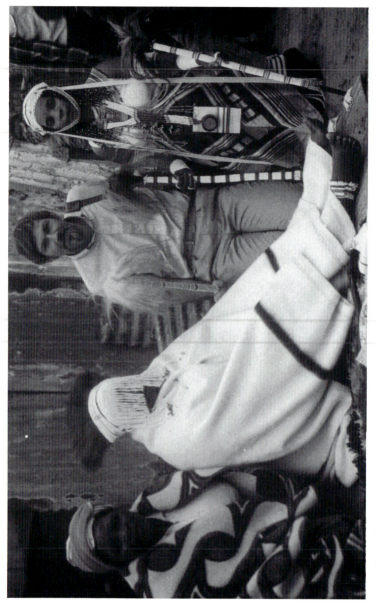

18. The author kneeling between the graduating still-veiled novice and her kinswoman (left) and her igqira healer (right), in Guguleto township. Photo by Reinhild Janzen, 1982.

Ngoma: I love Jesus, he set free my soul.

6. *Ukunqula*: Mzala, I thank what you've done, saying sorry after "sinning," consulting those above you.

Ngoma: I love Jesus, he set free my soul.

7. *Ukunqula*: We came to uncover the wound, and thereafter take some oil and anoint it. I, too, came to say: Let the wound be healed. The amagqira have spoken well.

Ngoma: I love Jesus, he set free my soul.

The basic call-and-response structure of the ukunqula/ngoma pattern is enriched by a rhythm between speaking and singing. Afrikaans, English, Xhosa, Zulu, and Swazi evocations and songs in these two sessions are a particularly poignant reminder of the cleavages and cosmopolitan diversity of South African society. Especially touching are the exchanges in Afrikaans (#3, #4) that may have been prompted by my presence with several members of my family. One of the senior igqira in evocation number 3 asks the others to tell "why we're here." That is followed by an ngoma in Afrikaans: "What's happening here?" The next *ukunqula* (#4) responds that it's a *kaffirdans*. This demonstrates the power of the medium to absorb the condescending attitude of white South Africa toward an African institution. The exchange is, however, intended to be ironic. *Ukunqula* number 2 also touches on the role of ngoma in helping these amagqira deal with the racial tension in their society. This woman was a domestic worker in a white home, and she complained to us of her low wages for long, hard working hours despite many years of seniority. She used the ngoma session to tell the others, and her ancestors, that this is what made her "on edge," or spiritually "sharp."

The repetition of the ngoma "I love Jesus . . ." from Zionist singing, demonstrates the influence of Christianity, but it also suggests that it is difficult to draw a line separating "African" from "Christian" reference points. However, ngomas 1, 2, and 7 are in a more conventional idiom.

After shaking off the *isimnyama,* pollution, as a result of the death, and singing-praying for the igqira, the second ngoma session follows for the novices. A just-graduated, fully qualified igqira (the woman in the blue and black striped sweater, plate 13) leads this session. (Plates 10, 11, and 12 portray this event.) She opens with a song-dance.

Ngoma: Simonwoya. We have spirit . . .

8. *Ukunqula* [by a boy novice]: Ka Ngwane [ancestors], hear me.

    Ngoma: Mombeleleni, unonkala, ngasemlanjeni. Sing and clap for the crab next to the river.

    Ngoma: He Majola [clan name], phuma e jele. Majola, come out of jail. *Ndinendabe zonzi wakho.* I have news of your house. (See fig. 10.)

    [One of the persons in the circle points to another who is sick, a novice.] We are giving [the song, ngoma] over to you mother, *camagu.*

    Ngoma: . . . eluhambeni. . . . in a trip [inaudible].

9. *Ukunqula:* I ask for protection from my people [ancestors], the Radebes and the Mtinikulus.

    Ngoma: [call] *Akulalwa ezweni akulalwa;* [response] *akulalwa akulalwa ezweni. . . .*

    Ngoma: He Majola phuma entelakweni, ndinendaba zonzi wakho. Majola come out of confinement (lit. "the pot"), I have news of your household. *Camagu!*

    Ngoma: Hey Majola, come out, I have news of your household.

10. *Ukunqula:* Let darkness be replaced by light. I call on my ancestors. This igqira was handed me by a parent while living. I take after my grandmother, and use one of the *eyezeni* medicines. I resemble an igqira of igqiras, a truly authentic one. The white bones over which death lies, I approached them with my back turned to them, that they not be resentful of me. May the drug be revealed to me, so that as an igqira I may be able to say the truth after kneeling before my clients.

    Ngoma: Khawuhibe igqira. Go, go igqira.

11. *Ukunqula:* Since I almost left this ceremony without coming forth to say something, I might fall sick after leaving this house. May I sing.

Figure 10. Spatial layout of "doing ngoma" in living room of home depicted in figure 9; (a) all participants in living room; (b) circle of amakwetha (novices); (c) fully qualified igqira (healer) who leads session; actors in the ritual unit once session has begun: (d) in left-hand scheme, novice presents *ukunqula*; (e) other novice or leader responds to self-presentation, and leads in song-dance, as shown in right-hand scheme.

Ngoma: Ndine thumba lam lokuthandaza. I have my time to pray.

Ndinendawo yam yokuthandaza. I have my place to pray.

12. *Ukunqula: Camagusha!* Let us remember what we are here for. To *ukuhlamba*, purification. I have very little with me. [Response] *Camagu.* Let the darkness be replaced by light! [Response] *Camagu.* I pray for a drug, that it may do its work. May it be there, as far as the caves, the river, from where it comes, and where its roots are ground on a stone to make medicine of it. I am also here to pray to God. May this home of the Makwayis have the darkness replaced by light.

Ngoma: Andimanto esandleni, ndize kanye Nkosi. Sendondele ekrusini, ekubethelweni. I have nothing at hand, I come once Lord . . .

13. *Ukunqula:* When I'm here, presenting myself, I think back to my mother's home, at the KwaNguni, and the way they said, "Let darkness be replaced by light." *Ndiyanqula ndiyathendaza, camagwini?* [Response] *Camagu.* I admit that I take pills when I come to a ceremony [*inthlombe*] because it makes me sick. May darkness be replaced by light. My people should not worry that I'm doing

this *ukunqul* presentation. I'll lead in my song and then hand the ngoma over.

Ngoma: *Andiyoyiki le ntwaza na ingangani.* I am not afraid of this girl who is as big as myself. [Response] *Camagu*.

14. *Ukunqula*: I am hard-pressed by rental fees and many other things. I had to take from my children, asked them to give me some soap, for the young women here to smell good.

Ngoma: Blessed be the name of the Lord [in English].

Ngoma: *Yomelelani kunzima emhlabeni.* Be strong because it's hard here on earth.

15. *Ukunqula*: I come from afar. My home is in Swaziland, and I'm a visitor. I call on my ancestors.

Ngoma: [call] *Unwoya wam*; [response] *wankhulul'umoya wam.* My spirit, he set my spirit free.

Ngoma: *Ndize kuwe, undincede.* I am coming to you Lord for help.

Ngoma: *Sicel'i camagu.* We are requesting a *camagu*.

16. *Ukunqula*: I call upon my ancestors to let darkness be replaced by light. I am glad that the darkness that has been hanging over here could be removed, that broken hearts have been consoled. I thank all of God's children present, in the name and authority of Jesus. Hallelujah, might God give us power. May Jesus give the woman Maradebe power. Things are as they are, the wearing of white beads [novices who are initiated], because there is no peace in the world. Hallelujah, beloved ones, may God bless you.

Ngoma: *Themba lam ngu Yesu, ndozimele ngeye.* My hope is Jesus, I'll hide in him.

17. *Ukunqula*: I wish to be a sincere, honest igqira. If I can't diagnose something, I'll kneel down and pray in order to tell the truth. I want to stand atop of Table Mountain and be light to the people. May the darkness be replaced by light!

The spoken calls (*ukunqula*) and sung responses (ngoma), with drum and dance accompaniment, demonstrate the complex basis of this institution. There is a keen desire on the part of these novices (amakwetha) to be in touch with each other, as they put it, to *camagusha*. The phrases "let's *camagusha*" or the call "*camagu!*" followed by the response *camagusha* indicates before each ngoma unit a kind of ritual positioning to follow through. This call announces, in effect, "let's do an exchange," or "we have heard," "we have agreed." These verbal signals are important as rhetorical framing devices in the ngoma work at hand.

There is also evidence of deliberately handing the ngoma around, as it were, "being it." In set number 8 someone, it is not clear who, hands the song over to another woman.

The content of the individual declarations and songs varies widely, the former for the most part relating to the lives of particular individuals, their call, sickness experience, environment, their aspirations, whereas the latter, the songs, are more culturally standardized. A number of *ukunqula* evocations call on ancestors for help and solace. We see from the names mentioned that this is a varied group of novices from across Southern Africa. Clan names such as Ka Ngwane from the Eastern Transvaal (#8), Radebe and Mtinikulu (#9), the generic KwaNguni (#13) are mentioned. One says she is from Swaziland. The ancestors are invoked in a general sense here, which differs from identification with particular ancestors in other regions of Central and Southern Africa (e.g., Fry among the Zezuru, or Turner among the Ndembu). There is also indirect and direct reference to natural domains of land and water and to mediators across these domains. The young boy (#8), following his *ukunqula*, sings out the "crab song" and others join in. This is a commonly heard ngoma both in Southern Africa and elsewhere (the term *nkala* for crab is very widespread, as is the reference to the crab as a mediator). The crab burrows in the beach sand and scurries into the water when discovered. It is the perfect natural reference for a spiritual metaphor bridging land, the domain of humans, with water, the domain of ancestors and spirits. Similarly, there is reference to plants and drugs (e.g., #12) found in caves and along rivers, mediatory zones, that are used to enhance the ngoma process of "coming out" and "sharing" and "presenting" oneself.

Most of the novices express a concern for articulating their inner conflicts, getting their words out. Songs in numbers 8 and 9 mention a Majola who is implored to "come out of his confinement"—literally a pot—because they have news to share with him. This image of a person being in a jail, or a prison, or a "pot," is an intriguing one for the person who is trying to clarify his situation. Another image common in this occasion was that of "replacing darkness with light," being able to "see" clearly.

Some of the *ukunqula* self-presentations have to do with personal problems. In number 10 the novice talks of her call from her grandmother and asks that she be able to follow in her steps as an igqira. In number 11, the novice feels compelled to share so that she won't become sick. The novice in number 12 prays for a medicine that will help her clarify her situation. Novice number 13 admits that she takes medicine prior to the sessions because they make her sick. In number 14, the singer confesses that she is so poor that she took from her children to be able to bring something to the sharing session. Another, in number 16, laments that there are so many igqira/ngoma novices because things are so hard, because there is no peace in the world. Several seem to be already thinking ahead to when they will be igqira. Novice number 10 prays that she will have effective medicines revealed to her by her grandmother. Novice number 16 prays that another woman may have power. Novice number 17 wishes to stand atop Table Mountain—the highest, most prominent point in the Cape—and be a shining light to her people.

References to God, to Jesus, and to the ancestors suggest that there is no dividing line in the minds of these people between what is "African" and what is "Christian." In fact, many of them have been in contact with the church and even continue to be members, but they are now participants in ngoma to come to terms with their sickness, their situation, and their *ukutwasa*, "call."

COMMON SONGS AND PERSONAL SONG IN NGOMA NARRATIVE TRADITION

The distinction between the therapeutic song and the coming-out song suggests that within the complex symbol "ngoma" there are at least two levels of narrative or performative understanding. The first is the importance of song-dance in defining and coming to terms with the suffering; the second is the importance of moving the sufferer toward a formulation of his or her own personal articulation of that condition.

In Victor Turner's account of Chihamba, a cult of affliction devoted to Kavula, the White Spirit, a doctor named Lambakasa "sings an *ngoma*" to Kavula on behalf of another woman asking to be relieved from barrenness:

> Completely white is that white clay
> You yourself grandparent [nkaka]
> All of you, you Nyamakang'a
> All of you, our dead.
> Today if you are making this person sick
> Today we will sing your drum
> This person must become strong.
> Completely white is that white clay. (Turner 1975:63)

This appears to be a generic ngoma, not Lambakasa's special song. Yet it fits the format of intercession of one ngoma participant for another, seen already in the case of the young Cape Town novice who could barely do his ngoma, or of the senior healer whose sister sang of her grief at the death of their mother, or of the participant who turned the song over to a particular woman who was very sick. This format is the quintessential act in ngoma, for it bonds the singer to the one being sung to, and shows the second how, when he recovers, he may begin to reformulate his own self with a creative new song.

Ngoma may take another form in which the individual begins to present self in a more active and articulate manner. This leads to the special personal song. An example of this is found in the work of psychoanalysts Vera Buhrman and Nqaba Gqomfa, who have studied Xhosa healing in the Transkei, South Africa. Every igqira (sangoma) and trainee has a personal special song that "came to him" during sickness and training (1981:300). Mrs. T., an igqira who is the main figure in the article, was healed by and trained with her igqira husband. She dreamed her song at the beginning of her sickness, when she was *twasa*:

> Ho, here comes an animal,
> It is clapping for me.

This song, like many among the amagqira, represents figures of the water or the forest ancestors, thus having an outer cosmological linkage. Further dimensions of Mrs. T's song, or songs, demonstrate her inner self-image, and the immediate events in her life, most recently a death in her family:

> I am sick, I am sick.
> News is bad about me in this location
> Things are bad with me,
> I am living by prayer.
> All things have gone wrong at my place.
> I am going.
> Things have gone wrong at my place. (1981:309–310)

Her husband's "special song" dwells on his medium, a horselike figure
that he calls Vumani:

> Here comes Vumani,
> I divine with him,
> My horse of news.
> I will die calling
> Ho! It is coming!
> Ho! My horse of news
> Is coming.
> Vumani. (1981:303)

An example of a strong, fully developed song comes from the Lemba
order of early twentieth-century inland Kongo society. Here entire
polygynous households were initiated to Lemba following affliction or
draft by the household head. Lemba's characteristic sickness afflicted
this mercantile elite, striking them with fear of the envy of their subordinates and the urge to redistribute their wealth to their lineage communities. The Lemba initiatory treatment created especially consecrated
polygynous households that served as nodes on the regional fabric of
alliances and routes through and over which the caravans moved on
their way to and from the ocean and the big market at Mpumbu above
the rapids on the Zaire River. One of the few personal Lemba songs
that has survived follows:

> That which comes from the sun
> the sun takes away.
> That which comes from the moon
> the moon takes away.
> Father Lemba,
> He gendered me, he raised me.
> Praise the earth,
> praise the sky.
> For I have been enhanced,
> I have gone far,
> From far I have brought [Lemba] back.

The initiate Lemba couple has taken a pilgrimage into contact with
the ancestors to bring back its Lemba insignia. It is also a symbolic pilgrimage song, declaring successful emergence into full Lemba status. A
further verse of the song addresses the sufferers this successful therapist
works with.

> Search in the ranks
> of the patrifilial children

of your clan.
KoKoKo [of the drum] . . . Ko! [response of drum]
Will you gain Lemba? . . . E [yes] Lemba!

The presiding healer refers to the source of initiatory revenue the client may bring, and the lineages of the matriclan's sons in whose ranks one may find preferred marriage partners to enhance community stability. Addressing the spirit, the healer sings:

Let go of the sufferer so he may be healed,
He will bring goods accordingly
Thereby offering a gift to your priests. (Janzen 1982:120–121)

A final example, from historic Sukuma in western Tanzania, from ngoma Ndono, shows that the ngoma song can take a collective, almost national turn. Here, a Christianized song from the time of World War I laments the drought that is raging and draws some wider implications.

We failed in our duty to Jesus the redeemer.
Our God, he is cross and sends no rain.
We see the clouds but they move away.
God hides the water and lets us die,
even the child in the womb of the mother.
What is our crime, O God?
Men arrived who taught us lies,
not to make the right sacrifices.
All countries are sad;
everywhere the sun is shining with such force.
Our God is very cross about adultery, witchcraft, lies, and
the crimes of theft.
The Mtemi Mkondo of Bulima has a good name,
but he does not succeed in making rain.
I hear that far toward lake Victoria there is rain.
The rain there moves stones,
it drives them quickly in front of it along the ground.
O Mother, wait, I shall sit on a log and
look at the world to see from where the rain comes.
Where is my father to teach me?
I am alone.
Though the ax of the rainmaker Migoma can be noticed,
I am alone, but not afraid. (Cory n.d.*a*)

The study of songs such as these in African healing has not come very far, since most scholars who have looked at them have concentrated on lyrics or on nonverbal symbols. They have not usually associated the content of these songs with social and cultural concepts. Yet the distinction between common and personal song appears to be very widespread in ngoma-type rituals. The significance and the role of self-presentation, or of others helping the sufferer learn to articulate self and ultimately compose his or her own song or song repertoire, have barely been outlined in field studies and in scholarship.

THE STRUCTURE OF NGOMA THERAPEUTIC COMMUNICATION

One way of comprehending the place of ngoma song in African healing is to take seriously the reference to text, texture, and context, and to look not only at the content of the songs but at the structure of these communications. The underlying and most pervasive structure of ngoma is the call-and-response pattern that is common in most African music. This is true not only of the songs, but of the very structure of the music and the ritual itself. There are numerous variations on this theme: sufferer and healer; sufferers among themselves; healers among themselves; sufferer, healer, and others; elements of sufferer's kin group; and spirits and humans. Since little collected therapeutic song material gives the relational context clearly, we need here to depend on the examples available from across the ngoma region.

The Western Cape example of "doing ngoma" offers a ready illustration of the call-and-response motif of song. The invocation, spoken, is followed by a song that is intoned by the speaker. The surrounding individuals join in with song. There are further amplifications of the call-response rhythm. There is the dialectic of speaking and singing. Within the singing there may be a call-and-response pattern. The sets of invocation (*ukunqula*) and song-dance (ngoma) are referred to by the set call "*Camugwini?*" and the response "*Camagusha!*" These two applications of the common verb "to agree," or "to have consensus, or affirm," pave the way for a well-understood routine that brings a sufferer into the group, sets him or her up to offer a few thoughts or concerns, and for the others to respond to them in an affirming, supporting manner. Throughout all of this, instrumental accompaniment is limited to the song-dance, and follows the vocalized, danced portion of the set. This is in keeping, everywhere, with the pattern of instruments becoming a secondary or tertiary voice in the sequence of voices entering in. According to Simha Arom's massive work *Polyphonies et polyrythmies instrumentales d'Afrique centrale* (1985), this feature is basic to musical styles across Africa. It is the foundation upon which the unique features of polyrhythmic and polyphonic patterns are built (see fig. 11a).

A more elaborate pattern of different voices is illustrated in the account of Lemba songs offered above. Here, senior priests and priestesses, the novice priest and priestesses, and the patrifilial children of the novice priest exchanged turns leading their songs in a "graduation" rite (Janzen 1982:114–121). These songs are intoned with the verbal call "Ko-ko-ko?" (suggestive of the drums) and the response "Ko!" Then the lead singer opens with a phrase such as "Will you gain Lemba?" and the chorus responds with "Yes—Lemba!" This is followed by the body of the song-dance performance of each particular song, with its recurrent internal call-and-response pattern.

A further, larger structure reflects the parties present in the rite. Throughout the event, the progression of lead singers is the following: (1) sponsoring healer or Lemba Father; (2) the other Lemba priests who are present at the event (sometimes the Lemba priestesses have a separate song); (3) the patrifilial "children" or offspring of the novice (that is, the offspring of males of his matriclan—a classificatory support group); (4) finally, the novice, after he and his wives have completed their initiations (see fig. 11b).

In the communication pattern of song in which divination is done, an even more complex exchange emerges at times. This can come in two ways. The first is in the presence of a third party who affirms or negates the interpretation of the diviner-healer; the second comes in those cases in which the diviner acts as a medium for a spirit. In Southern Africa the "third party," either an assistant to the diviner or a kin or friend representing the client-sufferer, responds to the divinatory interpretation of the diviner. After each utterance of the diviner, the third party intones "I agree" (si ya vuma) or "I do not agree." In the first case the diviner will continue the course of analysis of the case until reaching a conclusion. In the latter, the diviner will back up and try another track of analysis or will stop to discuss the case with the client. However, in Southern Africa and elsewhere, the diviner is often expected to establish the truth through a variety of convincing means, mechanistic or inspirational. Divination is not an empirical science based on questioning and the study of empirical evidence; it is held to be a mystical art, based on clairvoyant knowledge and wisdom. Thus, at the end of the session, there is agreement.[2]

When this clairvoyance is expressed in mediumistic form with the spirit invading and speaking through the diviner, in a sense the spirit

```
(a)  Primary voice (call)   > > > > > > > > > > > > > > > > > >

     Secondary voice (response)  > > > > > > > > > > > > > > > >
     or chorus

     Instrument I (drum or shaker)      >>>>>>>>>>>>>>>>>

     Instrument II                       >>>>>>>>>>>>>>>

     etc.
```

```
(b)  lead healer       >>>>>        >>>>        >>>>

     other healers          >>>>>       >>>>>

     novice's kin                       >>>>>

     novice and wives                          >>>>>
```

Figure 11. (a) The structure and sequence of voices and instrumentation in ngoma song, common to African music more widely; (b) the relationship of "roles" or "parts" in a documented ngoma event in North Kongo in the early twentieth century (Janzen 1982:106–124).

is the third party along with the diviner and the client-sufferer. In the ethos of possession divining, it is not appropriate to disagree with the spirit. One may not understand the spirit, but it is always right. Therefore the diviner becomes the third party, interpreting the utterances of the spirit as they are channeled through him or her, much as the diviner interprets the bones in Southern Africa, or the Ngombo basket objects on the Southern Savanna, or the shells of the Ifa oracle.

The combination of multiple communicative dimensions of vocal, visual, instrumental, and spatial and social domains enriches the overall "text" in ngoma, allowing it to articulate the complexity and contradictions of human experience. This process is enhanced by the addition of interpreters or the addition of points to the communicative structure (fig. 12) and of music to the communication, all of which we may speak of as "ritualization."

In several anthropological definitions of ritual inspired by communications theory (e.g., Leach 1966, 1976; Bateson 1958, 1972) the essence of ritualization is the process of adding channels or mediums of expression to a discourse so that there may be multiple, or redundant,

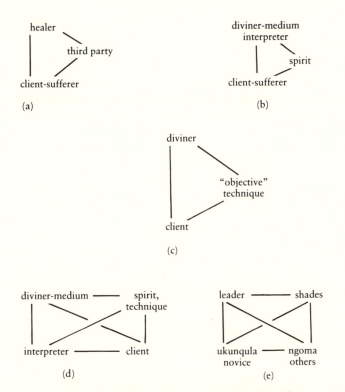

Figure 12. Modes of mediation in ngoma communication. These variations
model most of the cases presented in this work in terms of structures
between subjects or "players." Setting (a) shows a common clinical setting
with a therapy manager mediating between healer and sufferer. Divination
usually offers two types of structures, (b) and (c), in which the technique or
the shade/spirit become the message mode between healer and sufferer-
client. A more elaborate model emerges, (d) and (e), in which there is an
interpreter for the diviner and the spirit or technique (as in Nguni divining
where someone intervenes to "agree" or "disagree" on behalf of the client.
This model also applies to "doing ngoma" (e) in which there is a session
leader who mediates between spirits and novices, and a particular novice
at a given moment and the others who respond in ngoma.

levels of communication. Thus, in the example cited above, instrumentation would both repeat, and enhance, the primary level of vocal communication. For Bateson and Leach, ritualization occurs because of a
"block" or "static" in primary channels of communication and behavior. Redundancy helps to overcome or bypass these blockages. This
is not far from Turner's (1968) approach to ritual, which it is based
more on the importance of sign and symbol. In this perspective, ritual is
simply the greater degree of "density" in the meaning attached to par-

ticular sign referents. Ritual acts out relationships and meanings so as to heighten emotion and to articulate contradictory sentiments. These authors are not, however, overly concerned with the role of music in ritualization, although their theories do not contradict the focus upon music that is ultimately required to understand Central and Southern African ngoma.

OF MUSIC AND RITUAL IN NGOMA

Mahamoud Kingiri-ngiri, the Sufi Muslim mganga (healer) of Dar es Salaam who was introduced in chapter 1, rejected the use of ngoma in his healing work on the grounds that it was merely "happiness." Isa Hassan, who is also Muslim, utilizes ngoma because it is an essential method of getting the patient to "talk." Ngoma, especially the drumming, "heightens emotions." The theory behind this theme will be taken up in the next chapter, in which we explore "how ngoma works." Here I introduce the character and role of music in ngoma therapeutic ritualization.

A frequently mentioned feature of musical ritualization in this tradition is the "distinctive rhythmic pattern" of each ngoma. John Blacking, who has studied the music of the Venda people, traces this feature to the place of rhythm in the very distinction between song (u imba) and speech (u amba) (1973:27). As this distinction is also present in the KiKongo language in Western Bantu—singing being kuyimba, speech kukamba—we may assume it to be another very widespread Bantu language feature beneath therapeutic ritual. For the Venda, as for other Central African societies, ngoma and related therapeutic rites and techniques are designated by their distinctive rhythms. Of the nyimbo dza dzingoma, Blacking notes that these "songs for special rites accompany certain ordeals that the novices must undergo when they are in the second stage of initiation. Each one has a distinctive rhythmic pattern" (1973:41).[3] In Tanzania, Isa Hassan and other waganga and music experts also point to the association of spirits in ngoma and distinctive rhythms. Music, with the assistance of medicines, brings out the speech in the sufferer, which then indicates to the presiding mganga which spirit must be dealt with. For Botoli Laie, a mganga from Kilwa in Tanzania, specific instruments play distinctive rhythms appropriate to each spirit. This degree of specificity between spirit and rhythm, as well as the dance, is present as well in loa possession in Haiti (Courlander 1960:21), particularly in the Central and West African originating spirits.

We should be slow, however, to make a necessary connection between particular rhythms, instruments, and dances and spirits across the full gamut of African expression. As we have already noted, trance is not necessarily a corollary of the spirit or shade etiological hypothesis. In the Western Bantu Nkita society, the entire lineage is caught up in doing the rite. Its initiation is prompted by the sickness or death of infants and mothers in the matrilineage or by disputes at the time of protracted segmentation events. The "therapy" also entails restoring ancestral legitimacy in the lineage fragments. Even in settings such as the Western Cape recounted earlier in this chapter, the tightly regimented ngoma song-dance sessions do not prompt trance behavior, nor do there appear to be distinctive rhythms with the particular ancestral figures mentioned in the self-presentations and the songs. Gilbert Rouget's well-known work *Music and Trance* is based on the assumption that music is widely associated with trance, in some places triggering it, and in other settings calming it (1985:xvii). The relationship between the two is thus more complex than the reductionist arguments proposed by authors such as Neher (1962), Needham (1967), Huxley (1967), and others who suggest that percussion, drumming, or related pounding rhythmic music, by its intrinsic nature, stimulates or generates dissociative behavior.

These reductionistic theories of musical rhythm and trance behavior are very attractive in certain settings in Central and Southern Africa where trance occurs in connection with strong drumming. Attendants of a seance in which trance is accompanied by the participants' use of shakers and several types of drums, including the high pitched ngoma, with rhythm upon rhythm added to achieve the unique polyrhythmic effect that African music is so well known for, must in their "gut" believe in the theory of the neurological inducement of trance through rhythm. The effect of polyrhythmic percussion is not only the hammering, driving of the basic beats, which are like call-and-response patterns in conversation with each other, but the "metronome sense" (Chernoff 1979:49) of the "off beat" and the "hidden beat" that pulsates as a basic driving force beneath the surface (Thompson 1983:xiii). The supposition that this hidden beat sets up sympathetic echoes with the brain's alpha waves, which are at a comparable rhythm, seems quite plausible.

The problem, again, is that not all trance is touched off by strong rhythmic music—indeed, some is touched off by no music at all—and some strong polyrhythmic music when played masterfully does not induce trance. If there is a statistical prevalence of trance or possession behavior in the ngoma region in association with polyrhythmic music, with drumming, especially ngoma drums, despite the tempting reductionist hypothesis, the evidence and the logic of the case require us to conclude that it is a culturally mediated association.

Such a conclusion suggests that trance may be an analogy or a metaphor for the interpretation of life's experience but is not a driving or determining force that invariably shapes the course of sickness and healing.

CONCLUSION

"Doing ngoma" is the central feature of the institution we have called *ngoma* throughout this work; it is the ritual unit that defines the institution. Doing ngoma has been illustrated in this chapter by a Cape Town event in 1982, but it could have been equally well illustrated by events from throughout the wider region where, it seems, a great similarity of form prevails. This ngoma unit is structured around the call-and-response paradigm of communication, with spoken call often being echoed or answered by sung and danced response and the accompaniment of instruments. This communicative structure is the context within which the meaning of individual lives, among the ngoma practitioners, is articulated and where these individuals are urged to create a song of their own. Of course, there are counseling sessions and other types of conferrals between these semipublic ngoma gatherings that may occur whenever ngoma adherents meet. But it is the ngoma song-dance presented here that is the "minimal constituent unit" of the entire ngoma process.

Western scholarship has not known exactly how to categorize this unit, as was the case with the larger institution. Is "doing ngoma" music, or is it song, dance, or group therapy? Is it worship? In the theoretical push to identify the uniqueness of the institution, I have reserved judgment on this score by introducing the core notion as a translation of the indigenous name, "doing ngoma." Some of the principles of "ritualization" seem to apply to the manner in which ngoma is done and when it is done. More will be said in the next chapter about the amplification of messages and the role of metaphors within the song-dance communication, especially on the role of spirits in these communications.

A close look at "doing ngoma" reveals that it is the format and the setting in which highly individualistic perceptions are brought into the mirror of social reflection and subjected to reinforcement, repetition, and reaffirmation. The source of all the texts, dances, and rhythms is this individualized yet collective session in which the participant-sufferer-performer is urged to "come out of his prison" to full self-expression.

5

How Ngoma Works

Of Codes and Consciousness

The music enchants the sufferer . . . to reveal the spirit.
Isa Hassan, Dar es Salaam ngoma healer

This chapter and the next wrestle with the nature of knowledge—both personal and cultural—and the way it is utilized in ngoma. In previous chapters ngoma has been presented in a number of perspectives: the ethnographic present, the deep history of linguistic analysis and archaeology, and the close-up view of the core features and the main ritual, "doing ngoma." This chapter on "how ngoma works" seeks to understand how knowledge in this context is constructed and used. Indigenous theories of ngoma and a variety of analytical theories are brought to bear on the subject. The next chapter presents social and demographic perspectives and consequences on how ngoma works.

In evaluating the ngoma response to distress, scholars need to ask whether, and to what extent, our approach filters explanations in terms of the experience of individuals or of the cultural parameters that result from comparable outcomes among individuals within groups. For, although it has been established that there is indeed a widespread institution across Central and Southern Africa with distinct features, it is also clear that particular localized and regional foci of affliction may seem very disparate from one case to the next. The ontological problem of relating unique individual experience to cultural interpretation must now be confronted. This is particularly acute in regard to how the healer engages in intentional action toward the afflicted.

These questions take us to the heart of the issue of therapeutic "efficacy" as it has been debated in medical anthropology and related disciplines, which face the assessment of therapies studied comparatively

(Young 1977; Ahern 1979; Kleinman 1980; Devisch 1986; Csordas 1988). Since the test of efficacy depends greatly upon the criteria used, it is clear that there are many ways of claiming, as well as independently testing, efficacy. Some scholars have suggested that the pluralist array of therapies in the world is so vast that an assessment of efficacy is an impossible task (Sindzingre 1985:16). This relativistic perspective is consonant with another group of scholars who approach the question by stressing the cultural construction of efficacy, based upon people's beliefs, upon their fears of inefficacy of healing. The efficacy of a therapy may be established by studying therapeutic discourse on illness and the people's choices in seeking therapy. The present chapter deals with this type of efficacy of ngoma. A second group of scholars (Spring 1978, 1985; Corin 1979, 1980; Janzen 1980, 1989; Goblet-Vanormelingen 1988) insists that efficacy must be measured in absolute qualities of better health, which is defined in terms of survivorship, and mortality rates. We take up this perspective in the next chapter.

The questions of knowledge in ngoma and the efficacy of its actions come together in the sections of this chapter. We begin with a look at the distinction between individual and collective experience and knowledge. Most scholars who study African cults of affliction seem to dwell on the spirit phenomenon, around which there swirl many angles of interpretation. Some of the more important of these, for present purposes, are reviewed. Then we look at the conscious indigenous theories about ngoma, which are usually based on the hypothesis of spirit possession as the basis of the misfortune. From there, we turn to explanations that are more interested in the tacit or implicit knowledge of symbols and metaphors, and the way this allows for a more penetrating analysis of the rituals. Finally, because a number of the ngoma traditions demonstrate rather sophisticated knowledge about the empirical world, we must explore the relationship of scientific or empirical knowledge to ritual healing. The underlying leitmotif of this chapter and the next is that there are varied types of knowledge within ngoma; thus there are likely to be varying types of efficacy in ngoma as a ritual therapeutic enterprise.

PERSONAL EXPERIENCE AND CULTURAL REALITY

In a 1982 study of the Western Bantu cult of affliction, Lemba, I pressed to its ultimate conclusion the argument that the individual experience of each Lemba "afflicted" (individual or couple) could be grasped best in the contradictions and stresses confronting that person or persons. This contrasted, I suggested, with some interpretations of cults of affliction as standardized manifestations of affliction that led to predictable initiatory therapies into specified cults. Symptoms in the cases reported in connection with Lemba varied from headache, skin rash, verbal hysteria (loss of speech), stomachache, and a variety of heart afflictions, to loss of potency and to chaos in the community—in other words, a vague and ambiguous array of signs and symptoms—all being interpreted as "the Lemba sickness" by diviners or family members. By the time such an individual (or couple, since it was the couple/household that was initiated to Lemba) had gone through the course of Lemba initiation, the most idiosyncratic manifestation of affliction had been subjected to a standardized set of cultural classifications and ritual routines. As the initial ritual of purification, and the long middle course toward the final ceremony progressed, much of the symbolism and liturgy could be understood in terms of culturally standardized dichotomies and categories.

In one body of material from the Mayombe region of Lower Zaire, the medicine chest of the graduate priestly couple, in the organization of its contents, aligned classificatory oppositions about gender, color, cosmological ordering, and plants. In the medicine's symbolic structure, the "domestic abode" was contrasted to "public space," the former containing male and female elements, as well as the priestly hierarchy integrating the couple with the public realm of Lemba. These social dimensions were, in turn, expressed or amplified by spatial, animal, and vegetable objects or locations. The medicine, in effect, expressed the human dimension by projecting its inner parameters out onto other domains. The etiological myth accounting for Lemba's origin devoted attention to the composition of the medicinal satchel on a journey of the Lemba husband in search of a solution for his wives' health problems. The satchel's contents thus served as a mediatory vehicle between the human realm and the supernatural (Janzen 1982:257–272).

The point I wish to stress in reciting these details about the rituals, medicines, and myths of Lemba is that they are part of a dynamically patterned cultural code easily amenable to structural analysis. However, the less patterned, chaotic realm of personal experience as seen in distress or disease must not be ignored in the process of identifying the cultural codes to which they are subsumed. I emphasized that it was necessary to reconstruct, from all available bits of evidence, the historical setting within which the cult of affliction—the Lemba solution—had arisen, and to identify the questions and paradoxes that had been

asked and encountered at that time, and continued to be asked and encountered as individuals were drawn into it. These questions, or moments of crisis, I called "difficult experiences."

In this analysis of the setting at the basis of Lemba's origin, I used
Burridge's concept of the "true contradiction" (1967:105–106), developed in a critique of Lévi-Strauss's work on totemism. Burridge had
argued that a Lévi-Straussian opposition, at the basis of totemic representation of society's distinct groups, was not the same as a contradiction. A contradiction arose from contrary and clashing social norms,
conflicting goals or interests pursued by social segments, or conflicting
interests within individual lives, leading to paralysis and stress. The distinction between contradiction and opposition seemed to be an important one to make in the evaluation of Lemba, particularly if one wanted
to grasp the recurring existential context of distress of those individuals
who were steered toward the Lemba resolution, that is, those who may
have been involved in mercantile pursuits, who were possibly wealthy,
and who came to fear the envy of their subordinates in the kinship
arena. My analysis went out from the premise that there was a distinction between idiosyncratic, variable individual perception of chaos, distress, and anxiety, and the mechanisms of cultural order.

This point may be put another way. Just as experience constantly
meets and shapes culture, history constantly encounters myth. The two
are mutually shaped. Never is "living myth" a fixed canon. Lévi-Strauss
acknowledged that mythic structures may accommodate, even generate, new elements and combinations. But he did not well explain how
human experience continually generates new variations. His analysis
lacked the dimension of the contradictory in experience; it lacked the
dimension of the political manipulation of myth, which is commonly
called ideology. Both dimensions are important in our analysis of African ritual and lead directly to an understanding of "how ngoma
works." But we need to look at a range of theoretical approaches to
how this is explained. We begin with a look at ngoma as religious and
psychoanalytical explanations; then we turn to symbolist and metaphorical explanations; finally, in this chapter, we look at the possibility
of other types of knowledge in ngoma, including scientific knowledge.

SPIRIT LOGIC AND THERAPEUTIC DISCOURSE

This section will survey and evaluate a number of theories on and
explanations of the relationship of spirits to the therapeutic process.
Both scholarly and practitioners' views will be considered.

SPIRITS, A SCHOLARLY BUGABOO?

The majority of writers about cults of affliction have simply subordinated the phenomenon to another called "spirit possession." On the subject of spirits indwelling people, scholarship itself seems to have been obsessed with a bugaboo—a peculiar fascination, a fear, a concern—a word perhaps derived from the Western Bantu notion *buka lubuka*, to divine, to treat.[1] So pervasive has been this fixation on spirit possession that it has apparently become a sui generis category of Western scholarship, one that has given rise to entire bibliographies on the subject (Crapanzano and Garrison 1977; Zaretsky and Shambaugh 1978). The Western bugaboo has certainly gotten in the way of clear understanding of the African institution.

A part of the problem has been the use of the term *shamanism*, both in the use and in the breach. Although many authors on African spirit possession make a routine reference to the difficulty of using the term *shamanism* to refer to the African setting, the use of *spirit possession* tends to serve as a euphemism for shamanism. Authors such as I. Lewis (1986, especially his chapter "The Shaman's Career") and De Heusch (1971, especially his articles "Possession et chamanisme" and "La folie des dieux et la raison des hommes"), who do use African material in their general discussions on spirit possession, and use the term *shaman,* do not lay to rest the definitional issue. Other authors offer less charged descriptive distinctions in their writing on African spirits. Van Binsbergen and Schoffeleers (1985:39–40) distinguish between shamanistic and mediumistic divination. In the former, the diviner is said to go on a spiritual visionary quest from which he returns with his revelations; this is rare in Africa. In the latter, the diviner is locally considered to be entered or possessed by an external, invisible revelatory agent. This form is said to be prevalent in Africa.

A distinction between those societies that reflect possession belief and those that practice possession trance was introduced by Erika Bourguignon (1976:44–46) to account for another important dichotomy in relation to spirits. According to Bourguignon, the distinction between the two can be accounted for in terms of types of social organization. Less complex societies in which individuals take initiatives are less likely to utilize trance states than more complex societies in which religious expression is controlled or channeled.

Structural interpretations, such as these provided by De Heusch and Bourguignon, offer comparisons of differing valences of spirit presence between entire societies. De Heusch's distinction between *adoricisme* and *exorcisme* emphasizes the alleged pattern that in the first case creates a permanent bond between human and spirit, and in the second leads to the cleansing, or casting out, of the possessing spirit. In the first case the sufferer becomes a vehicle, or medium, of the spirit; in the second the sufferer needs to be cured of possession (De Heusch 1971:235). The first is "good" possession; the second "bad."

In practice, what do these structural surveys of possession types reveal? How helpful are they? For De Heusch, the Kongo (in the Nkita possession) and the Thonga feature possession sickness and trance, thus calling for exorcism or healing. The Sukuma and Lovedu reflect sickness possession, from which therapy is the only solution. Mediumistic possession is found among the Sukuma, Kuba, Luba, and Nuba, thus approaching shamanism. But only the Vandau, a small group living among the Thonga, have what De Heusch calls "authentic shamanism" (1971:258–276).

This approach, which lumps entire societies into structural types, has been correctly criticized by a number of writers (e.g., I. Lewis 1986), who point out that these ideal types are in fact usually moments in individual "careers." The typologies are based on rather inadequate ethnographic information that generalizes to the entire society. They need to be given a more historical and contextual interpretation in order to explain why some sectors of a society, at particular junctures in history, are prone to possession.

Ian Lewis's earlier approach to this question, developed from his work among Somalian pastoralists in the Horn of Africa, has become widely known for its emphasis on the "marginal cult," which stands in contrast to the "central" or dominant cult in a society. Spirit possession, he argued earlier, was an expression of crisis, impasse, or confinement, and the only legitimate or permissible outlet by members of society—often women—in subordinate or marginal positions. Nature spirits, the source of their possession, were marginal in the cult of the dominant—that is, Islam, controlled by men.

Later (1986) Lewis elaborated on this hypothesis of the "epidemiology of possession" with a more dynamic model that stressed the individual course from "uncontrolled" to "controlled" mystical experience. In social sectors that were marginal, the career of possession led from membership in a cult of affliction by a peripheral spirit in the dominant pantheon to a kind of permanent accommodation with the mystical force. In social sectors that were more central to power in society, possession led to control and even exorcism of the mystical force. If control, or channeling, of the force was the outcome, such holders of mystical power were generally thought to possess witchcraft—that is, mystical—power over others. This, of course, could lead to the use of this power in social control and government. For Lewis, the main difference between witchcraft (malefic mystical power) and possession had to do with whether it was handled "obliquely" in cult accommodation or "directly" through exorcism by the dominant religion or utilized in social control (1986:60).

De Heusch's and Lewis's approaches to possession in African religion offer a sketch of the work of a major school of writers who view it as a compensatory effort to come to terms with misfortune, suffering, and evil. There are many reasons why spirit possession might be a dominant hypothesis of difficult experience in Central and Southern Africa. In societies that are acephalous, either today or historically, individuals who claim original knowledge are vulnerable to envy and criticism. Thus, just as such individuals are often code-labeled as witches, in keeping with Lewis's approach, so cultural norms offset this by fostering as the source of all original knowledge and of change the realm of spirits, especially ancestral spirits or shades, the custodians of societal core values.

Other authors have questioned the wider applicability of Lewis's marginality model of possession cults. Linda Giles (1987) has studied the interface of ngoma and Islam on the Swahili coast of Tanzania, where there is a far greater interpenetration of the two than Lewis might allow. In any event, she suggests that not only are ngoma and related rituals practiced by Muslims but the Muslim waganga are often among the most devout adherents of Islam in Swahili society. A feminist scholar of Central African ritual healing, Anita Spring, who has studied ngoma rituals among Luvale women of western Zambia, offers that Lewis and other "marginalist" interpreters of cults of affliction have generally failed to consider the real presence of disease in connection with spirit possession and entrance to an ngoma order. Spring argues that the predominantly male scholars of ritual in Africa have imposed on African experience the nineteenth-century Western view of woman that accounts for women's mystical experience as their failure to cope with social conflicts (Spring 1978, 1985). I return in the next chapter to Spring's important study of the epidemiology of possession in relation to demographic and social profiles.

Whereas the former interpretations of African possession are characterized by their reduction of the phenomenon to social or structural themes, other approaches take the explanation in the direction of psychological theories. Bührman and Gqomfa (1981–82) have studied Xhosa healers in the Transkei of South Africa and are persuaded that the amagqira of the Transkei, whose work in most respects resembles that of the Cape Town therapists presented in chapter 1, can best be explained by Jungian psychotherapeutic models, and that the "sickness" (twasa) that ngoma treats is largely psychopathology, with schizophrenialike symptoms of excessive dreaming (1981). The similarity of dreams and dream therapies, and the songs derived from dreams, to those of other cultural and civilizational settings offer Bührman what she suggests is convincing case material for a Jungian approach (1978).

Another type of psychotherapeutic interpretation is offered by psychologist Ellen Corin of the Western Bantu rite Zebola, reported in chapter 1 as an Equateur Province Zairian rite brought to Kinshasa. Corin relates her understanding of Zebola to the approach of the "Dakar group" working under Henri Collomb, with a generally psychoanalytic orientation. A major concern in African psychotherapy, suggests Corin, is the differentiation of the self within a tight kin setting. This leads frequently to a diagnosis of witchcraft, with the identification of a specific other as the source, such as a mother's brother in a matrilineage, or an uncle in a patrilineage. However, etiologies in African therapies are often presented in a chainlike sequence, such that culturally standardized etiologies such as witchcraft and spirit possession are invoked to explain quite a variety of particular signs and symptoms.

This is the case with Zebola, in which all cases are ultimately explained by possession of the spirit of Zebola, a type of upriver nature spirit. Yet, on studying the sign-symptom sets of particular members of Zebola in Kinshasa, Corin demonstrated that a majority were recommended for recruitment due to transgressions of social rules (28 percent) and interpersonal conflicts (55 percent), whereas witchcraft (8 percent), meeting an evil spirit (2 percent), and direct possession by the Zebola spirit (7 percent) were relatively insignificant immediate causes (1980:150).

Corin's method of relating the individual experience to the culturally standardized cause offers important correctives to the problems of the structural reifiers as well as the psychological reductionist explanations of spirit possession. Corin suggests, first, that there is a loose, accommodating, link between sign-symptom and etiology and, second, that the spirit possession nosology is, as I have suggested throughout this work, a kind of cultural hypothesis about misfortune (Corin 1980:152; see also Crapanzano and Garrison 1977, whom she cites). The narrow psychopathological interpretation of ngoma offered by Bührman not only seems forced, it does not allow for the "recruitment to leadership" understanding of ngoma that appears in the indigenous model of the amagqira themselves.

Yet other approaches to spirit possession in Africa move away from the sociological and structural perspective entirely on the grounds that this fails to take into consideration the terms of the experience itself. These authors, such as Lambek (1981) and Comaroff (1981, 1986) work with an approach that is generally called "phenomenological" or "hermeneutical." Lambek's work on the island of Mayotte in the Indian Ocean between Mozambique and Madagascar especially typifies the approach. Rather than presenting spirit possession as a phenomenon to be explained in terms of society or its own cultural structure, this approach presents it as a text that needs to be "read" in its own terms and categories. As Lambek points out, on Mayotte possession is presented in terms of "curing," but it really has little to do with "disease." The spirits, who are for the most part spirits of the dead, are related to as separate, almost human, beings. Interaction with these spirits can be differentiated by distinctive codes of food and gesture exchange, incense, the topics of conversations, and the role of third parties (1981: 11). Although Lambek approaches the question of the "epidemiology of possession"—that is, the frequency of possession and social categories of the possessed, who are mainly women—he rejects any direct sociological inference to their roles as marginal to Islam or to their distinctive role in society. Rather, he insists that possession is a culturally autonomous domain that must be seen in its own terms and its own logic.

Csordas (1988) has recently provided a comparable picture of religious healing in a non-African setting, namely charismatic Christian healing in the United States. However, he goes beyond the mere phenomenological portrayal of healing to attempt to explain the criteria for "efficacy" in its outcome. With penetrating case study comparisons, he has identified the following criteria as important variables in predicting the outcome: the sufferer's prior disposition toward the treatment, whether positive or skeptical; the quality and character of the particular religious experience; the possibility in the mind of the sufferer as to the outcome; the occurrence of personal changes in incremental steps (Csordas 1988:138). Csordas's application of these criteria to charis-

matic Christian healing takes us directly to evidence for ngoma therapy's efficacy as established by healers and sufferers themselves. After
reviewing the literature and my own fieldnotes on this point, I am
amazed that so little is available. Also, those with personal involvement
in ngoma and who are divined to be possessed do not speak with one
voice. Still, it is important to discern an indigenous "theory of ngoma"
that can be generalized from particular settings to the entire range of
manifestations.

HEALERS' VIEWS OF NGOMA THERAPY

Muchona, the Ndembu doctor whom Victor Turner relied on extensively for his understanding of Ndembu ritual, including cults of affliction, is depicted as a veritable sage of esoteric lore of the Southern
Savanna. There is not a ritual symbol or a gesture that he cannot interpret. Muchona's knowledge is the principal source of our extensive
appreciation of Central African ritual color symbolism, of the choreography of the affliction cults, and of our understanding of the way
individuals move through the stages of their therapeutic initiations.
However, there are very few passages in the exegetical commentary of
Muchona in which we actually hear him developing his own views on
how the cults of affliction are supposed to work. Usually he is respond-
ing to Turner's questions about the interpretation of particular ritual
symbols. The closest we come in Turner's *Drums of Affliction* to a
theory of the system is in appendices in which a number of Ndembu
men expound on the character of shades (*mukishi*), shadow or reflection (*mwevulu*), ghost (*musalu*), and a dead person (*mufu*), the constituent elements of a person, and how these elements can cause disease
in others and need to be dealt with. Success in the hunt, according to
one, should prompt the hunter to offer an offering to his ancestral
shrine tree and to distribute the meat to others. Failure in the hunt may
require one to take white clay (*mpemba*) to the same shrine tree to invoke assistance from God through the mediation of the shade. Several
others emphasize the serious consequences of dreaming (*lota*) about the
shades, who are normally invisible. Such a dream, or persistent dreams,
will cause sickness and require the dreamer to seek out a doctor (*chim-
banda*) to help the person drink the appropriate medicine. To have identified one's shade is to have a mystical helper who can come to one's
assistance. At other times the shades come in dreams and request beer
or food offerings. If one does not satisfy these demands with appro-

priate responses, one will be stricken with disease. Usually a diviner is needed to identify the shade and what must be done about it. Becoming a shade is part of the process of dying and having the body, the ghost (*mufu*), separated from the shadow and shade (1968:284–290). In this, the role of the ngoma cult of affliction is to be the organized effort to establish appropriate relationships between individuals and their shades. It is also the organized effort to restore health where disease or misfortune have been interpreted by divination as being caused through dreaming of shades. Obviously much is left to the diviner. It is important to note here that what other writers call "possession" or "trance" behavior is mentioned by Turner with reference to only three of the twenty-three cults of affliction: Ihamba, entailing the extraction of the ancestor's tooth; Kayong'u, in which the mode of affliction is respiratory disorders, and the patient dreams of a deceased diviner relative; and Tukuka, wasting or respiratory troubles, in which the patient dreams of spirits of Europeans and speaks with tongues, simulating European behavior (1968:300–302). Why has Western scholarship emphasized possession so much, when it is only a minor feature of the entire ngoma system, in the sense of trancelike or out-of-consciousness behavior?

Elsewhere, as well, demonstrative possession and trance are either absent in the overall system of shade or spirit involvement or they are one way among others of expressing communication with spirits. Or, possession on the part of mediumistic divining or in ritual therapies is a phenomenon that emerges in the context of ngoma institutions at a particular point in history, or declines similarly in other settings. Each of these possibilities needs to be reviewed to accurately understand what the shades or spirits in ngoma mean and how they are used as active presences in ritual.

The ngoma-related role of shades and spirits where demonstrative possession-trance is altogether absent is illustrated in the Western Cape, and perhaps in Natal, thus among most Xhosa, Mpondo, Zulu, and some Swazi settings. Not only is divination done without paraphernalia, there is no demonstrative trance expression of *ukutwasa,* the state of being "called" by ancestors.

The second condition, in which demonstrative trance-possession moves into a setting, is illustrated by the "red" takoza-sangoma method of mediumistic divining seen in Swaziland and apparently in regions of Mozambique. Most sources, as well as takoza such as Ida Mabuza, said the appearance of this type of divining is of recent origin, having come from the Thonga, quite possibly the Vandau to whom De Heusch attributed "authentic shamanism."

In actual divination this meshing of the less demonstrative technique with possession-trance divining takes the form of a hierarchy of modes. Ascending from two to thirty-five emlangeni in price are ranged (1) the basic bone-throw divination, (2) bone throw with expert translation by a mediator between the diviner and client; then, in increasing expense and degrees of power, (3) the client's recourse to mediumistic divination with Swazi water spirits, victims of Swazi wars, and alien spirits. Having presented a Western-style family issue to levels 1 and 2 of this system, and having seen the hierarchy of level 3 in operation, I saw that counseling and problem-solving may go on alongside the more formal divination hierarchy. I have similarly seen various mechanistic methods of divining put aside for counseling and interpretation in Kongo settings. It is apparent, however, that although any mode of knowledge is recognized in this African context, ancestrally sanctioned knowledge often has greater legitimacy.

The third possibility, that of the decline of possession-trance in ngoma, may be illustrated in the Tanzanian context, where ngoma, although associated with groups of spirits, is usually done strictly as a dance and therapeutic technique. A form of routinization and control of the ritual, as well as a hierarchization of the organization of healers who practice a particular ngoma, has apparently contained, or controlled, open manifestation of the spirit.

The analytical thread that runs through all these "transformations of spirit" is that they are part of a worldview or ideology of order and misfortune, of health and disease, in which individual experience is brought together with culturally normative knowledge. It is not an exaggeration to speak of particular spirits as specific paradigms and the realm of spirits as a generalized paradigm.

Ngoma needs to be understood as the institutional form that frequently emerges as Central Africans pick up the pieces of their lives following a common and recurring misfortune. Part of this form has to do with the assumption that misfortunes may originate in the realm of human beings or former human beings and spirits, as understood in the proto-Bantu cognate *dòg*. The particular combination of causal imputations of misfortune and the social context with which this is dealt with does not rule out combining "empirical" or "practical" knowledge with spirit knowledge. Also, because of the social dangers of exposure of individuals with knowledge to envy and accusation, spirit legitimation is a preferred legitimation of both new problems and new solutions. It in no way substitutes for common-sense knowledge or ad hoc problem solving. It is thus a serious oversimplification to restrict what I call the "spirit hypothesis" to possession and trance.

In several of the rare conversations I held with ngoma therapists in which the "theory" was discussed, emphasis was placed on the sufferer's acceptance of the condition and the calling, as interpreted by the diviner or healer, and upon the relationship between the sufferer's song and spirit. One of these accounts is from Cape Town, the other from Dar es Salaam. These lead us to look for other types of analytical models to understand "how ngoma works" than have been sought so far.

Adelheid Ndika, with whom I had the pleasure of speaking on various occasions about her work, spoke of the importance of understanding the sufferer's dreams. They could indicate the nature of the call, and of the spirits, as well as the appropriateness of the sufferer's choice of a sponsoring healer. The acceptance of the challenge, call, or sickness (*uvuma kufa*) was the beginning of recovery. (This is similar to Alcoholics Anonymous rehabilitation, or to Csordas's "predisposition.") Physical symptoms such as headache and nosebleeding, and mental symptoms are often the expression of resistance to the sickness. Ndika was not willing to speak of them as the displeasure of the spirits. Acceptance, rather than exorcism, was the preferred mode in which she and other Cape Town healers approached "spirits."

Medicines in the first stage of the initiatory therapy, suggested Ndika, are usually intended to calm and purify the sufferer, to cleanse the thoughts, and to "drive away the darkness." This medicine, which may contain analgesics and hallucinogens, is usually "white," whether it is a plant-derived liquid (*ubulau*) or white chalk (*ikota*), because the ancestors are of a "white" disposition. Incense used in the early rites of initiation is intended to gain favor with the ancestors. She stressed the importance of the goat sacrifice in her work, in terms of the disposition of the sufferer and the relationship with others and the ancestors. Her theory of the songs emphasized the formation of a strong self through self-presentation in the ngoma sessions.

However, it was in Dar es Salaam, in conversations with the leaders of the coastal healer's association Shirika la Madawa, that a theory of ngoma in relation to spirits emerged. Song was stressed as central to the ritual. Omari Hassan, Muslim mganga and practitioner of ngoma Msaghiro for sufferers of chronic and severe headache caused by the coastal or beach spirits (sheitani) Maruhani, Subizani, Mzuka, and Kinyumakero and also of headaches caused by Warungu "inland" spirits of the hills, baobab trees, or mountains, offered this:

> The aim of healing ngomas is to make the patient talk, to heighten emotions. If that fails, you go to the forest for roots, give them medicine. Either way, talking is important. The purpose of the drumming is to know the particular spirit, so it speaks out in the patient, so the healer knows how many, which, where they come from, what it wants. When the patient speaks, it's the spirit [speaking]. Spirit and person are one and the same. After medicine is taken, and ngoma is played, the patient must sing in increasing tempo, the song of the particular spirit. It's thus the patient who directs the healer on the type of treatment.

Isa Hassan, also a Muslim healer and officer of the organization, added that:

> The spirits like the music, so they may make themselves manifest, so they may talk [through the sufferer]. A specific type of music is for a specific type of spirit; only this way will each spirit reveal ways of releasing the patient. Once the healer has established the type of spirit before him, in the person, he begins the corresponding type of music. The lyrics are the healer's [or sufferer's] own. It is impossible to give lyrics of a particular ngoma because there is so much improvisation and variation, so much depends on the individual case. How then does an ngoma help a person? The music enchants the sufferer so he can express himself better, and reveal the spirit.

"Accepting the sickness," "confessing dreams," "presenting one's self," "the spirits talking," "sufferer and spirit being the same thing," "patient directing the healer" are some of the expressions that get to the core of ngoma discourse. In terms of the communicative structure of this discourse, we have seen (in the previous chapter) how important is not only the two-way discourse between healer and sufferer but that a third pole, a third party, is also common. This may be the therapy manager of Kongo society, the diviner-assigned assistant who says "I agree," in Swaziland, or the small group in the ngoma session who listen and sing back to the sufferer the song just intoned. Spirit, here, may be considered another type of third party in the discourse, which may or may not be dramatically manifested. In other words, spirit is a manner of speaking, a hypothesis, a format.

NGOMA AS THERAPEUTIC DISCOURSE

The analytical theory that seems to be most consonant with this view of ngoma ritual healing may be found in the recent writing of

Tullio Marañhao, *Therapeutic Discourse and Socratic Dialogue.* Marañhao is interested in finding out what it is about verbal therapy that cures. Is it a "science of the psyche" or a "rhetoric of communications"? To organize his inquiry he selects Freudian psychoanalysis and family therapy as two extreme opposed approaches on a continuum of approaches to language in therapy. The first, with its theories of transference, of condensation, of the subconscious and the libido, finds language as a surface manifestation of deeper psychic and physical forces in the individual. Therapeutic speech is to reveal and correct these forces. Family therapy, by contrast, is far more surface-oriented, with family members talking together, with the therapist's guidance, to reveal and to agree on problems, misunderstandings, contradictions, and approaches to common mutual reinforcement. Yet in family therapy there is a further element that is often blamed for contradictions and faulty relations, namely, the force of power and manipulation. Is it possible to bring the varied therapeutic schools together under one umbrella?

Marañhao (1986) sees the diverging strategies of verbal therapy—exemplified in psychoanalysis and in family therapy—as part of a Western cultural struggle that has gone on for several millennia between two fundamentally opposed approaches to public knowledge: the first, caught up in deep dark secrets of the soul; the second, in a struggle for consensus of knowledge that is out in the open. Socratic discourse, which appeared as Greek society was making the transition from a predominantly oral society to one that depended on writing, provided a method for working out many of the tensions that opposed, or contrasted, the two approaches to language use. Through the use of questions and answers—dialogue—these discourses showed public knowledge, and knowledge of the self, to be elusive, transitory, and bound up in socially embedded relationships.

There are just enough resemblances between African ngoma uses of verbal knowledge in therapy and what Marañhao is saying about Western verbal therapy, that we may disagree with him that this is a uniquely Western struggle. In ngoma there is knowledge of the spirits as found in dreams, above all. In order to identify which spirits are at work—which deep dark demons—it is necessary to "let the sufferer talk" (or sing). When the pattern or the mood becomes apparent, the appropriate drums can respond with appropriate rhythms. Psychoanalysis stops with the revealing. African therapy follows through with the song-clarification. In family therapy knowledge is brought out through the grid of social relations. In ngoma the grid of discourse, through which knowledge is revealed, is quickly subjected to the test of agreement or disagreement, a kind of Socratic questioning and answering.

These are, then, the approaches to spirit in African and Western religious and therapeutic thought. They are an important point of departure for our understanding of how ngoma works. However, they are not the end of that journey for understanding. We carry some of these perspectives into the next section on symbols and metaphors in ngoma therapeutic discourse. This takes us beyond consciousness.

FROM SPIRIT TO SONG-DANCE: ARTICULATING METAPHORS OF DIFFICULT EXPERIENCE

Although we have now brought our understanding of ngoma therapeutic technique around to focus squarely on song and dance, which is to say a conscious verbal expression and performance, there is value in retaining something of the psychoanalytic appreciation for the "deep, dark forces" of the soul. Although we have relegated "spirit" to the status of a divinatory or diagnostic hypothesis, or paradigm, we must still try to account for the types of anxieties and perplexities, impasses and "intractable dilemmas," associated with the spirit hypothesis. Ngoma songs, especially the personal songs, make references to personal experiences, as in the songs cited in chapter 4: the "sickness all around in this place" of Mrs. T. in the Transkei; of lack of rain in historic Tanzania; of the pain of segmenting lineages in Kongo society; of the infertility of a close friend of Lambakasa, the Ndembu woman.

There are allusions to the natural universe, the cosmological grounding of images, metaphors, or tropes. The "animal calling me" of Mrs. T's song; the medium horse, Mr. T's Vumani; the sun and the moon taking and giving in the Lemba priest's special song; the whiteness of ancestral resolution in Lambakasa's song; the crab that scuttles back and forth from water to land on the Indian Ocean beach. The images in the Yaka version of the Nkita rite, as related by Devisch (1984), include numerous uses of natural metaphors such as chickens laying eggs and hippos rising from the water.

The manner in which experience is connected with these stock cultural figures has been persuasively explained in the work of such schol-

ars as James Fernandez and Renaat Devisch. Inchoate personal distress
and feeling are pulled out, given valence and clarity through association
with exterior images.

My favorite example of this process comes from a marvelous Lemba
song, which weaves together inner personal images of pain with the
path of Lemba opportunity, death of personal frustration with new life,
and the allusion to the rising and setting of celestial bodies:

> That which was a "stitch" of pain
> Has become the path to the priesthood.
> It has caused to rise
> The sun of Lemba.
> My death occurred
> In the Lemba Father.
> Now there is life in Lemba. (Janzen 1982:118)

The cosmological background knowledge reveals that the celestial bodies of sun and moon cycle endlessly in their courses, and that similarly,
individual life may cycle from despair to hope, death to life. These cosmological images are part of a widespread Bantu-African use of threshold metaphors relating personal and social experience to nature, to the
invisible forces in nature, especially as conceptualized in water, earth,
and sky. The metaphoric operation may relate to the natural categories,
as in this Lemba song:

> Praise the earth
> Praise the sky.

Or it may attach the experience to "movers"[2] within, or more commonly across, these categories, such as, again, the "sun of Lemba":

> What Lemba gives, Lemba takes away
> What the sun gives, the sun takes away.

Similar are Mr. T's horse medium, which brings him messages, or
Lambakasa's "whiteness," which brings her friend fertility from the
ancestors, or Mrs. T's "animals," which call her. In ngoma thought,
some of these "metaphoric movers" are, of course, spirits, sometimes
accepted (adored, in De Heusch's words), other times rejected (exorcised). The process is hardly mechanistic, nor is it fixed as positive or
negative in an entire society. The question is, to cite Zairian philosopher
Valentine Mudimbe, "how does one read and interpret these procedures as metaphorization?" (1986:280–281) That is, how might one

read the "mythologization of history and the historicization of mythical narratives"?

In Lemba, this process was the effort of individuals, kinfolk, and diviners to interpret the sufferer's intractable situation, that is, to find a metaphor in the stock of culturally ordered ideas to interpret and deal with that situation. Lemba did not force the experience of the Lemba sickness into a single mold. Rather, I suspect that the presiding Lemba father took as his point of departure the dreams, symptoms, complaints, and aspirations of the Lemba son—the patient—and his wives, and worked from there. Accordingly, there are important variations in song versions from the same region and period, suggestive of individualized ritualization. Thus, while the particular individual situation of the patient-novices varied according to their experiences and surroundings, the process of interpreting through the construction of metaphors was common to all.

Metaphor, as seen here, is a verbal or nonverbal—performed—process by which a given set of terms or figures is associated with another set so as to give the first ideational, emotional, or dramatic amplification contained in the second set, or in the combination of both. This process was at the core of the Lemba experience.

The song-dances of the "drum of affliction," which define the existential moment of the sufferer-novice, the psychological state of the sufferer, are aligned with another set of terms that vividly reflect the experience and cast it into a wider frame of reference.

The foregoing examples are relatively straightforward. Others, which are drawn from the vocabulary and prose of Kongo myth cycles, reflect a more grandiose manipulation within culturally standardized material and settings. Although Lemba's association at this level has been noted in every region, and with a series of mythic figures, I illustrate my point with the excellent case of Lemba's use of the Moni-Mambu trickster cycle.

As all who have read an African trickster cycle will know, this African figure plots many surprises and transformations, some with violent, others with socially redemptive outcomes. Many of the trickster's deceitful deeds are based on punning, with ambiguous verbal allusions, or on ambiguous social terms. In the Kongo trickster cycles there comes a time when the people, or their judges, rise up to take the villain trickster to court. At first they are inclined to forgive him because his intentions appeared to have been noble. Later, however, when it becomes

apparent that he has cunningly used cultural ambiguities—contradictions—to mislead and deceive and destroy others, he is regarded as a
criminal and a witch. Ultimately he is killed. Thus the standard trickster
cycles.

In a cultic setting, as in the trickster who brings Lemba, the trickster
turns cultural hero, turning these same ambiguities around, fetching the
appropriate medicine with which to resolve the dilemmas and contradictions of those caught in them. In the text presented in the book,
much is made of the composition of the satchel in which are found the
helpers who will aid Moni-Mambu gain the recognition of his father,
God, who ultimately presents the Lemba medicine, just as the Lemba
father extends the medicine to his Lemba son.

It would seem, then, that in a cultic setting such as Lemba, or of
another ngoma, the consciousness found in lyrics is manipulated so as
to create a positive, conjunctive, outcome to those dilemmas which,
in noncultic versions, are given a negative, disjunctive portrayal. Or
perhaps this manipulation in the interest of a positive narrative outcome
is the mark of ruling class consciousness that seeks to contain or over-
ride contradictions that beset the society. This would have been a fitting
analysis of Lemba performances because its ranks were filled with the
mercantile and power elite of the society who sought to gain wealth
from the coastal trade *and* at the same time maintain, through gen-
erous ceremonial distributions, the egalitarian ethic in North-Kongo
kin-based society. Whatever the case, it is clear that this manipulation
within Lemba of standard cultural narratives lends support to the hypothesis of Lemba's concern for social control, of its use of ideology.

Lemba's medicines and nonverbal rituals become important in seeing
how "contradictions" were dealt with. I have shown, in detail, that the
contradictions or social ambiguities that are edited out of the mundane
version of myth for cultic purposes are in nonverbal metaphors associated with medicinal compositions, as in the Lemba medicine box
(*nkobe*). The contradiction metaphors are allowed to remain in all their
antithetical forces, and are transformed and converted, in the Lemba
rituals, into social power. In this sense one may speak here of metaphoric healing and transformation, or of the efficacy of ritual healing
(see also Devisch 1984:140–148).

This scholarly understanding of metaphor as active agent is appropriate because allusion to spirits is, in the African setting, also a
hypothesis, an analytical exercise. The misfortune of Lambakasa's
friend is not made significant until it, and the solution, are contex-

tualized with reference to Chihamba. Mrs. T's sadness at the death of her son-in-law and her generally miserable situation are focused in the diviner's encouragement to join an igqira/ngoma singing group in the context of South African apartheid.

We know very little of the actual choreography of these metaphors of difficult experience, sung and danced out—that is, as performance. Ngoma as historical material, with the song text, dialogic though it may be, offers a bias of a cognitive model of ngoma therapeutic ritual. The transformation of the metaphor to a medicinal material level is a very tempting interpretation that shows the "power" or "efficacy" of the rite. However, from watching ngoma sessions in Kinshasa, Dar es Salaam, Swaziland, and Cape Town, my overwhelming impression is that the song texts, in order to be effective metaphors of the difficult experience, must be staged in a context of support that permits the full release of emotional pain and tension. This may include the enactment of anger or tension, as with the young woman in Kinshasa who nearly beat her infant child's head on the concrete, or the young man in Cape Town whose pain at having to lead his song was visible in his taut face and body (see plate 12).

These metaphors or tropes, sung, thought, danced, and felt, are of course sometimes identified as the work of the spirits. It is important to emphasize that the outside analysis, just as the internal theory, recognizes that the spirit explanation of misfortune and its denouement is one available option, which comes in a compelling manner to some through dreams—which must be interpreted—and in a less compelling manner to others. Possession thus is an available hypothesis, a culturally learned behavior. Although it may be a major framework within which ngoma knowledge is couched, it is by no means the only one, and it should not be construed as overdetermining the content of ngoma knowledge.

NGOMA AND SPECIALIZED KNOWLEDGE

The "working" of ngoma has been presented here as a format for generating, articulating, and applying knowledge about misfortune. Although spirit possession is often given as a framework for ngoma ideas and is then said to have come through dreams or in divination, at other times the knowledge of ngoma resembles more the working concepts of a profession, or the crafts of a specialized guild. Snake-handling ngoma of western Tanzania illustrate this type of knowledge. It is loosely and formally associated with possession, but rarely with trance.

The western Tanzanian snake-handling ngoma must come to terms with technical recipes of venom and antidotes, handling snakes, and treating snakebite, as well as with hysteria and fear that accompanies, even in Tanzania, attitudes toward snakes and vipers. Historically, the Sukuma, Nyamwezi, and neighboring societies have had to cope with some of the world's most poisonous vipers and other frightening snakes. The bite of the black mamba, for example, will kill its victim within half an hour. The cobra can spit poisonous venom and blind its victim. Boa constrictors and pythons, which strangle their victims, are formidable creatures too.

The Sukuma approach to dealing with snakes is through ngoma-style dance groups. On one front, there are the societies, dances, and initiations. Carried by the ritual is the scientific knowledge of antidotes and snakelore. The members of the snake-handling ngoma make antidotes with venom "milked" from the viper's fangs and come to the aid of people who find snakes in their houses.

Norbert Chenga, novice of a Sukuma snake-handling ngoma and who works at the Ministry of Culture in Tanzania, related the character of the cultural knowledge of snake handling, although not its technical secrets, which are kept within the ngoma order. First, I was struck with his positive attitude toward snakes. "Tanzania really has quite nice snakes, you know," said Chenga. Second, in speaking about the snakes, he took their viewpoint. The black mamba is very lazy, he said, but has a very good poison. The snakes get acquainted with their trainers and recognize their distinct smell. If you've been good to them they know after a while that you won't harm them, so they can be handled. The snake-handling dance serves to lessen fear of snakes, since during the dance all types of snakes are handled, and in the one I saw, a "volunteer" allowed himself to be bitten.

How does this training and knowledge of snake venom and antidotes relate to the ancestor possession ideology of the ngoma organizational mode in general? We know little about recruitment to the snake-handling ngoma, nor whether recruitment fits the notion of a "call" by ancestors. However, the one account of a historic initiation into a snake-handling ngoma that we possess, namely the Sukuma Buyeye (Cory 1946), shows that the linkage between the experience with snakes and the conceptual order is handled through the juxtaposition, in the initiatory lodge, of three legendary cosmic serpents with the three ritual colors: red, white, and black (Cory 1946:165–166).

The songs of ngoma Buyeye, for snake handling, reflect the same fusion of existential concern for the "difficult issue"—here those "quite nice" snakes—the invocation to the ancestors, and a concern for the protection of special knowledge.

> You mothers of the ant-hills [the snakes]
> with the glaring eyes,
> do not hurt us.
> We are your children.
> Look down, you ancestors of the Buyeye,
> Look down at us.
> Whoever looks at us with envy,
> May they become blind.
> Whoever pursues us, the Buyeye,
> May die;
> May he burst like clouds.

Possession, if this be it, backs up the normative codes that call for legitimation of skilled and esoteric snake-handling knowledge by the ancestors.

Given this integration of multiple modes of knowledge and evidence in a series of ngoma, the prospects for further evolution of the ngoma format, with application to a variety of "difficult issues," is likely. We should not be surprised to find in ngoma the possibility of a shift of legitimating ideologies from one mode of knowledge to another, or of the insertion of new knowledge into old legitimacy.

CONCLUSION

The efficacy of ngoma ritual therapy is, as we have seen, many-sided. In order to establish criteria for efficacy, we have had to identify some of the types of knowledge that are found at the basis of ngoma. These have been grounded in the different kinds of "difficult personal experiences," which have been interpreted through divination, diagnosis, and other procedures to fit culturally standardized categories and explanations. The "spirit" hypothesis is what brings the individual experience into the orbit of ngoma. However, spirit is not what it appears to be, nor is it equally strong in all expressions. This expression ranges from a mere divinatory hypothesis that may or may not be accepted to a full-blown trance. This, in turn, may be long lasting and pervasive or fleeting in time and place. The consensual basis of knowledge is important, both in Western and African healing, as Marañhao (1986) has shown. This consensual basis of knowledge provides for a social handle, a social forum, for understanding the deep, dark secrets in the souls of individuals. It provides a framework to deal, publicly, with the things that individuals find fearful, with the ways they would manipulate knowledge—witchcraft, in the Africanist's idiom.

The consensus of knowledge in an ngoma format may also provide the basis for rational or technical understanding of the natural world, for the empirical application of techniques to common problems, as we have seen in the use of antidotes for venomous snakebites.

Song, which provides the format for public scrutiny of these secrets and a forum for remembering, also provides us with text that contains the metaphorization of these experiences into culturally standardized forms. Difficult experience, inchoate feelings, emotions, and hidden meanings are given standardized expression in the songs. If they are representative of the experience of many, they catch on, are sung repeatedly, and become part of the common culture.

6

How Ngoma Works

The Social Reproduction of Health

Is it good for the children?
Rick Yoder, Planning Adviser, Swaziland Ministry of Health

Exploring the issue of efficacy continues in this chapter, in terms of the survivorship of at-risk sectors of society and the role of ngoma in the creation and maintenance of a social fabric that contributes to health. Whereas in the previous chapter I identified practitioners' and analysts' theories of how ngoma rituals are intended to work, here I shall examine the consequences of ngoma upon the "social reproduction" of health. Social reproduction as used here refers to the maintenance of a way of life and the commitment of resources to relationships, institutions, and support organizations that directly or indirectly maintain health.

Four widely different ngoma settings illustrate the social-reproduction-of-health model of analysis: the historic coastal Congo Lemba order in the context of the mercantile trade at the Atlantic coast; the Southern Savanna natality-enhancing ngoma orders of Zambia and southern Zaire; the township ngoma orders of Cape Town; the professionalized ngoma institutions of Dar es Salaam.

The questions that are at the heart of this inquiry are these: What type of social fabric is created, reinforced, or reproduced by a particular ngoma order? How does it address health issues and needs? Can this be assessed in terms or definitions that health planners or practitioners could use?

HEALTH AND HEALTH INDICATORS

The analysis of ngoma ritual healing in terms of health requires both a distinctive perspective on definitions of health and a bridge to the definitions of health commonly used by demographers and health planners. Health is a universal human goal, like virtue or enough to eat, but it eludes definition except in terms of specific negative or positive criteria. Myriad definitions of health exist.[1] This is not the context in which to present an exhaustive review of them. For present purposes, we require, rather, a selection of those that seem to fit the phenomenon.

It has been observed that good health is not necessarily determined by medicine, especially not curative biomedicine, narrowly defined (Navarro 1974; World Health Organization 1978; Dawson 1979). Rather, a range of factors such as nutrition, housing, environmental quality, social order, and mechanisms for coping with stress are important (Gish 1979). Further, if improvement of health on a societal scale is to be attained, then health policies must be appropriate so as to avert health catastrophies or gradual declining levels of health.

One way to describe health, suitable for present purposes, is that it is embedded in a set of structured relationships, rights, and practices rooted in a worldview of values, truths, and ideals. In a stable situation this would include hygiene (although methods would vary), adequate and clean water, sufficient and clean food (although this would vary from nearly all-meat to all-vegetable), rules of social interaction and organization (varying enormously), and rituals spelling out the coherence and interconnectedness of things. As we will see, this understanding of health could be "paraphrased" in terms of the ecologist's concept of the "adaptive system," in which the human community obtains its food source through a given technology, a given social order, and a structured flow of energy from the environment to the human community and back into the environment (Janzen 1980:7–8).

More focused in scope and scale would be a description of health based on the society's self-conscious efforts to treat disease and restore health—that is, its medical or ritual systems. Here we would find at work "an explicit theory (or theories) of disease causation, a corresponding set of therapies, and a focus directing the scale of application of such theories and therapies. These aspects of the medical system will be evident in symptoms, complaints, and verbalized statements about illness and health, in the cultural premises used to evaluate the meaning of affliction, and in practices of healers" (Janzen 1980:9).

Despite the appropriateness of such conceptualizations of health for the purpose of understanding ritual healing, it is useful to begin this discussion with the types of health assessments that have generally been done with more precise measures of fertility, mortality, and morbidity—the demographer's stock in trade. We learn from a World Development Report issued by the World Bank (1985), that crude birth rates and crude death rates in Sub-Saharan Africa's "low income countries" and its "middle income countries" have declined from 1965 to 1983. For 1965, the birth rate in low-income countries was 48/1000 and the death rate 22/1000; for middle-income countries the birth rate was 50/1000, the death rate 22/1000. This produced a population gain per annum of about 2.7 percent. By 1983 both had declined, to 47/1000 births and 18/1000 deaths for low-income; 49/1000 births and 16/1000 deaths for middle-income—a population gain per annum of 3.3 percent. Thus, death rates declined faster than birth rates, leading to an overall growth in population increase rates.

A good portion of this decline in crude death rate came about through the decline in infant mortality rates. In 1965 IMR was 156/1000 in low- and middle-income countries in Sub-Saharan Africa. This was a great improvement over the 350/1000 IMR that had prevailed in the continent earlier in the century. In a few countries, such as Kenya, IMR had been brought down to under 100/1000 by the late 1980s. These "improving" health figures were, however, offset by 6 to 7 percent decline in food production, which translated in the lower-income countries into a nearly 10 percent decline in calorie intake (the middle-income countries saw a slight improvement in this category). Insofar as one can then extrapolate from these composite statistical figures, survivorship has increased, although real income and food production has decreased.

Morbidity patterns in the ngoma region, as measured by agencies such as the World Health Organization and standardized measures, indicate that although some of the major contagious diseases such as smallpox, cholera, and measles had been eliminated or brought under control, others such as diarrhea and respiratory infection continued to be the greatest killers of infants. Generally, the disease profile continued to be that of contagious diseases rather than of degenerative and other "diseases of civilization."

What do these figures mean in terms of our understanding of the backdrop of ritual healing, or the status of health in the region with which we are concerned? Does ngoma relate to these population measures?

There is a discussion that concerns our agenda, perhaps indirectly, having to do with whether Sub-Saharan Africa's health measures represent a conventional pattern of demographic transition, comparable to that which has been seen in Europe and Asia. There, following the decline of mortality and morbidity earlier in this century, fertility measures declined as well. In Africa, although mortality and morbidity have declined, fertility has probably increased. This pattern may be related to what ngoma does.

One set of analysts argues that the demographic profile of Sub-Saharan Africa is to be explained by the peripheralization of the subcontinent in the world capitalist system, and by capital's need for a large, cheap, surplus labor pool (Gregory and Piche 1982; Cordell, Gregory, and Piche 1992; Stock 1986). Another group (e.g., Lesthaege and Eelens 1985) evaluates what they call "demographic regimes," characteristic profiles, with an interest in the fate of socioeconomic and cultural mechanisms such as child spacing, household structures, and number and composition of family members available for childcare, which might affect overall demographic trends. They document the apparent collapse in recent decades in Africa of a number of these long-term historic structures and the consequent increase in fertility rates. A related perspective has suggested that much of Central and Southern Africa's social priorities are derived from a lineage base and a particular technology of hoe agriculture (Goody 1976; Caldwell, Caldwell, and Quiggin 1989) and that so long as these institutional structures prevail, health and fertility measures will be affected in distinctive ways.

The outcome of this debate on Africa's demographic transition will not be clear for some time. We know health has improved considerably in the past half-century, but there is still much room for improvement in diseases and conditions for which cures are available. We know fertility has not begun to decline, and in some areas it has probably increased. Clearly many of these factors affecting health status have to do with knowledge, access to resources, and social policies. Therefore, in our assessment of the role of ritual healing in affecting health status, we do well to keep "hard" demographic data in mind but to develop social theories of the ways health-related resources are generated and utilized. This is why it seems appropriate to bring the notion of "social reproduction" to bear upon the analysis of health and healing.

THE SOCIAL REPRODUCTION OF HEALTH

The definition of social reproduction with which this chapter began—the maintenance of a way of life and the commitment of resources to relationships, institutions, and support organizations that directly or indirectly maintain health—was a generic statement derived from a number of writers whose work on this concept may be presented more fully here.

In assessing a "social reproduction" concept of health, it is important to identify the social units or sectors involved and to identify some indices of this process that are separate from biological reproduction and the reproduction of labor. Meillassoux's work offers one perspective on this type of analysis. He separates the "domestic community" as a social formation from both biological reproduction and the reproduction of labor for capitalist needs (1981). This analytical model distinguishes the energy or "social product" needed (a) to reconstitute productive adult producers, (b) to nurture future producers, that is, "not yet productive" children, and (c) to maintain the postproductive elderly and the sick (1981:51–57). The sum of these products offers an indication of what is required to socially reproduce the domestic community. Relative surpluses enhance and enrich the community; relative deficits erode it. Over several years one can in theory determine the level at which a community reproduces itself or falls below a minimal replacement level.

Other authors go beyond Meillassoux's approach to include more than material needs in the calculus of social reproduction. The distinctions between social, biological, and symbolic reproduction are further developed in Pierre Bourdieu's well-known study of the Kabyle of Algeria, published in his *Outline of a Theory of Practice* (1977). Here the patrilineage, composed of households headed by brothers, is the principal social institution. Various centrifugal forces are at work to bring disintegration to the lineage. Strategies to pull the lineage together, to maintain the family—socially, symbolically, and biologically—concentrate on the appropriate marriage. This is often a marriage of a man to his father's brother's daughter (*bint amm*), so common in pastoral nomadic societies. Such a marriage serves materially to keep the herds and other aspects of the estate intact. However, Bourdieu points out that such a strategy involves far more than just economic management (1977:60). The ethos of honor attaches to the unity of the land, to equal status alliances, and the unity of the agnatic group, the prestige of the house. Bourdieu says it is impossible to separate ends and means in the collective matrimonial strategies. Every marriage tends to reproduce the conditions that have made it possible. "Matrimonial strategies, objectively directed towards the conservation or expansion of the material and symbolic capital jointly possessed by a more or less extended group, belong to the system of *reproduction strategies,* defined as the sum total of the strategies through which individuals or groups reproduce the relations of production associated with a determinate mode of production by striving to reproduce or improve their position in the social structure" (1977:70).

These issues of threshold levels of household and community maintenance are addressed in Colin Murray's work "The Work of Men, Women and the Ancestors: Social Reproduction in the Periphery of Southern Africa" (1979), in Lesotho communities that are deeply involved in oscillating labor migration to the mines, cities, and factories of South Africa. As has been abundantly documented, Lesotho has moved from being an autonomous agrarian society earlier in this century, which exported grain, to being a society now largely dependent on wage labor, and which imports most of its food. Disease levels have risen during this period; tuberculosis in particular constitutes a major endemic disease (Murray 1981). Aggregate demographic data for Lesotho are comparable to data elsewhere in the continent, with crude birth rates having remained constant at 42/1000 per annum, and death rates having declined from 18 to 15/1000 from 1965 to 1983, resulting in an increase in population growth over that time from 2.4 to 2.7 percent per annum (World Health Organization 1979; World Bank 1985).

Murray's careful anthropological fieldwork suggests that these aggregate demographic data mask the significant intra-community and household disparities, having to do with household makeup, related mortality and morbidity, and overall health rates. Up to 70 percent of the households are managed by women who are almost entirely dependent on their husbands' wage labor for survival. Only 6 percent of household income came from the sale of farm produce. At highest risk for disease were those families of single household heads, and children in families in which the spouse of the resident head did not provide a cash stipend (Murray 1979:346). In these homes infant mortality often reached 50 percent, far higher than the 120/1000 average. Although these "at risk" households reproduced the labor pool for the South African industries and contributed to population increase, they were not "socially reproducing themselves." In Meillassoux's equation of social reproduction, they plainly reflected a social product deficit.

In Murray's account, social mechanisms most often utilized in Lesotho society to achieve social reproduction were "inter-household income transfers," such as cash and in-kind remittances, bridewealth transfers, share-cropping arrangements, and other contractual and reciprocal arrangements connected with agriculture; also, informal sector transfers such as beer brewing, petty trading, and concubinage, all of which maintained a wider scale of social relations than the household, and thus extended viable social support links for those in short-term or long-term need. In noting a further feature of Lesotho society that is directly related to the way ngoma reproduces society, Murray demonstrates how the exchanges and feasts of ancestor rituals, often in connection with leaving for, or returning from, migrant labor, play an important role in forging and renewing the alliances needed to survive the absence of the family head (Murray 1979:347). Although ngoma in a narrow sense is absent in historic Sotho-Tswana society, perhaps because of its centralized judicial institutions, the initiation case in chapter 1 is that of a Sotho man whose family is caught up in labor migration.

A further noteworthy author who has taken a view comparable to "social reproduction of health," without utilizing these exact words, is Steven Frankel, an M.D.-anthropologist who has worked among the Huli in New Guinea. Frankel's medical anthropological study of the Huli of New Guinea (1986) develops both the negative indices of health, the "absence of disease," and the positive concept of "social effectiveness." The elaboration of rhetorical skills, esoteric knowledge, ritual practices, and cosmetic decorations are considered essential in the ability to be effective in social exchanges. These are seen as prerequisites in soliciting others' generosity and ultimately enabling an individual to care for a family and to lead the community. For the Huli, and for Frankel, social effectiveness is seen as operating at a level to include not only the household but larger societal levels as well, and not merely the material basis of existence but the symbolic exchanges needed to extend public institutions.

In sum, the concept of social reproduction offers a model of how therapeutic rituals such as ngoma might prove efficacious in enhancing health. Can it be tested?

PROFILES OF NGOMA
SOCIAL REPRODUCTION

The social networks and therapeutic cell communities formed through the long-term association of master-healer and novice, as well as the "lay" clients and the assemblies of people at ritual events, may well offer, in their ability to recreate society, the most pronounced characteristic of ngoma therapy in achieving and maintaining health where it has collapsed. The structure of these emergent social forms shows the social reproduction around sufferers and former sufferers, healers and the healed. The four illustrations of this process that follow will focus, as noted earlier, on the type of social fabric that is created, reinforced, or reproduced by the particular ngoma ritual so as to more effectively address health needs.

RECONCILING LINEAGE AND TRADE
IN PRECOLONIAL KONGO SOCIETY

In the setting of the ancient Lemba cult of affliction in Lower Zaire, the local lineage was challenged to come to grips with the mercantile wealth of the great trade with the coast without having its egalitarian ethos shattered. I have suggested, in chapter 1 of the present work and elsewhere (1982:70–79), that this was possible through the judicious creation of alliances between lineages, which forged links across the countryside along the trade routes, and through adequate exchange and distribution within these nodes of society, thereby assuring that Lemba members could safely travel from market to market, and to the coast with their caravans.

The demographic profile of coastal Kongo society during the seventeenth to early twentieth centuries, during which Lemba existed, is known to have suffered from an overall decline of about 50 percent of what it had been in the sixteenth century (Sautter 1966:2–71). An objective assessment of the factors involved in this would include not only the slave trade, which drew the best young adults out of the society, but the compounding influences of societal breakdown resulting from raids and epidemics.

Lemba initiation rituals approached these conditions at several levels. One was the divination and treatment of specific symptoms and signs related to the fear of subordinates' envy. However, a more important criterion of the initiates' acceptance was their ability to pay for the final stages of the initiation rite, the "graduation," whether with their own or their lineage's patronage. Effectively, Lemba was a cult of affliction of the elite households of north bank Congo River society, in the face of the disintegrative forces of the mercantile trade with the coast.

The social structural particulars of this arrangement are well known. Of strategic significance in the whole Lemba scheme of social reproduction was the Lemba household, which brought together two types of groups. One was the alliance that linked major landowning freeholder lineages in adjacent communities; the second was the alliance that bonded such freeholder lineages with client lineage fragments. In the first instance, the marriage tended to be of the patrilateral, cross-cousin type between lineages of equal status, between whom equal exchange marked successive marriages of this type. In the second setting, they were often, from the perspective of the marrying male in the dominant lineage, matrilateral cross-cousin marriages. This pattern expressed the unequal exchange between the two lineages, serving nevertheless to weld the community of several exogamous lineages together in a hierarchic local society. The Lemba marriages between freeholders assured a regional network for the trade and peaceful relations in a region where no historic state extended its hegemony. The Lemba marriages between unequal—master and client, or slave—lineages enhanced the local community by enlarging its population and political base. Indeed, the rhetoric of Lemba stated that the lineage in possession of Lemba "could not die out."

In these two ways Lemba helped to socially reproduce the society in the face of the centrifugal forces unleashed by the coastal trade from 1600 on, economic divisions within lineages, slave raids, feuds and wars, and epidemics. We have no way of knowing whether Lemba diminished the episodes of fear of envy by subordinates, either through protective medicine or through redistribution of goods and food. However, it is clear, and north Kongo informants stress, that Lemba was usually an important deterrent to local feuds and thus averted the bloodshed, loss of property through burned houses, and chaos that otherwise resulted from local wars. In this sense Lemba did have a measurable effect on the well-being of the region where it was implanted.

We have only glimpses of the numbers of individuals in a region involved in Lemba. In terms of the percentages of marriages that might have been "Lemba marriages," extrapolating from historical data in the village on which I have such records, it appears that less than 5 percent were involved. Yet as the elite, they were influential, and the impact of Lemba was considerable.

SAVING LIVES OF MOTHERS AND INFANTS ON THE SOUTHERN SAVANNA

Another area in which we may usefully examine the "social reproduction" hypothesis of the efficacy of ngoma rituals is in the enhancement of conception and successful birthing and the survival of healthy children. Although ngoma-type intervention has been studied in the Western Bantu Nkita rite described earlier, and although Victor Turner studied certain ngoma rites among the Ndembu, these studies do not focus on epidemiological or demographic variables. However, we now know that the region from the Atlantic coast inland to western Kasai in Zaire, and the Southern Savanna to western Zambia, and northward to Congo and Gabon, constituted—and in some areas still constitutes—the widespread "infertility zone" (Gaisie 1989).

The work by Anita Spring (1978, 1985) and Veronique Goblet-Vanormelingen (1988) on this ngoma-style institution on the Southern Savanna of northwestern Zambia and southern Zaire, respectively, is exceptionally valuable for its attention to the demographic and epidemiologic indicators associated with the purported goals of ngoma. Spring has studied the Kula rite and related *mahamba* (generic shrines) among the Luvale; Goblet-Vanormelingen has studied an institution called Mbombo among the Mutombo Mukulu Luba of Shaba Province in Zaire. These are similar in their emphasis on reproductive difficulties in the cults of affliction of Wubwangu, Isoma, and aspects of Nkula which Victor Turner (1968) described among the Ndembu of Zambia.

The core features of ngoma identified in chapter 3 may all be found in the reproductive enhancement rites on the Southern Savanna. The mode of affliction is identified as spirit-originated threat to the newly conceived fetus. After an initial rite of entrance, the pregnant woman leaves her husband and enters seclusion in a special enclosure constructed in the homestead of her sponsoring healer-gynecologist-midwife, where she is taken care of with anti-abortive medication, special diet, and hygienic attention. Upon the successful birth of the child, in some variants, and as much later as the first steps of the child in others, seclusion ends with a second-stage ngoma graduation and final entry of the mother into the order. In Mbombo, as described by Goblet-Vanormelingen, the end of seclusion comes shortly after the birth of the child, at which time the mother and child are washed in a nearby river and presented to the father. Ngoma music accompanies this "coming out" of the new child with its mother.

Both Spring and Goblet-Vanormelingen are interested in the "efficacy" of these birth-enhancing procedures. Spring criticizes Turner for paying little attention to this question and for assuming that Isoma (for miscarriages, abortions, stillbirths, barrenness, menstrual disorders, illness of infants), Wubwangu (for twin pregnancies, infant disorders, barrenness, miscarriages, menstrual disorders) and Nkula (for menstrual disorders, barrenness, miscarriages, ill health of infant) were primarily social, symbolic, and religious in nature. She is interested, first of all, in the "epidemiology of ritual participation" and in whether the seclusion procedures enhance survivorship. One important predisposing issue to be taken into account in the Luvale region of Zambia is that although the continuity of the lineage and family is highly valued, infertility and subfecundity of women is common and survivorship of infants is low. About 20 percent of Luvale women in Spring's sample of forty-five-year-old women had been barren during their adult lives. A high percentage were subfecund, that is, had gone five years without a live birth during reproductive years. Further, infant mortality was about 150/1000. This resulted in a completed family size on average per woman of only 2.05 children for the society, which is barely a replacement level (Spring 1978:175–176). The Luvale were understandably concerned with fertility enhancement.

Reasons for the high infertility included high levels of genital and urinary-tract disease, much barrenness, and fetal wastage. These are in part reflected in the high level of abdominal pains, dysmenorrhea, and fevers probably caused by bilharziasis, gonorrhea, and nonspecific bacterial infection, in addition to malaria, hookworm, and amebiasis, which are endemic (1978:176).

The isolation therapy at the time of conception is part of a more general cultural strategy of the Luvale to improve the chances of offspring. Childless women are first of all given treatment for barrenness. If they become pregnant, they receive the performances of several *mahamba* cults at a number of possible points in their reproductive years. If a pregnant woman has a miscarriage or delivers a stillborn child, she is a likely candidate for the seclusion ritual. If she has menstrual dysfunctions, she will receive herbal treatments, which, if unsuccessful, will be followed by further ritual treatment. If a woman's child becomes sickly, both mother and child will be secluded. If a woman's small child dies, she will receive seclusion. If a woman becomes ill with problems unrelated directly to childbirth, she will be a candidate for the seclusion ritual. "Possession" cult initiation may thus occur at any one of a number of points in the course of a woman's reproductive years. The etiology of spirit or shade involvement is usually made official by the diviner. Rarely does it involve trance, although the ngoma-type song-dance, a variety of particular medicinal and technical treatments, food prohibitions and special diets, the "white" symbolism of seclusion, and the two-stage passage are integral features of the rites.

Fully half of the women in Luvale society are initiated to one or another manifestation of reproductive cults by the time they reach the end of their childbearing years. In Turner's Ndembu sample, women's reproductive issues were by far the most frequent encounters of individual Ndembu with the ngoma system. In his sample from two areas, Turner noted that nineteen of twenty-six women had gone through Nkula; twelve of twenty-four through Isoma and Wubwangu each (1968:303). Goblet-Vanormelingen, whose work is still in process, gives no statistical information of this type. Spring emphasizes that these reproduction enhancement rituals are thus responses to both generalized physical ill health and particular concerns of Southern Savanna families for effective biological and social reproduction.

How effective are the rituals and their related interventions? Goblet-Vanormelingen judges as "truly beneficial" the following aspects of Mbombo ritual: the continuous assistance of the healer and the woman's husband, creating an encouraging atmosphere for her; some rules of behavior, particularly the necessity of living away from the stresses of family life, the dangers of exposure to contagious diseases and work-related infections, and having complete rest; and, after childbirth, seclusion to reinforce the mother-child bond. More dangerous to the health of mother and child are certain practices in preparation for birth and delivery, which, because they are nonsterile, may increase the risk of infections or tetanus, and certain food prohibitions that appear to restrict intake of nutritious food. On balance, believes Goblet-Vanormelingen, the Mbombo rituals appear to enhance the chances of well-being of both mother and child.

Spring's analysis of Luvale womens' reproduction rituals, although it does not lend itself to a precise statistical evaluation, does suggest that the isolation therapy and the maintenance of networks of ngoma orders probably improve the health of mothers and children, that is, increase survivorship. Spring's evidence suggests that most women who are divined to require ngoma rituals do enter them, and in their later years these women become the doctors of these cults. This means that because they are at risk, survival ratios of the infants of those women who are members of, involved in, and leaders in the ngoma orders will be lower than among nonmembers. Survivorship must be counted in terms of pregnancies saved that might otherwise have been lost and surviving infants who might otherwise have been lost.

Anita Spring focuses her discussion of efficacy—although she does not use the term—around the structure and the strength of the network of women active in reproduction enhancement, and what this does for their self-image, social role, and the structure of the community. The sequence of being a sufferer-novice, an apprentice, and finally a cured-doctor results in a cooperative system of social relations permitting women to gain, and perpetuate through practice and teaching, the knowledge of how to deal with women's reproductive concerns. As in other ngoma contexts, adversity is turned into strength, anxiety into specialized knowledge, suffering into healing. The institutional framework brings spirit possession, as an ideology, into the set of etiological beliefs, although the type of knowledge needed to deal with infertility, threatened miscarriage, stillbirths, sick children, and the rest, is highly practical, what in the West we would call empirical and rational knowledge, rather than a trance state.

Not all ngoma attention to children is as salutary as that of the Southern Savanna. On two occasions in the 1982–83 survey I witnessed practices that I thought might lead to the child's death, rather than to its recovery. Both had to do with divinatory possessions. The first occurred in Kinshasa as Mama Kishi Nzembela, the Luba Bilumbu medium, allowed her apprentice medium to flail about with her child pressed between her legs, shouting that it was evil and that she had an evil spirit. Obviously the young woman was unhappy, and in a reckless abandon she took her misery out on her child. The child escaped that episode unscathed, but the mother nearly smashed its tender skull on the cement floor, with which it came into very close proximity on several occasions. The other time was during a divining session in Swaziland when the most elaborate and high-priced mediumship divination was done to determine the cause of the sickness of a small child. Granted, in both cases, the infants were born to women who were not married, or whose marriages had ended. Thus, ancestral and spirit displeasure as cause of a small child's respiratory infection was a type of diagnosis that should have been abandoned in favor of adequate clinical and parental care. Although these two mediumship divinations may have enhanced family solidarity, they did not contribute to the well-being of the infants involved.

Rick Yoder's concern, "Is it good for the children?" was not an idle one with regard to ngoma rites.

REGIONAL NETWORKS OF THE ISANGOMA/ AMAGQIRA OF SOUTHERN AFRICA

The demographic profile of South Africa reflects both third world and first world conditions. White society has low mortality and fertility, on par with Western Europe, and a morbidity profile in keeping with

an industrialized, affluent society. The leading causes of death are degenerative and cardiovascular diseases. By contrast, the society of the
black townships reflects conditions of high mortality and fertility; the
leading morbidity causes are infectious diseases and accidents. Among
adults, tuberculosis is a serious problem. Among children, respiratory and intestinal infections and contagious diseases are the leading
causes of death. South African homelands, whose health statistics are
often not published in official records because some of them are "independent," have the highest infant mortality rates in Africa, near
300/1000.

Ngoma is well-represented in the black townships of the Western
Cape, as noted in earlier chapters. However, its relationship to the
foregoing health indicators is not well understood. Little work has been
done on the subject. The composition of ngoma cells is not as strict or
well-defined as in Central Africa. Ngoma activity, as noted, exists in a
single inter-ethnic mode, rather than being thematically specialized and
ethnically distinctive. Cells may be organized as informal friendship alliances between healers (sangoma, amagqira). One igqira with whom
I discussed the composition of her group of collaborating healers,
suggested that she met with "her friends," whom she invited to her
events with about a week's advance notice, on the basis of friendship
and compatibility, that is, that they did not drink excessively. It was
along such lines that information would be passed and mutual help and
gifts exchanged over divination, counseling, and healing-initiating.

In five related events I observed in Cape Town, a loosely linked "star"
network pattern emerged, suggestive of overlapping sets of fully initiated sangoma or amagqira (see fig. 13). To the skeletal network of Western
Cape diviner-healers, one must add an array of, on average, ten novices
allied with each healer, plus the novices' families and friends. For the
five amagqira with whom I was able to discuss this, each had nine,
twenty, ten, ten, and six apprentices respectively. These novices regularly attend purification events on the occasion of a death in the family
or kindred of any one of them and also of their master-healer; they attend all events put on by their master-healer, such as initiations and
graduations. The novices' own families are to some extent involved, if
not directly in the events, then indirectly in the benefits of the regular
food distributions made at the time of goat, sheep, and cattle sacrifices
and feasts. The attendance at one typical event, the initiation mentioned
in figure 13, included six master healers (three Xhosa and one Zulu
woman, two Zulu men), two female Xhosa senior novices, six Xhosa

Event Type	Full Amagqira/Sangoma and Novices Present
(1) "Washing of beads" for B, sponsored by A	
(2) Initiation *nthlombe* for novice of B	
(3) "Washing of beads" for novice of G	
(4) "Washing of beads" for novice of B	
(5) Graduation *nthlombe* for novice of L	

Figure 13. Pattern of association of individual healers and their novices in five events in Western Cape ngoma networks, late 1982. Capital letters refer to senior healers present at particular events; clusters of enclosed *x*'s refer to these healers' novices in therapy/training with them.

female novices and one male Xhosa novice, a Sotho male initiate, and seven unidentified additional novices. Several dozen observers were on hand, including the initiate's family and neighbors.

The strength and depth of this type of organization in Cape Town township society is not easy to generalize without adequate survey information. However, a rough estimate may be projected from numbers of master healers in the two streets in Guguleto and Nyanga where *ngoma* participation was assessed. One street had four full igqira residents; the other had two, plus an *ixwele* herbalist. I was told that this was a common degree of representation for the townships. This average of 3.5 amagqira per street, however shaky its statistical significance, times the 153 equal-length streets and houses in two townships, would suggest that there are 535 fully qualified sangoma/amagqira in Guguleto and Nyanga. This figure, doubled to include the townships Langa and Crossroads, would yield an estimate of over a thousand healers of the ngoma type in the townships of Cape Town. If the Western Cape Regional Authority's figure of 200,000 African inhabitants is used, there would be approximately one ngoma healer for 200 inhabitants.

However, to estimate the full extent of ngoma networks in the populace, this figure must be multiplied by ten, for the average number of each master healer's apprentice-novices. Assuming five to seven individuals in each household, this would indicate ngoma involvement, as master healer or apprentice, in one in four households.

Such brandishing of statistical information is admittedly of dubious value. The claim that ngoma cells and networks socially reproduce relations needs to be given context not only in the ngoma setting but also in the domestic setting out of which the individuals originate. Evidence for this is again somewhat anecdotal and case-study specific. A review of one igqira's roster of current (1982) apprentice-novices, their family settings and domestic relations, and work records showed the following. Novice one, a married woman with five children in the house, had entered ngoma seven years earlier. With a secondary school degree, she worked for her husband's boss at a construction company. She was a "five to" (midnight), that is, near completion, and was assembling goods for her graduation. Novice two, also married to a man with "good work," and with children in the home, worked as a cleaning woman. She had begun seven years earlier and was gathering resources for her graduation. Novice three, married to a man with steady work in a blanket factory, also worked as a cleaning woman. Her children were small when she entered ngoma nine years earlier. She was trying to collect goods for her graduation. Novice four had children at home and was married to a taxi-bus owner who employed other drivers. She did not work outside the home. She had begun ngoma nine years earlier, having been a Zionist, and was a "five-to" assembling goods for her graduation. These four women, with seven to nine years experience as novices, were the mainstays in ngoma sessions under the direction of their master healer.

A second group of four novices in this cell seemed to have greater difficulty moving "through the white." They were all single mothers working outside the home. Novice five worked as a domestic and had three children. She had begun ngoma nine years earlier but had only progressed to the status of junior novice. Novice six, a single mother of one daughter, also worked as a domestic. She had problems with alcoholism and was not progressing well in her therapeutic initiation. Novices seven and eight were a mother-daughter set, living together without husbands. The daughter was a schoolteacher. Both were junior novices.

Two new apprentices were both parents in relatively stable marital relationships with small children at home. Novice nine, a member of the Bantu Presbyterian Church, was married to a man with a good job. Novice ten was a married man with children and stable employment.

Few generalizations may be drawn from this set of ten novices in one healer's group of apprentice-novices. One common factor is that they enter ngoma as young or middle-aged adults, and most require from five to ten years to move through the novitiate. But little is known about the "epidemiology" of ngoma involvement in South Africa.

Janet Mills, however, has sought to identify factors within the household that might be associated with the appeal to ngoma (1982). Although the explicit reason commonly given for entering an ngoma cell is the "call" (twasa) from ancestors, she has investigated the possible correlation between this support seeking and active tuberculosis cases in the household. She found tuberculosis to be slightly more frequent in ngoma-related than in non-ngoma households. Although no conscious or explicit linkage is made in ngoma participants' explanations between tuberculosis and the call to join ngoma, the possible basis for such a link may be hypothesized. It is unlikely that ngoma healing is directly beneficial for tuberculosis. Rather, it may be that just as tuberculosis—endemic in its latent state—has erupted in active infection, the energies of productive individuals have been so strained as to lead to support seeking in an ngoma or similar network. Tuberculosis is endemic in South African blacks, and a variety of stressors, such as inadequate nutrition, poverty, lack of adequate shelter, can bring on an active episode. Also, prolonged rest along with medication is required to recover from an active episode. Participation of the care providers—that is, spouse—in an ngoma cell or network would provide the requisite support, additional contacts, and sources of aid needed to deal with the long-term crisis of tuberculosis in the family.

Although one could figure the nutritional intake offered to participants in the ngoma network events as a possible point of departure for the analysis of its existence, more significant may well be the social investment in ngoma therapeutic structures. If one in four households is involved, this network covers the entire urban society, as well as connecting it to other cities and rural areas.

This significance of social reproduction, which I argue is also health-building efficacy, would seem to make an impact at three levels: the nucleus of the master with apprentices; the broad network spanning the whole society; and those households that are connected with ngoma. During the years of apprenticeship-initiation-therapy, the master healer serves as role model, counselor, therapist, guide; in return, the master may expect services and some goods from the novices. Although the novices or their family pay their masters a goodly sum of money for the sacrifice animals and for their own costume, they stand to benefit in the reshaping of their lives, in sorting out problems, finding contacts to jobs, and referrals of all sorts. Intense resocialization occurs within the group of novice-peers. The possibilities go beyond this, to the more public network into which the master healer is the "hub" of the wheel, radiating out along "spokes" to many households, and ultimately, to the entire society. A case can be argued that twasa is not madness, but the call to social reproduction. It is, as Harriet Ngubane has suggested (1981), a pan-societal network extending across Southern Africa, and, as we now know, well beyond.

PROFESSIONAL AND STATE CONTROL OF NGOMA ON THE SWAHILI COAST

The final example of the social reproduction of health through ngoma is from coastal Tanzania and shows yet another variation of the therapeutic focus and organizational structure of the institution. Among Zaramo and Zigua peoples of the Swahili coast, the coastal healers have utilized their ngoma networks to create a centralized institution, the Shirika la Madawa ya Kiasili, with officers, books, a treasury, and a "director," that is, a representative of government to be a liaison with appropriate ministries. Local ngoma performances draw, as everywhere in ngoma, a shifting set of senior participants with their apprentices and novices. At another level, there are individual waganga who belong to patrilineages, which in the Swahili coastal setting have often passed their therapeutic skills from generation to generation.

The Shirika had about five hundred members in 1983, with strongest representation in Dar es Salaam, Tanga, Bagamoyo, and Morogoro, and in the new capital, Dodoma. They were trying to create branches in other localities. Tanzania had earlier experimented with a national organization of healers, but this was abolished when it became too politicized, that is, fractured and powerful. The links between the Shirika and the government revealed some of the same forces of economic interest, of political strength, and of party and government control that had surfaced in the national organization. Why was the state interested in ngoma?

The Shirika had official recognition through the Ministry of Culture, which generally handled licenses for ngoma entertainment groups and conducted research on song-dance. Why, though, should therapeutic dancing be controlled by the Ministry of Culture and not the Ministry of Health? The power of ngoma as a resource, especially one so large and well organized, was indicative of its symbolic power in society at large. The role of a party-appointed "director" with affiliation to the national political party hinted at some of the potential tensions between the organization and the state's interest. The director in effect controlled the recruitment of new ngoma cells to the Shirika, thereby exercising restrictions on its overall influence. This would avert what had occurred in the case of a cattle-rustling ngoma that had arisen in response to the need to locate stolen livestock. The government had heard about it only after it was fully constituted and then belatedly tried to gain its allegiance. Somewhat similarly, the ngoma for entertainment organized by the National Service indicated the effort to connect the state to the powerful symbolism of socially focused song-dance.

These details of the relationship between state and ngoma illustrate a significant general principal. A resource such as ngoma, which may arise in response to a need, and which symbolically, socially, and materially reproduces itself, by that very fact attracts the state, which seeks to co-opt power and legitimacy unto itself.

The resources to be drawn from the Shirika—an umbrella organization of therapeutic ngoma—were also apparent to the individuals and families who made their living from these performances. Unlike the populistic networks of reproduction-enhancing ngoma of the Southern Savanna or the township ngoma of the Western Cape, here by no means everyone who was brought into the initial stage of treatment followed through with the full initiation. In fact, according to the records and testimony of the Shirika leaders, only about 3 to 4 percent of the sufferers who entered ngoma dispensaries for treatment were fully initiated. This is corroborated by research of a decade earlier, in which only three of sixty waganga had entered their healing profession through spirit calling (L. Swantz 1974:203).

In Dar es Salaam, the recognition of healers and the opportunity for them to organize into associations has led to the strengthening of their control of resources (Unschuld 1975). On the one hand, this has led to full-time practice, the utilization of therapeutics as income, and to the control of the therapeutic and symbolic resources, in this case divination, the diagnosis of spirit possession, and the performance of authorized therapeutic song-dance. On the other hand, this has led to the restriction of access to the role of the ngoma healer and to the consolidation of membership in the Shirika.

The effect of professionalization of health care elsewhere has been the codification of methods and the regulation of access to the ranks of those who practice (Last and Chavunduka 1986).

CONCLUSION

This chapter has offered an approach to the study of the relationship between social organization and the allocation of resources, and to their impact on health in the context of ngoma-type healing. Social reproduction theory, as put forward by Meillassoux, Bourdieu, Murray, and Frankel offers tools for a more rigorous analysis of the manner in which society itself structures the resources of health.

Unfortunately, very little research has been conducted to actually test propositions about the efficacy of ngoma-type therapy in terms of measurable health indicators. In the cases we have reviewed here, only the work by Anita Spring and Veronique Goblet-Vanormelingen on fertility-enhancing rituals of the Southern Savanna approaches the question in such a way as to offer clear comparative results. Ngoma structured care and isolation from the stresses of household duty appear to make a difference in survival of at-risk pregnancies.

A retrospective hypothesis for the controlled study of health as social reproduction would need to provide the following minimal information. What is the nature and extent of social support and its allocation to health-related arenas in the household, the extra-household networks, and society at large? Are there measurable differential effects upon survival of at-risk segments of society or the improvement of perceived health?

Conclusion

A major goal of this work has been to explore the basis for the institution variously known as the "ritual of affliction," "cult of affliction," or "drum of affliction," the latter term being derived directly from the widespread notion ngoma, a Bantu language cognate. Utilizing a variety of historical, linguistic, archaeological, and comparative sources, the case was made that ngoma may have emerged as part of the classical Bantu expansion over two millennia ago, although some evidence points to a more recent Eastern Bantu origin.

Nineteenth-century culture historians might have said that we had perhaps identified a health and healing "complex," a set of interrelated traits and practices, and unique characteristics. Others might have sought to explain it in terms of its origins. One reader of this manuscript noted that if ngoma was as old as suggested, it must have responded to a distinctive need during the original Bantu expansion.

Unfortunately, to unearth such an original purpose is beyond our reach. Perhaps one day very sophisticated sociolinguistic history or semiotic analysis of bodily motion will divulge the prehistory of ngoma. This work does not rest its case for ngoma's existence solely on a rigorous cultural-historical approach to ritual. Rather, utilizing a broad survey approach, I have demonstrated certain underlying common properties—linguistic, behavioral, and structural—that seem to make it appropriate to speak of ngoma as an institution, in the tradition of Durkheim, Weber, and Marx.

The formal properties of this institution were quite readily identified: the phased rite of passage, an approach to classifying misfortune which emphasizes the place of the social context—of people; the role of the shades and spirits in the outcome of dealing with that misfortune; the release of the sufferer from normal social obligations, and the progression of the sufferer-novice through the "white" liminal sick role and initiation to full membership in the order; the pervasiveness of sacrifice, which sets in motion an exchange between the living and the supernatural, as well as creating the bonds and networks among the living through the cooking and distribution of the sacrificial animal; finally, the empowerment of the initiate as qualified healer.

However, these features do not hold together as an institution until they are identified in their performance context, that of "doing ngoma." In this setting, a far more dynamic set of features is at work. The actions, described and analyzed in chapter 4, bring together every level of participant—novice, trainee, senior qualified person, as well as whoever else is present—to share of themselves and to respond to one another. Doing ngoma sets the stage for each and every individual in the order to work on self-transformation through song, as if before a constant mirror of others also seeking the same goal. Together, they seek renewed self-definition, in personalized song statements that resonate with the common terms of the ritual. Western institutional analysis has all too often crushed and distorted ngoma-type phenomena by forcing them into its own familiar slots and categories. In the present work I have tried to interpret the uniqueness of the institution in a number of other ways.

Ritual analysis offers one approach. Ritual may be defined as the amplification of layers upon layers of meaning, of levels or mediums of expression, or as the addition of more lines of communication to those normally used between individuals. Ritualization may occur because of "clogged channels" or contradictions in the individual's life, or in the household unit or society around the individual. Or it may result from unique ruptures within the social environment or from chronic suffering of sectors of society, such as women with children or working men alienated from their families. It may result from constant segmentation of the lineage basis of society.

Our task would have been facilitated had there been a conscious awareness in Central and Southern Africa of an overarching institutional presence. In my survey work in Kinshasa, Dar es Salaam, Swaziland, and Cape Town I encountered little or no evidence of this among patients and healers, nor among scholars. Healers did have an awareness of regional networks, of common ties. In western Zaire, there was awareness of the comparability of Nkita, Bilumbu, Zebola, and the other *grands rites,* and in Tanzania, of the existence of other ngoma than the ones practiced, including those from other regions. In Southern Africa, there was a greater degree of mixing and cross-fertilization of ngoma or the work of the amagqira than anywhere else. In some ways, scholars were more provincial than the healers, in that they often limited the focus of their research to tribal and national entities, for example, the Zulu diviner, the Zigua rite of affliction, the Ndembu cult of affliction.

This absence of the awareness of a larger institution and its character called for a further ontological query of whether the overlapping levels of evidence—the verbal cognates, the behaviors—could provide us with a clear picture of what ngoma was all about. Healers and scholars alike were intrigued by the possibility that their local institution might be part of a larger entity. They were able to point out recognizable common practices or features in photographs and musical recordings, as well as differences between their own practices and those of others. Some asserted that the version from afar was "wrong" in terms of the way they did it. Nevertheless, there emerged in practitioners' accounts of "how ngoma worked" a more or less common theory that words and spirit etiologies—often as expressed in song—provided the core working principle of ngoma. This aspect of ngoma needs extensive further research, as very little case material exists on the way in which individuals reach creative self-expression through the crucible of affliction.

But we are getting ahead of ourselves. What finally is going to be the name of this newly identified, widespread, apparently ancient institution? The name is no trifling matter, for on the choice of name will hang much of the identity of the institution. "Cult of affliction," "possession cult," "divination," "rite of affliction," "drum of affliction," and ngoma have been used more or less interchangeably. The first several are recognized analytical names; the last, an indigenous term that has multiple meanings and is therefore ambiguous. The advantage of utilizing an analytical term is that we can say it exists even if the locals give it another name. However, the advantage of utilizing the African name, *ngoma,* or another variant, *ngoma za kutibu* ("therapeutic ngoma," in the words of E. K. Makala in Tanzania's Ministry of Culture), or "ngoma-type ritual" or therapy, to cite Anita Spring, is that we tie into the conscious level of awareness of it. This offsets certain scholarly excesses that have distorted the identity and definition of the institution in the literature.

This perspective helps us overcome particularly the Western preoccupation with "trance" and "possession" as the central definers of the institution, which the term *cult* denotes. Fixation upon natives with upturned eyes grunting unintelligible spirit talk and dancing about in a frenzy has seduced scholars from the important task of looking at the context, structure, history, intention, and change of an ancient instituted process. As has become clear in the course of this study, trance behavior is but an occasional corollary of the etiology that attributes misfortune to ancestors and spirits. The spirit possession etiology is a type of ideology or hypothesis, usually invoked by diviners, to interpret a range of usually vague symptoms or signs, although at other times it is used in very clear-cut expressions of distress. The spirit hypothesis, as I like to call it, rarely blurs the practical exigencies of day-to-day life. It is rather a framework that sets up and legitimates an institution that may bring together many kinds of perspectives and theories. To limit ngoma expression to possession trance is particularly unfortunate because its outcome is the exact opposite of possession, namely, creative self-expression. Trance, when it does make an appearance, is usually an aspect of the performance ritual and needs to be seen in the context of dialogical music, confessions, and divinatory sessions in which problems are being worked out. Only occasionally do trance and possession join as a shamanic-type journey of the analyst.

For these reasons, this work has stressed the centrality of discourse in ngoma interaction and knowledge. The "doing ngoma" process is a format for the identification of sources of misfortune, for bringing out and articulating, energizing, and transforming individual identity and purpose, and for gathering others who are in a position to vicariously help with these tasks. It is a process that may address any type of situation in which the form is servant to the content. It may accommodate a great latitude of types of knowledge: common sense, the hypotheses embedded in spirit fields; technical knowledge of the natural world, scientific knowledge based on propositions, social principles in kin and non-kin society, and other types of "survival knowledge," to cite Lihamba (1986). Gregory Bateson long ago emphasized that one of the functions of ritual was the preservation and utilization of knowledge.

Readers will have recognized the similarity between ngoma-type healing orders in Africa and Western self-help institutions such as Alcoholics Anonymous, Weight Watchers, Parents Anonymous, networks of organ transplant subjects, parents of sudden infant death syndrome victims, cardiac rehabilitation groups, and many more. These, in the West, have often had the benefit of biomedical consultants or liaisons, although in their organizational character they have been independent of direct medical institutional control. Part of their success in the lives of members is the transformation of the self in the very area of prior weakness or failing.

Out of this process emerges a further agenda of this work, namely, to define health, to test the institution's impact on health, and to determine its efficacy in either preventing deterioration of health or in restoring health where it has deteriorated. There is much variability in the criteria by which health inventories are judged. The theoretical terrain of this discussion is fraught with philosophical dilemmas about the identification of sets of variables used in defining health. In this work, criteria that have been brought forward have had to do with words and consciousness, labeling of diseases, and the predisposition of the sufferer; with the role of metaphor and symbol and the amplification of these expressions in ritual performance; with the creation of communities of the afflicted and the importance of sharing one's problems with others.

Because of the prevalence of a trance and possession definition of ngoma in much of the scholarly literature and popular culture, or the implication that ngoma's therapeutic orientation is psychological only, there has been a certain resistance on the part of scholars and policymakers to consider ngoma's role as it addresses epidemiological and demographic definitions of disease. Yet as we have seen, there appears to be significant evidence that ngoma rites such as the Tanzanian snake handling or the Southern Savanna fertility-enhancement procedures for mothers and children at risk may directly address these issues.

Given the promise of significant ill-health risk reduction in some particular ngoma institutions, what are the prospects that they can be engaged more intentionally in the agendas of health ministries and other agencies? One issue that has emerged in this regard is the struggle over the organizational matrices of ngoma entities. For the most part, *ngoma* organizations represent an "uncaptured" power base whose leaders and resources, decentralized as they are, resist co-optation by the nation-state. Where there has been centralized organization, as in coastal

Tanzania, struggle for the control of ngoma resources has remained a problem.

Ngoma resources have been effectively integrated into national institutions in Swaziland, where the king has personally endorsed, and underwritten the care and training of, skilled healers such as Ida Mabuza. It is possible, but difficult, to generalize this model of integration in the modern state, where bureaucratic rules and decisions are prevalent. It might work to the extent that leadership remains personalized within the mantle of bureaucratic rationality. However, in such a patrimonial system there is enormous competition for the legitimation that such personal support entails, and it hardly provides a basis for consistent and equitable distribution of resources to a needy populace.

It appears most appropriate to seek integration of ngoma-type institutions, and their overall enhancement, at a less bureaucratic level, such as has been sketched in Zaire. There, the state health service has recommended general hygienic instruction for all healers to upgrade their contribution to health without eroding their power base. Public health and hygiene instruction of healers in Ghana and Sierra Leone has produced significant reduction of infant mortality rates.

As the Southern African ngoma networks show, there are transnational channels of information at work that tend to distribute new knowledge. Ngubane writes that the shifting cell composition at successive sessions of the sangoma uniquely serves to spread insight about healing techniques and solutions to problems. In theory, it should be possible to introduce knowledge of hygiene, public health, and other areas of public concern at any point in such a network and see it spread throughout the system. Of course, ngoma knowledge, as we have seen, has its own assumptions and structures. Ancestral or spirit legitimation, rather than individual legitimation, must remain prior. This is Africa's way of stressing the moral basis of useful knowledge in the institutional process. Yet the distinction between common and personal songs allows for the introduction of new personal knowledge. To the extent that personal knowledge, or messages about personal transformation, are generalized and taken on by others, and then become common knowledge, ngoma settings may serve as channels of new outside knowledge and information.

Ngoma, an apparently classical institution of Central and Southern Africa, deserves our consideration, whether we are interested in its dance and discourse format, its therapeutic instrumentalities, or its applicability to the resolution of societal problems. We do well to consider ngoma as a uniquely ngoma instituted combination of processes and attributes that the West puts together in other ways, or leaves undone.

Appendix A
Partial Listing of Guthrie's Inventory of Bantu Languages

These groupings, mapped on the following topographical charts suggestive of their geographical relationships (see appendix B), are arranged according to morphological and lexical features of Bantu languages. Although some of Guthrie's genetic relationships are disputed, this listing and the cognate summary is a widely accepted overview of language and culture relationships.

A.10	LUNDU-BALONG GROUP [Cameroon]
A.11	Londo
A.20	DUALA GROUP
A.24	Duala
A.30	BUBE-BENGA GROUP
A.32a	Banoo (Nohu, Noko) [Cameroon]
A.32b	Bapoko (Naka, Puku)
A.34	Benga [Gabon, Rio Muni]
A.40	BASA GROUP [Cameroon]
A.42	Bakon (Abo)
A.43a	Mbene (Basa, Koko, Mvele)
A.60	SANAGA GROUP
A.63	Mangisa
A.70	YAUNDE-FANG GROUP
A.71	Eton
A.72a	Ewondo (Yaunde)
A.72b	Mvele
A.72c	Bakja
A.72d	Yangafek
A.73a	Bebele
A.73b	Gbigbil

A.74	Bulu
A.75	Fang (Pangwe)
A.80	MAKA-NJEM GROUP
A.81	Mvumbo (Ngumba)
A.83	Makaa
B.10	MYELE CLUSTER [Gabon]
B.11a	Mpongwe
B.11b	Rongo (Orungu)
B.11c	Galwa
B.11d	Dyumba
B.11e	Nkomi
B.20	KELE GROUP
B.22a	W. Kele
B.22b	Ngom
B.24	Wumbvu
B.25	Kota (Shake, Mahongwe)
B.30	TSOGO GROUP
B.31	Tsogo (Mitsogo, Apindji)
B.50	NJABI GROUP
B.52	Nzebi (Njabi)
B.60	MBETE GROUP [Congo]
B.61	Mbete
B.62	Mbaama (Mbamba)
B.70	TEKE GROUP [Congo]
B.71a	Tege-Kali
B.71b	Njininji
B.72a	Ngungwel (Ngungulu)
B.72b	Mpumpu
B.73a	Tsaayi
B.73b	Laali
B.73c	Yaa (Yaka)
B.73d	Kwe
B.74a	Ndzindziu
B.74b	Boo (Boma)
B.75	Bali (Tio, Teke)
B.76a	Mosieno
B.76b	Dee
B.80	TENDE-YANZI GROUP
B.81	Tiene (Tende)
B.82	Boma
B.83	Mfinu (Funika, Mfununga)
B.85a	Mbiem (W. Yanzi)
B.85b	E. Yans (Yanzi)
B.85c	Yeei
B.85d	Ntsuo

| B.85*e* | Mpur |
| B.87 | Mbuun (Mbunda) |

C.10	NGUNDI GROUP [North Zaire]
C.11	Ngondi
C.12*a*	Pande
C.12*b*	Bogongo
C.13	Mbati
C.20	MBOSHI GROUP
C.23	Ngare
C.30	BANGI-NTOMBA GROUP
C.31*a*	Loi
C.31*b*	Ngiri
C.32	Bobangi
C.35*a*	Ntomba
C.35*b*	Bolia
C.36*a*	Poto
C.36*b*	Mpesa
C.36*c*	Mbudza
C.37	Buja
C.40	NGOMBE GROUP
C.41	Ngombe
C.45	Angba (Ngelima, Beo, Tungu, Buru)
C.50	SOKO-KELE GROUP
C.52	So (Soko)
C.54	Lombo (Turumbu)
C.55	Kele
C.56	Loma
C.60	MONGO GROUP
C.61*a*	N.E. Mongo
C.61*b*	N.W. Mongo (Nkundo)
C.63	Ngando
C.70	TETELA GROUP
C.71	Tetela
C.73	Nkutu
C.74	Yela
C.75	Kela (Lemba)
C.80	KUBA GROUP
C.82	Songomeno
C.83	Bushong

D.10	MBOLO-ENA GROUP
D.14	Enya (Genya, Ena, Zimba)
D.20	LEGA-KALANGA GROUP
D.21	Bali (S.E. Bua, Bango)
D.24	Songola
D.25	Lega (Rega)

D.27	Bangubangu
D.28*a*	W. Holoholo (Guha, Kalanga)
D.28*b*	E. Holoholo [Tanzania]
D.40	KONJO GROUP
D.42	Ndandi (Nandi, Shu)
D.50	BEMBE-KABWARI GROUP
D.54	Bembe
D.60	RUANDA-RUNDI GROUP
D.61	Ruanda
D.62	Rundi
D.66	Ha

E.10	NYORO-GANDA GROUP
E.11	Nyoro (Gungu, Kyopi)
E.12	Tooro
E.13	Nyankoro (Hima)
E.15	Ganda
E.16	Soga
E.30	MASABA-LUHYA GROUP
E.32*a*	Hanga (Luhya)
E.32*b*	Tsotse
E.40	RAGOLI-KURIA GROUP
E.41	Logooli
E.42	Gusii (Guzii, Kisii)
E.50	KIKUYU KAMBA GROUP [Kenya]
E.51	Gekoyo (Kikuyu)
E.52	Embo
E.53	Mero
E.55	Kamba
E.60	CHAGA GROUP
E.61	Rwo (Meru)
E.62*a*	Hai (Chaga, Moshi, Machame)
E.62*b*	Wunjo (Marangu)
E.62*c*	Rombo
E.64	Kahe
E.65	Gweno
E.70	NYIKA-TAITA GROUP
E.71	Pokomo
E.72*a*	Giryama
E.72*b*	Kauma (Nika, Nyika)
E.73	Digo
E.74*a*	Dabida (Taita)
E.74*b*	Sagala (Taita)

F.20	SUKUMA-NYAMWEZI GROUP [Western Tanzania]
F.21	Sukuma
F.22	Nyamwezi

F.30   ILAMBA-IRANGA GROUP
F.31   Nilamba (Iramba)
F.32   Remi (Nyaturu)

G.10   GOGO GROUP [Tanzania]
G.11   Gogo
G.20   SHAMBALA GROUP
G.21   Tubeta (Taveta)
G.23   Sambaa (Shambala)
G.24   Bondei
G.30   ZIGULA-ZARAMO GROUP
G.31   Zigula (Zigua)
G.32   Dhwele
G.33   Zaramo (Dzalamo)
G.34   Ngulu
G.40   SWAHILI GROUP
G.41   Tikuu (Tukulu)
G.42a Amu
G.42b Mvita
G.42c Mrima
G.42d Unguja
G.44a Ngazija [Comoro Is.]
G.44b Njuani (Hinzua)
G.50   POGORO GROUP
G.51   Pogolo
G.60   BENA-KINGA GROUP
G.63   Bena

H.10   KIKONGO GROUP [Zaire, Congo, Angola]
H.11   Bembe
H.13   Kunyi
H.14   Ndingi/Woyo
H.16a S. Kongo
H.16b C. Kongo
H.16c Yombe
H.16d W. Kongo
H.16e Bwende
H.16f Laadi
H.16g E. Kongo
H.16h S.E. Kongo
H.20   KIMBUNDU GROUP
H.21a Mbundu (Ndongo)
H.21b Mbamba
H.30   KIYAKA GROUP
H.31   Yaka
H.33   Hungu

K.10   CHOKWE-LUCHAZI GROUP [Angola, Zaire, Zambia]
K.11   Ciokwe (Cioko, Djok)
K.14   Lwena (Luvale)
K.15   Mbunda
K.20   LOZI GROUP
K.21   Lozi (Kololo)
K.30   LUYANA GROUP
K.31   Luyana (Luyi)
K.32   Mbowe
K.40   SUBIYA GROUP
K.41   Totela
K.42   Subiya [Botswana]

L.10   PENDE GROUP [Zaire]
L.11   Pende
L.20   SONGE GROUP
L.21   Kete
L.22   Binji
L.23   Songe (Yembe)
L.24   Luna (Inkongo)
L.30   LUBA GROUP
L.31a   Luba-Kasai
L.31b   Lulua
L.33   Luba-[Shaba]
L.34   Hemba
L.35   Sanga
L.40   KAONDE GROUP
L.41   Kaonde
L.50   LUNDA GROUP
L.52   Lunda

M.30   KONDE GROUP
M.31   Nyekyosa (Konde, Kukwe, Sokili)
M.40   BEMBA GROUP
M.41   Taabwa (Rungu)
M.42   Bemba (Wemba)
M.50   BISA-LAMBA GROUP
M.51   Biisa
M.52   Lala
M.60   LENJE-TONGA GROUP
M.61   Lenje (Ciina Mukuni)
M.63   Ila
M.64   Tonga

N.10   MANDA GROUP [Malawi]
N.12   Ngoni
N.13   Matengo

N.15	Tonga (Siska)
N.30	NYANJA GROUP
N.31*a*	Nyanja
N.31*b*	Cewa (Peta)
N.31*c*	Manjanja
N.40	SENGA-SENA GROUP [Mozambique]
N.41	Nsenga
N.42	Kunda
N.43	Nyungwe (Tete)
N.44	Sena

P.10	MATUMBI GROUP [Malawi, Mozambique, Tanzania]
P.11	Ndengereko
P.20	YAO GROUP
P.21	Yao
P.22	Mwera
P.23	Makonde
P.24	Ndonde
P.25	Mabiha (Mavia)
P.30	MAKUA GROUP
P.31	Makua
P.33	Ngulu

R.10	UMBUNDU GROUP [Angola]
R.11	Mbundu (Nano)
R.20	NDOMGA GROUP
R.21	Kwanyama (Humba) [Angola, S.W. Africa]
R.22	Ndonga (Ambo)
R.23	Kwambi
R.24	Ngandyera
R.30	HERERO GROUP
R.31	Herero
R.40	YEYE GROUP [Botswana]
R.41	Yei (Yeye, Kuba)

S.10	SHONA CLUSTER [Zimbabwe]
S.11	Korekore
S.12	Zezuru
S.13*a*	Manyika
S.13*b*	Tebe [Mozambique]
S.14	Karange
S.15	Ndau
S.16	Kalanja
S.20	VENDA GROUP [South Africa]
S.21	Venda
S.30	SOTHO-TSWANA GROUP [Botswana, Lesotho]
S.32*a*	Pedi (N. Sotho)

S.40	NGUNI GROUP [South Africa, Swaziland]
S.41	Xhosa
S.42	Zulu
S.43	Swati & Ngoni [Malawi, Swaziland]
S.44	Ndebele
S.50	TSWA-RONGA GROUP
S.51	Tswa [Mozambique, Zimbabwe]
S.60	CHOPI GROUP [Mozambique]
S.61	Copi (Lenge)
Z.1	TIV GROUP [Nigeria]
Z.1	Tiv
Z.2a	EKOID GROUP [Nigeria]
Z.2b	Baleb
Z.2g	N. Etung
Z.2r	Nkim

Appendix B
Distributions of Terms in Bantu Languages Pertaining to Therapeutic Concepts and Actions

The verbal cognates in these maps are reconstructions of common ancestral terms derived from modern phonetic resemblances and presumed semantic shifts from an original basic sound and meaning. The distributions are based mainly on the work of Malcolm Guthrie, as published in his *Comparative Bantu*; the numbers given with most terms are from his Comparative Series (C.S.). Following his convention, the asterisk indicates a reconstructed ancestral or "proto-" form derived from contemporary phonetic and semantic variations. It must be emphasized that these reconstructions are based on a limited number of languages for which glossaries and dictionaries were available in the 1950s and 1960s when Guthrie did his work; thus the distributions shown are approximations and may have gaps. Maps 2, 7, and 19 are based partially on other work.

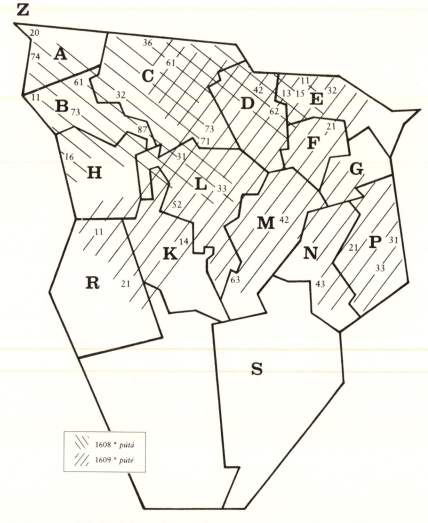

B.1   C.S. 1608 * -*pútá*- wound
           C.S. 1609 * -*púté*- wound, boil

This distribution indicates a proto-Bantu cognate, with B.14 coequal in the Eastern Bantu region.

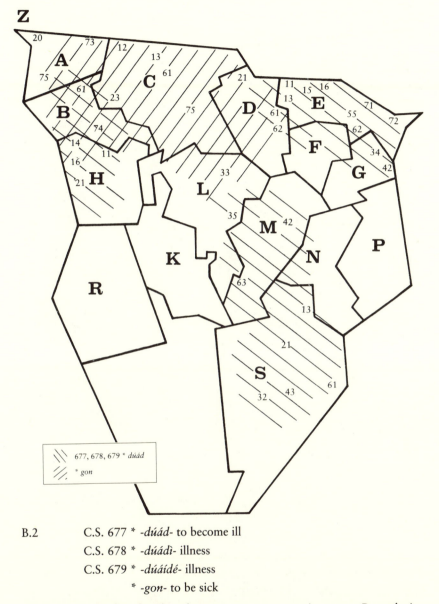

B.2   C.S. 677 * -*dúád*- to become ill
            C.S. 678 * -*dúádì*- illness
            C.S. 679 * -*dúáídé*- illness
                      * -*gon*- to be sick

The cognate -*dúád*- is distributed so as to suggest an ancient proto-Bantu lexical item that has been partially replaced by *kon* or *okon* in the Western Bantu forest area (Obenga 1985:196; Huygens 1987:86–93).

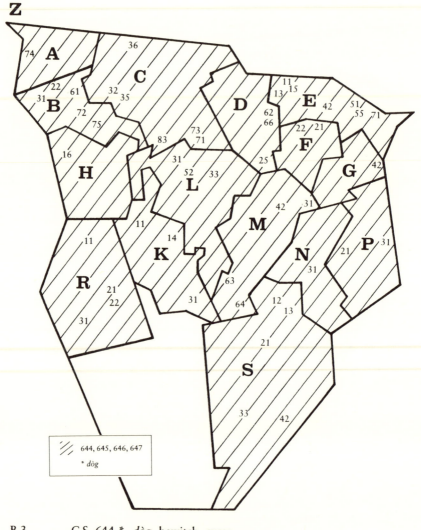

B.3   C.S. 644 * -dòg- bewitch, curse
           C.S. 645 * -dògá- witchcraft
           C.S. 646 * -dògí- witchcraft
           C.S. 647 * -dògò- witchcraft

A widespread term in many societies of the subcontinent, an ancient proto-
Bantu and central contemporary concept in therapeutic thought systems.

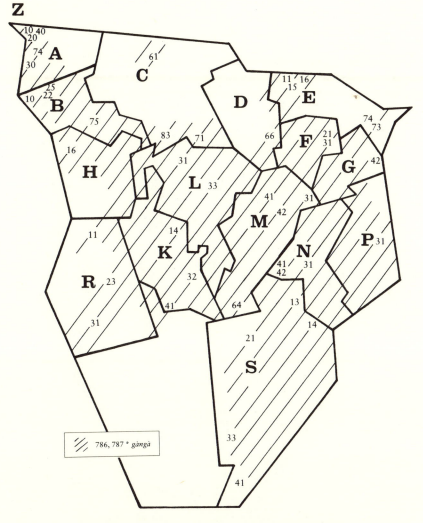

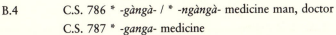
786, 787 * gàngà

B.4   C.S. 786 * -gàngà- / * -ngàngà- medicine man, doctor
           C.S. 787 * -ganga- medicine

Both healer and medicine are derived from this widespread and presumably proto-Bantu cognate.

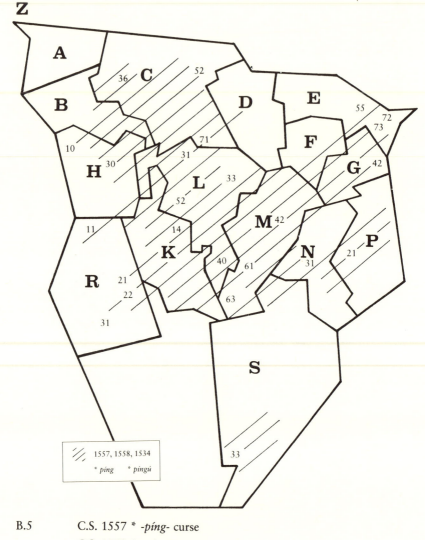

B.5   C.S. 1557 * -*píng*- curse
           C.S. 1558 * -*píngö*- curse
           C.S. 1534 * -*píngú*- fetish, charm, omen

Guthrie suggests that C.S. 1534 was proto-Bantu and is part of a set including
two synonymous cognates—293 * -*càngó*-, East Bantu (B.17); and 1072 * -*kítì*,
West Bantu (B.12)—that emerged where the original item disappeared.

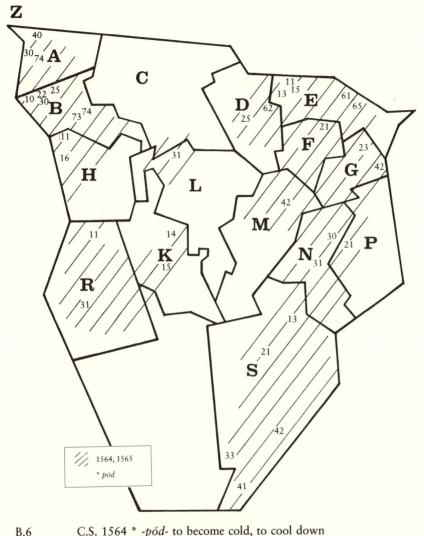

B.6   C.S. 1564 * -pód- to become cold, to cool down
             C.S. 1565 * -pód- to become cured, to get well

This bifurcated Western and Eastern Bantu distribution suggests a proto-Bantu
status for this cognate, and the pervasiveness of the notion of "the cool" in
connection with health, purification, or cleansing and by implication, of heat
with sickness, disorder, and pollution.

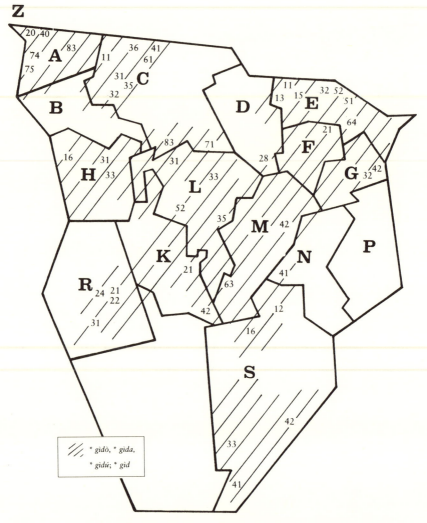

B.7   C.S. 826 * -gìdò-, -gìda-, -gìdú- substantive form of interdiction,
               prohibition

           C.S. 822 * -gìd- verbal form indicating to interdict, to refuse, to
               create an interdiction, to abstain from food, activities,
               contacts

The reconstruction of this cognate is based primarily on Huygens's recent work
(1987) in the Tervuren Bantu languages project, which is a continuation and
extension of Guthrie's work, as well as his intensive study of the Fang and Beti
languages. Its pervasive distribution suggests it as a part of the proto-Bantu
health conceptual scheme, although there are other terms for this concept.

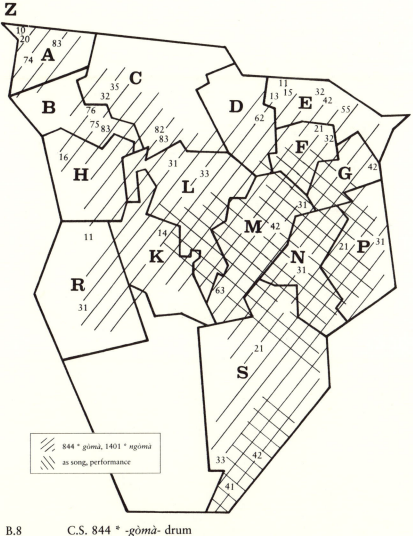

B.8   C.S. 844 * -*gòmà*- drum
           C.S. 1401 * -*ngòmà*- drum

Distribution of *ngoma* as song or performance:

The central cognate of this book, *ngoma* (drum), is distributed widely throughout the Bantu language areas, with the exception of the forest regions C and
D. This, and the distribution of the additional meaning of "song" and "performance" supports the hypothesis of an Eastern Bantu origin of the therapeutic
ngoma that is the subject of this work.

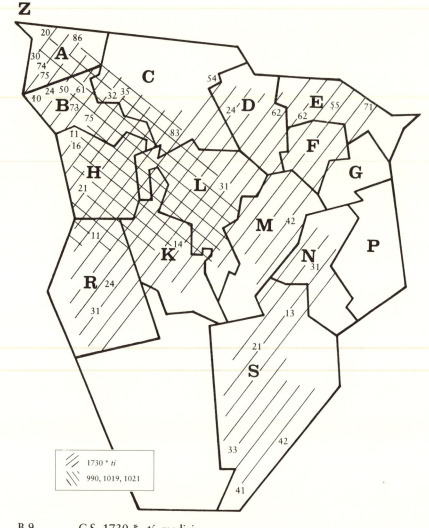

B.9   C.S. 1730 * -tí- medicine
             C.S. 990 * -kàg- to protect with medicine
             C.S. 1019 * -káyá- leaf, tobacco
             C.S. 1021 * -káyí- leaf

Of these two cognates for plants, or medicinal plants, the more widespread,
-tí-, proto-Bantu, is also identified as "tree" (C.S. 1729) and "stick" (C.S.
1731). The other terms denote medicinal uses of plants or the process of pro-
tecting with medicine, -kàg-. Tobacco, introduced from America, was assimi-
lated to the Western Bantu cognates, -kaya-, -kayi-.

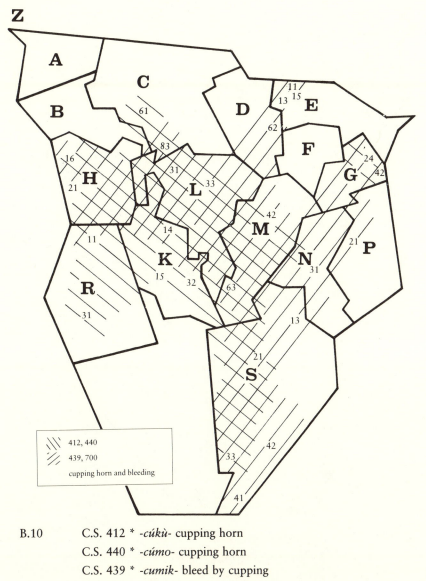

B.10   C.S. 412 * -cúkù- cupping horn
            C.S. 440 * -cúmo- cupping horn
            C.S. 439 * -cumik- bleed by cupping
            C.S. 700 * -dumik- bleed by cupping

Eastern and Western Bantu terms for the cupping horn and for the process of
bleeding by cupping suggest that these are part of an old system of therapy,
although there may have been an even older cognate that is now lost.

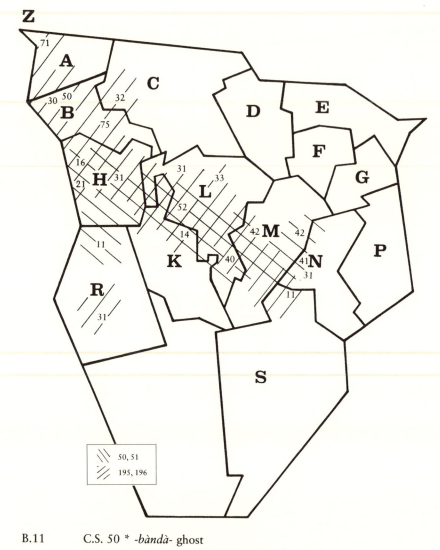

B.11   C.S. 50 * -bàndà- ghost

             C.S. 51 * -mbàndà- medicine man

             C.S. 195 * -búk- to cure

             C.S. 196 * -búk- to divine, to cure by divining

There are two related Western Bantu terms for healer, divining, or the process of healing. *Mbanda* suggests mediumship in some settings. The distribution of the term *búk* suggests an earlier expansion in Western Bantu.

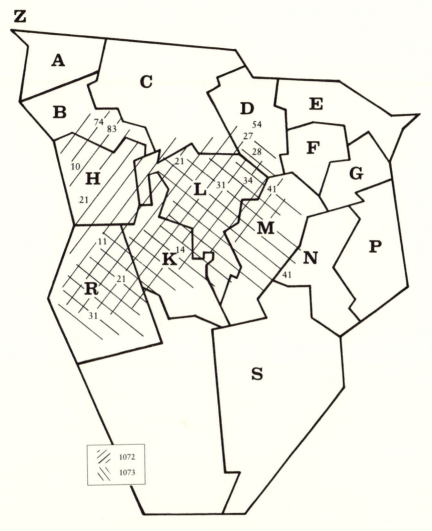

B.12   C.S. 1072 * -kíti- fetish, charm
            C.S. 1073 * -kíti-, or -kíci-, spirit

This Western Bantu concept and practice is present as a visible medicine or object in its western distribution. At its south and eastern expansion, or frontier,
it comes to be identified mainly as spirit. Its eastern-most occurrence is due to
the expansion of Luba influence in the sixteenth century among the Senga-Sena
linguistic group (Waite 1987).

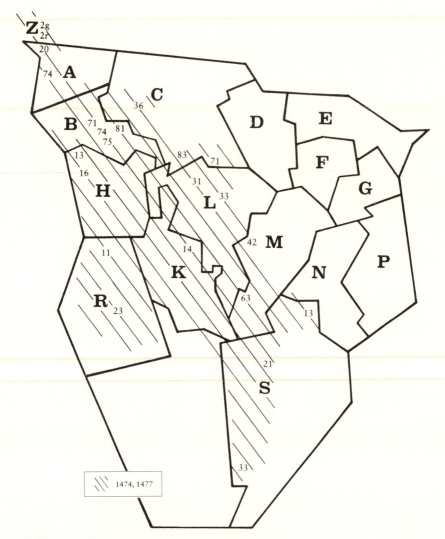

B.13   C.S. 1474 * -pémbà- white clay
            C.S. 1477 * -pémbé- white clay

The use of white clay or kaolin is pervasive in Sub-Saharan ritual, but this term for it is Western Bantu. That this cognate is ancient is seen from its presence among the Tiv of Eastern Nigeria, in the putative origin area of Bantu languages.

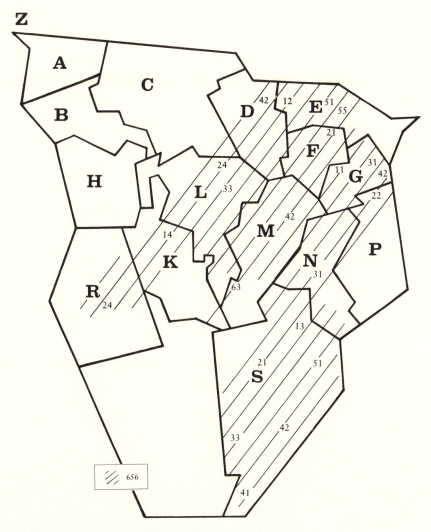

B.14   C.S. 656 * -*donda*- sore

A common cognate of Eastern Bantu origin.

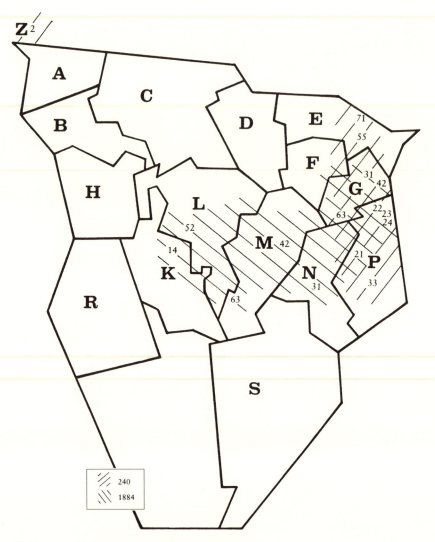

B.15   C.S. 240 * -cábi- witch, witchcraft

C.S. 1884 * -yábi- ordeal, poison

These two related cognates of Eastern Bantu origin may be related to the Tiv notion *tsav*, or *tsawi* (see Bohannan 1958), the evidence of witchcraft substance in the bowels of a corpse.

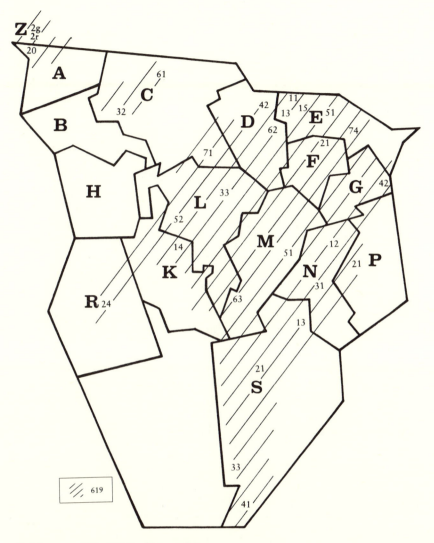

B.16   C.S. 619 * *-dímu-* spirit

This apparently ancient and proto-Bantu cognate for spirits, usually ancestral, is widespread in ngoma rituals. *Kulu* may be the Western Bantu counterpart for this.

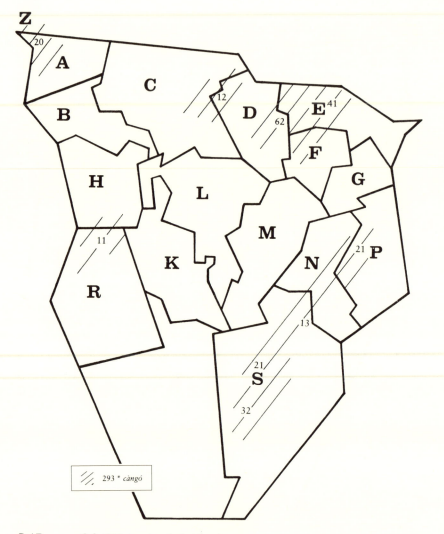

B.17   C.S. 293 * -càngó- fetish, charm

The Eastern Bantu counterpart of -kícì- (B.12), both of which, according to
Guthrie, may have replaced píngö (B.5).

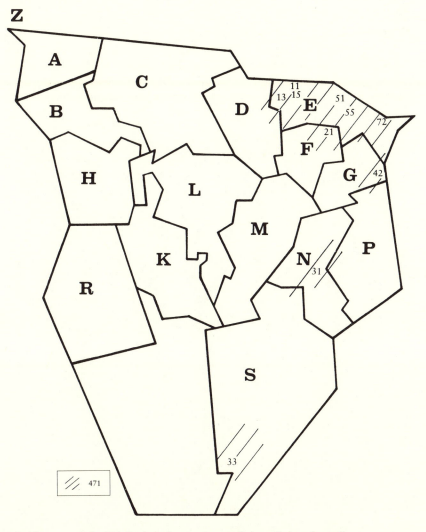

B.18   C.S. 471 * -*dagud*- practice medicine, divine, foretell

Dagud is the Eastern Bantu counterpart to *mbàndà* and *búk* (B.11), which together supplanted -*gàngà*- (B.4) in certain instances.

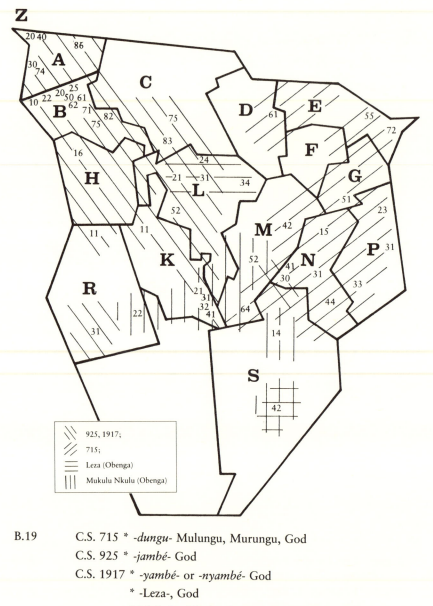

B.19   C.S. 715 * -dungu- Mulungu, Murungu, God

            C.S. 925 * -jambé- God

            C.S. 1917 * -yambé- or -nyambé- God

                    * -Leza-, God

                    * Mukulu, Nkulu, Ancient One, God

These are examples of numerous terms for God used in the attribution of illness etiologies that contrast to human-caused or spirit-caused etiologies. Obenga (1985:152–153) is the source for the distribution of the last two terms.

Appendix C
Instrumentation Accompanying Healing Rituals in Central and Southern Africa

Initial names refer to ethnic entities; numbers in parentheses refer to Guthrie's linguistic groupings shown on map C.1 and related maps in appendices A and B; names in quotation marks refer to therapeutic ritual or association, or name cited in text; vocal arrangement and instrumental combination are in order of type: idiophone, membrophone, aerophone, and chordophone. Sources are given at end of entry.

EQUATEUR

Mongo-Ekonda (C.61*a*) "Elima": voice + *bokwasa* rasp/ *elepo* rattles/ whistle/ *lokombe* zither
(IMNZ [Institute des Musées Nationaux du Zaire] recording 75.3.3/1 by Boilo)

Mongo-Ekonda (C.61*a*) "Elima": voice + *bokwasa* rasp/ bell/ *elepo* rattles/ whistle/ *lokombe* zither
(IMNZ recording 75.3.7/1 by Boilo)

Mongo-Ekonda (C.61*a*) "Elima": voice + *ingengele* bell/ *bokwasa* rasp/ *ilongo* kettle drum
(IMNZ recording, 75.3.8/1 by Boilo)

Ntomba (Kinshasa) (C.35*a*) "Elima": voice (1 female healer, 2 female novices) + 4 rasps/ *ilongo* kettle drum
(IMNZ recording, 75.7.2/3 by Ludiongo)

Mongo-Ngelentandu (C.61*a*) "Zebola": voice + bell/ double gong/ drum
(IMNZ recording, 75.3.11/1 by Boilo)

Mongo-Nkundo (C.61*b*) "Nzondo": voice + *bakwasa* rasp/ *ilongo* kettle drum
(IMNZ recording 75.3.15/6 Boilo)

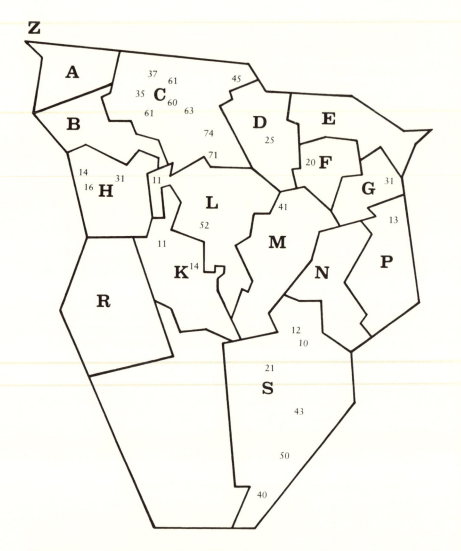

Mongo-Batwa (C.60) "Nzondo" (Ilako): choir
    (IMNZ recording 76.3.20/2 by Boilo)
Mongo (C.60) "Bongita": 2 soloists + choir + rattles
    (IMNZ recording 75.6.1/4 by Quersin and Esole)
Tetela (C.71) "Wetsi": 1 male/ 2 females + 2 *diwolo* calabash rattles/ *lokombe*
    trapezoid drum
    (IMNZ recording 75.8.7/3 by Quersin and Esole)
Tetela (C.71) "healing song": 2 females/ choir
    (IMNZ recording 75.8.7/5 by Quersin and Esole)

Mongo-Bagandu (C.63) "Nkanga": 2 soloists/ 5 healers/ choir + 3 *isanga* rattles/ *elonza* bell/ *mopati* horn
(IMNZ recording 74.6.5/2 by Quersin)
Mongo-Bagandu (C.63) "Nkanga": vocal/ handclapping + *isanga* rattles
(IMNZ recording 74.6.7/1 by Quersin)
Boyela-Malemadja (C.74) "Wetsi W'okonda" (Balimo): 1 female + 2 males + choir + *elanja* gong/ *isanga* rattles/ *ifange* horn
(IMNZ recording 74.6.23/3 by Quersin)
Boyela-Makandja (C.74) "Wetsi W'okonda" (Balimo): 1 female/ 1 male/ choir + *boyende* rattles/ *elondja* gong/ *lokombe* trapezoid drum/ *basuli* sticks
(IMNZ recording 74.6.16/4 by Quersin)
Boyela-Makandja (C.74) "Wetsi W'okonda" (Balimo): 3 females/ female choir + rattles + *ilonja* gong + *nkombe* drum + *ifonge* horn
(IMNZ recording 74.6.23/5 by Quersin)
Boyela-Makandja (C.74) "Ekata" "Lokote": 3 females/ choir/ handclapping + bell/ rattles/ trapezoid drum/ 2 membrane drums/ *ifonge* horn
(IMNZ recording 74.6.25/1 by Quersin)
Boyela-Makandja (C.74) "Lokote": 1 female/ choir + *ifonge* horn
(IMNZ recording 74.6.19/3 by Quersin)
Boyela-Makandja (C.74) "Wetsi W'okenda": 2 females/ female choir + *isanga* rattles/ *nkombe* trapezoid drum
(IMNZ recording 74.6.30/2 by Quersin)
Ngbaka-Mabo (C.45) "Nzombo": vocal solo/ 30-voice choir
(IMNZ recording 75.6.32/1 by Quersin and Esole)
Budja (C.37) "music of healing": 4 males + 1 *sanza* hand piano/ 2 rattles
(IMNZ recording 75.6.56*b*/6 and 7)

EASTERN ZAIRE

Warega (D.25) "Butii": adult male choir + large drum/ small drum/ percussion stick
(IMNZ recording 74.14.6/6 by Kishilo)

SOUTHERN SAVANNA

Lunda-Tshokwe (K.11) "song of healing": 1 female soloist/ choir + *lubemb* double gong/ *ngom* drum/ *kakakasj* drum sticks
(IMNZ recording 75.2.13/4 by Gansemans)
Lunda (L.52) "healing songs": 4 females
(IMNZ recording 75.2.14/6 and 15/1 by Gansemans)
Pende (L.11) "Ngombo" divination: 1 female + *dimba* xylophone
(IMNZ recording 80.2.2/43 by Malutshi)
Pende (L.11) "Hamba": female vocal + *ngoma* drum
(IMNZ recording 80.2.2/34–42 by Malutshi)

Yaka (H.31) "divination": diviner/ assistant/ choir + *nkoko* trapezoid drum/
ngoma drum
(IMNZ recordings 74.4.2/13 and 74.16.4/5)
Luvale (K.14) "Hamba": female vocal/ choir + *ngoma* drums
(Spring 1978)
Ndembu (L.52) "drums of affliction": solo/ choir + *ngoma* drums
(Turner 1968)

KONGO-ATLANTIC

Woyo (H.14) "divination song": female and male vocal + *ngondji* double
gong/ *binthakidi* rattles/ 2 *ngoma-ngoma* trapezoid drums/ *pitu* whistles
(IMNZ recording 81.2.9/3 by Quersin)
Woyo (H.14) "Nkazi Mbumba Maveko" *nkisi* song: female and male vocal
+ *tshingoma* trapezoid drum
(IMNZ recording 81.2.5/1 by Quersin)
Woyo (H.14) "Malembe Nyenda Kwamiye Lali" *nkisi* song: female vocal/
handclapping
(IMNZ recording 80.1.1/11 by Quersin)
Kongo-Mpangu (H.16g) "Nkita": 8 females + rattles/ 2 *ngoongi* double
gongs/ *moondo* single membrane drum
(Ciparisse 1972)

EAST AFRICA

Sukuma (Dar es Salaam) (F.20) "Mungano": solo/ choir + *ngoma* drums
Matumbe (Dar es Salaam) (P.13) "Manianga": solo/ choir + shakers/ *ngoma*
drum
Matumbe (Dar es Salaam) (P.13) "Mbungi": vocal + wood gongs/ 5 *ngoma*
drums
Zigua (Dar es Salaam) (G.31) "Maruhani": vocal + shakers/ 5 double mem-
brane drums
Zigua (Dar es Salaam) (G.31) "Msaghiro": vocal + shakers

SOUTHEAST AFRICA

Zezuru (S.12): vocal + *mbira* hand pianos/ rattles/ *ngoma* drums
(Fry 1976:118)
Taabwa (M.41) "Lumbu": vocal choir + rattles/ 2 *ngoma* drums
(Roberts 1988:fig. 2)
Shona (S.10) "Bira *dza vadzimu*": vocal + *mbira* hand pianos with gourd
resonators
(Berliner 1981)

SOUTHERN AFRICA

Venda (S.21) *"ngoma dza vadzimu"*: soloist/ choir + shaker/ *ngoma* drums (Blacking 1973)

Swazi (S.43) "sangoma": soloists/ choir + *tigomene* metal and membrane drums

Western Cape (S.40 and 50) *"amagqira"*: soloists/ choir + metal and membrane drum

Notes

1. SETTINGS AND SAMPLES

1. This is one of numerous references throughout this work to the interface of ngoma and Christianity. Later, in the account of Tanzanian ngoma, a similar interface appears between Islam and ngoma. In a survey overview work of this type, I have not been able to explore systematically the many ways in which there has been interpenetration of ngoma with the world religions. Local histories, particular mission policies, reactions of local authorities, and particular decisions by influential individuals would be elements affecting the interfaces.

2. It is possible that the *ubulau* drink taken by the novices just prior to this moment was a hallucinogen based on a plant ingredient used in the drink. However, I was unable to pursue this or other uses of medication in ngoma in any detail because of the survey nature of the project. The pharmacopoeia of ngoma is of course an entire additional project related to African medicine in general, beyond the scope of this work.

2. IDENTIFYING NGOMA

1. Lexicostatistics is the methodology by which phonetic, morphological, and morphophonological features are correlated across a number of presumably genetically related languages. Higher frequencies than random clusters of correlated features are held to demonstrate genetic or historic commonality. The Swadesh list of 100 lexical items, common to all known world languages, has also been used in this research on Bantu languages.

2. The most significant continuation of Guthrie's work has been carried on by the Tervuren lexicostatistical project, initiated by André Coupez, Alfred Meeussen, and Jan Vansina in the 1950s and headed today by Yvonne Bastin of

the Linguistic Department of the Musée Royal de l'Afrique Centrale, Tervuren, Belgium. Additional research work in the Bantu paradigm is being conducted by the Centre International des Civilisations Bantoues, of Libreville, Gabon, including some coastal archaeological research to establish the lower threshold of the Iron Age in the Western Bantu expansion.

3. Obenga's chapter "Tradi-pratique et santé chez les Bantou" (1985:195–217) concentrates on a comparative reconstruction of Mbochi and Mbulu and related languages of Western Equatorial Africa, essentially Western Bantu, and does not benefit from the work of Guthrie.

4. DOING NGOMA

1. I am indebted to Thembinkosi Dyeyi of East London, South Africa, for translating and interpreting the transcription of this Western Cape event.

2. In some interpretations of Zulu divination, this agreement, contained in the verb *vuma,* is turned into confession, *ukuvuma,* which is extracted from the client by the diviner after a series of interrogations. Axel-Ivar Berglund offers a vivid account of a divination of this sort in the context of Zulu independent Christians (Berglund 1989:113–115).

3. Blacking's identification of other song styles in the universe of all Venda initiation music includes: *nyimbo dza u sevhetha,* songs for dancing round, sung by girls dancing counterclockwise around the drums, including a "song of dismissal" and a "recruiting song"; *nyimbo dza vhahwira,* songs of the masked dancers, with varying tempo to accompany different phases of the dance and distinctive rhythms to mark various steps; and *nyimbo dza milayo,* songs of the laws of the school, sung by novices and any graduates present (1973:40–41).

5. CODES AND CONSCIOUSNESS

1. The term *bugaboo,* or *boogaboo,* has a Central African origin drawn directly from the Western Bantu religion and healing vocabulary. Vass (1979:106) traces it to *buka lubuka,* to divine, or consult a diviner.

2. In semiotic parlance, appropriately called "shifters."

6. SOCIAL REPRODUCTION OF HEALTH

1. I have explored definitions of health elsewhere (Janzen 1985:64–67; 1989, in Sullivan, ed.; and Feierman and Janzen: forthcoming). The first two of these discussions concentrate on a series of health concepts, including "health as what physicians do," "health as the absence of disease," "health as functional normality," "health as adaptation," "positive health," and "health utopias," along with "the social reproduction of health." In Sullivan, ed., 1989, these are interlaced with "verbal concepts" in African healing. Positive health indicators are difficult to encapsulate or codify since they depend upon particular programs to carry them out. Most national biomedical health programs are

defined in terms of "the absence of disease" and lend themselves to demographic indicators of mortality, morbidity, and fertility. I have tried to develop the "social reproduction" definition of health because it seems uniquely suited to evaluate ngoma ritual healing.

Bibliography

Ahern, E.
1979   The problem of efficacy: Strong and weak illocutionary acts. *Man* (n.s.) 14:1–17.

Arom, S.
1985   *Polyphonies et polyrythmies instrumentales d'Afrique centrale.* 2 vols. Paris: Société d'Etudes Linguistiques et Anthropologiques de France (SELAF).

Augé, M., ed.
1985   *Interpreting illness.* Special issue of *History and Anthropology* 2, 1:1–13.

Augé, M., and C. Herzlich, eds.
1984   *Le sens du mal: Anthropologie, histoire, sociologie de la maladie.* Paris: Editions des archives contemporaines.

Bastin, Y.
1983   Essai de classification de quatre-vingts langues bantoues par la statistique grammaticale. *Africana Linguistica.* 9:11–107. Tervuren, Belgium: Musée Royal de l'Afrique Centrale (Sciences Humaines 110).

Bastin, Y., A. Coupez, and B. de Halleux
1981   Classification lexicostatistique des langues bantoues (214 relevés). *Bulletin des Séances de l'Académie Royale des Sciences d'Outre-Mer* (n.s.) 27, 2, 173–199.

Bateson, G.
1958   *Naven.* Stanford, Calif.: Stanford University Press.
1972   Redundancy and coding. In *Steps to an ecology of mind,* 411–425. New York: Ballantine Books.

Beattie, J., and J. Middleton, eds.
1969   *Spirit mediumship and society in Africa*. London: Routledge &
            Kegan Paul.
Berger, I.
1981   *Religion and resistance: East African kingdoms in the precolo-
            nial period*. Tervuren, Belgium: Musée Royale de l'Afrique Cen-
            trale (Annales No. 105).
Berglund, A.-I.
1989   Confessions of guilt and restoration to health: Some illustrative
            Zulu examples. In *Culture, experience and pluralism: Essays on
            African ideas of illness and healing*, ed. A. Jacobson-Widding,
            109–124. Uppsala, Sweden: Acta Universitatis Upsaliensis (Stud-
            ies in Cultural Anthropology 13).
Berliner, P.
1981   *The soul of Mbira*. Berkeley, Los Angeles, London: University
            of California Press.
Bibeau, G.
1981   The circular semantic network in Ngbandi disease nosology.
            Social Science and Medicine 15B, 3:295–308.
Bibeau, G., ed.
1977   *La médecine traditionnelle au Zaire*. Ottawa: Centre de recher-
            ches pour le développement international; Kinshasa, Zaire: Cen-
            tre de Médecine des Guérisseurs.
Blacking, J.
1973   *How musical is man?* Seattle and London: University of Wash-
            ington Press.
1985   Movement, dance, music, and the Venda girls' initiation cycle.
            In *Society and the dance*, ed. P. Spencer, 64–91. Cambridge:
            Cambridge University Press.
Blakely, T., and P. Blakely
1986   Personal communication.
Bohannan, P.
1958   Extra-processual events among the Tiv of Nigeria. *American
            Anthropologist* 60:1–12.
Bontinck, F.
1984   Review of *Lemba, 1650–1930*. *Revue Africaine de Theologie*
            15:111–118.
Boone, O.
1951   *Les tambours du Congo belge et du Ruanda-Urundi*. Tervuren,
            Belgium: Annales du Musée du Congo Belge, (n.s.) Sciences de
            l'Homme, I.
Boorse, C.
1977   Health as a theoretical concept. *Philosophy of Science* 44:542–
            573.
Booth, N., Jr.
1977   The view from Kasongo Niembo. In *African Religions: A Sym-
            posium* 31–67. New York: Nok Publication.

Bourdieu, P.
1977   Outline of a theory of practice. Cambridge: Cambridge University Press.
Bourgeois, A.
1984   Review of Lemba 1650–1930. International Journal of African Historical Studies 17:4.
Bourguignon, E.
1976   Possession. San Francisco: Chandler and Sharp.
Bourne, D., and B. Dick
1979   Mortality in South Africa 1929–74. In Economics of Health in South Africa, Vol. I, ed. Francis Wilson and G. Wescott, 57–78. Johannesburg: Ravan Press.
Bührman, V.
1978   Tentative views on dream therapy by Xhosa diviners. Journal of Analytical Psychology 23, 2:105–121.
Bührman, V., and Nqaba Gqomfa
1981–82 The Xhosa healers of Southern Africa. Journal of Analytical Psychology, 26(1981):187–201, 297–312; 27(1982):41–57, 163–173.
Burridge, K. O.
1967   Lévi-Strauss and myth. In The structural study of myth and totemism, ed. E. Leach, 91–119. London: Tavistock Publications (ASA Monograph 5).
Byamungu Lufungula wa Chibanga-banga
1982   Les plantes médicinales, les rites thérapeutiques, et autres connaissances en médecine des guérisseurs au Kivu. Manuscript, Centre de Médecine des Guérisseurs, Kinshasa, Zaire.
Caldwell, J. C.
1982   Theory of fertility decline. London: Academic Press.
1988   Personal communications.
Caldwell, J. C., P. Caldwell, and P. Quiggin
1989   Disaster in an alternative civilization: The social dimension of AIDS in Sub-Saharan Africa. Canberra, Australia: Health Transition Centre Working Papers No. 2.
Chernoff, J. M.
1979   African rhythm and African sensibility. Chicago and London: University of Chicago Press.
Ciparisse, G.
1972   Le chant traditionnel: Une source de documentation orale, chants des Bampangu (Zaire). Les Cahiers du CEDAF, 1, 1.
Comaroff, J.
1981   Healing and cultural transformation: The Tswana of Southern Africa. Social Science and Medicine 15B, 3:367–378.
1986   Body of power, spirit of resistance: The culture and history of a South African people. Chicago: University of Chicago Press.
Cordell, D., J. Gregory, and V. Piche
1992   The demographic reproduction of health and disease. In The

social basis of health and healing in Africa, ed. S. Feierman and J. Janzen. Berkeley, Los Angeles, Oxford: University of California Press.

Corin, E.
1979   A possession psychotherapy in an urban setting: Zebola in Kinshasa. *Social Science and Medicine* 13B, 4:327–338.
1980   Vers une reappropriation de la dimension individuelle en psychologie africaine. *Révue Canadienne des Etudes Africaines* 14, 1:135–156.

Corin, E., and H. B. M. Murphy
1979   Psychiatric perspectives in Africa, I. *Transcultural Psychiatric Research Review* 16:147–178.

Cory, H.
1936   Ngoma ya Sheitani. *Journal of the Royal Anthropological Society* 66:209–217.
1938   Sukuma secret societies (Mwanza). Manuscript, East African Library, University of Dar es Salaam, Cory 191.
1946   The Buyeye: A secret society of snake charmers in Sukumaland, Tanganyika Territory. *Africa* 16, 3:160–178.
1949   Baswezi (disciples of Lyangombe). Manuscript, East African Library, University of Dar es Salaam, Cory 45.
1955   The Buswezi. *American Anthropologist* 57:923–952.
n.d.*a*   Sukuma songs and dances. Manuscript, East African Library, Dar es Salaam, Cory 192.
n.d.*b*   Sukuma dances. Manuscript, East African Library, Dar es Salaam, Cory 192.
n.d.*c*   Migabo. Manuscript, East African Library, Dar es Salaam, Cory 138.

Coupez, A., E. Evrard, and J. Vansina
1975   Classification d'un échantillon de langues bantoues d'après la léxicostatistique. *Africana Linguistica* 6:133–158. Tervuren, Belgium: Musée Royal de l'Afrique Centrale (Sciences Humaines 88).

Courlander, H.
1960   *The drum and the hoe: Life and lore of the Haitian people.* Berkeley and Los Angeles: University of California Press.

Crapanzano, V., and V. Garrison, eds.
1977   *Case studies in spirit possession.* New York, London, Sydney, Toronto: A. Wiley Interscience Series.

Csordas, T. J.
1988   Elements of charismatic persuasion and healing. *Medical Anthropology Quarterly* (n.s.) 2, 2:121–142.

David, N.
1980   Early Bantu expansion in the context of Central African prehistory: 4000–1 B.C. In *L'Expansion Bantoue,* ed. L. Hyman and J. Voorhoeve, 609–645. Paris: SELAF.

Dawson, M.
1979   Smallpox in Kenya, 1880–1920. *Social Science and Medicine.*
            13B, 3:245–250.
DeCraemer, W., J. Vansina, and R. Fox
1976   Religious movements in Central Africa: A theoretical study. *Jour-
            nal of Comparative Studies in History and Society,* 18, 4:458–
            475.
De Heusch, Luc
1971   *Pourquoi l'épouser?* Paris: Gallimard.
1985   *Sacrifice in Africa.* Bloomington: Indiana University Press.
DeMaret, P.
1980   Bribes, débris et bricolage. In *L'Expansion Bantoue,* ed. L. Hy-
            man and J. Voorhoeve. Paris: SELAF.
1984   L'archéologie en zone bantou jusqu'en 1984. *Muntu* 1:37–60.
DeMaret, P., and F. Nsuka
1977   History of Bantu metallurgy: Some linguistic aspects. *History in
            Africa* 4.
Devisch, R.
1984   *Se recréer femme: Manipulation sémantique d'une situation d'in-
            fécondité chez les Yaka du Zaire.* Berlin: Dietrich Reimer (Collec-
            tanea Instituti Anthropos 31).
1986   Le sacré et le symbolisme du corps dans une culture de l'Afrique
            centrale. *Archivio di Filosofia* 54, 1–3:565–586.
Douglas, M.
1970   *Natural symbols: Explorations in cosmology.* New York: Pan-
            theon, Random House.
Doyal, L.
1979   *Political economy of health.* London: South End Press.
Dubos, R.
1968   *Man, medicine and environment.* New York: Mentor.
Ehret, C.
1967   Cattle-keeping and milking in eastern and southern African his-
            tory: The linguistic evidence. *Journal of African History* 8:1–17.
1968   Sheep and central Sudanic peoples in southern Africa. *Journal
            of African History* 9:2113–2121.
1973–74   Patterns of Bantu and central Sudanic settlement in central and
            southern Africa. *Transafrican Journal of History* 3:1–71; 4:1–
            25.
1974   Agricultural history in central and southern Africa, ca. 1000 B.C.
            to ca. 500 A.D. *Transafrican Journal of History* 4.
Ehret, C., et al.
1972   Outlining southern African history: A reevaluation A.D. 100–
            1500. *Ufahamu* 3:927.
Ehret, C., and M. Posnansky, eds.
1982   *The archaeological and linguistic reconstruction of African his-
            tory.* Berkeley, Los Angeles, London: University of California
            Press.

Eliyahu, P.
  n.d.   *Punywa, Ngoma ya Kiarusha*. Dar es Salaam: Tanzanian Minis-
                try of Culture.
Feierman, S., and J. M. Janzen, eds.
  1992   *The Social Basis of Health and Healing in Africa*. Berkeley, Los
                Angeles, Oxford: University of California Press.
Feldman, P.
  1988   Review of *Lemba 1650–1930*. *Medical Anthropology Quarterly*
                17, 4:106.
Frankel, S.
  1986   *The Huli response to illness*. Cambridge: Cambridge University
                Press.
Freidson, E.
  1971   *Profession of medicine: A study of the sociology of applied
                knowledge*. New York: Dodd, Mead & Co.
Fry, P.
  1976   *Spirits of protest: Spirit mediums and the articulation of con-
                sensus amongst the Zezuru of southern Rhodesia*. Cambridge:
                Cambridge University Press.
Gaisie, S.
  1989   Personal communications.
Geertz, C.
  1988   *Works and lives: The anthropologist as author*. Stanford, Calif.:
                Stanford University Press.
Giles, L. L.
  1987   Possession cults on the Swahili coast: A re-examination of the-
                ories of marginality. *Africa* 57, 2:234–257.
Gish, O.
  1979   The political economy of primary health care and "health by the
                people": An historical exploration. *Social Science and Medicine*
                13C:203–211.
Gluckman, M.
  1962   *Essays on the ritual of social relations*. Manchester: Manchester
                University Press.
Goblet-Vanormelingen, V.
  1988   Traditional organization for the survival of children at high risk
                in rural Zaire. Manuscript.
Goody, J.
  1976   *Production and reproduction: A comparative study of the do-
                mestic domain*. Cambridge: Cambridge University Press.
Greenberg, J.
  1955   *Studies in African linguistic classification*. New Haven, Conn.:
                Yale University Press.
  1963   The languages of Africa. *International Journal of American Lin-
                guistics* 29, 1:6–7, 30–33, 35–39.
  1972   Linguistic evidence regarding Bantu origins. *Journal of African
                History* 13, 2:189–216.

Gregory, J. W., and V. Piche
    1982   African population: Reproduction for whom? *Daedalus* 3,
              Spring.
Guthrie, M.
    1953   *The Bantu languages of Western Equatorial Africa*. London:
              International Africa Institute.
    1962   Bantu origins: A tentative new hypothesis. *Journal of African
              Languages* 1, 1:9–21.
    1962   Some developments in the prehistory of the Bantu languages.
              Journal of African History 3:273–282.
    1967   *The classification of Bantu languages*. London: International
              Africa Institute.
    1967–71   *Comparative Bantu: An introduction to the comparative linguis-
              tics and prehistory of the Bantu languages*. 4 vols. Farnborough,
              Hampshire: Gregg.
Hammond-Tooke, W. D.
    1980   *The Bantu-speaking peoples of Southern Africa*. Boston: Rout-
              ledge & Kegan Paul.
    1989   *Rituals and medicines: Indigenous healing in South Africa*. Jo-
              hannesburg, South Africa: A. D. Donker.
Hartwig, G. W., and K. D. Patterson, eds.
    1978   *Disease in African history*. Durham, N.C.: Duke University
              Press.
Harwood, A.
    1987   Symbol, tool, and statement. *Medical Anthropology Quarterly*
              (n.s.) 1, 1:3–5.
Heine, B.
    1984   The dispersal of the Bantu peoples in the light of linguistic evi-
              dence. *Muntu* 1:21–35.
Heine, B., H. Hoff, and R. Vossen
    1977   Neuere Ergebnisse zur Territorialgeschichte der Bantu. In *Zur
              Sprachgeschichte und Ethnohistorie in Afrika*, ed. W. J. G.
              Moehlig, F. Roffland, and B. Heine, 57–72. Berlin: Dietrich
              Reimer.
Hiernaux, J.
    1968   Bantu expansion: The evidence from physical anthropology con-
              fronted with linguistic and archeological evidence. *Journal of
              African History* 4:505–515.
Huxley, F.
    1967   Anthropology and ESP. In *Science and ESP*, ed. J. R. Smythies.
              London: Routledge & Kegan Paul.
Huygens, P.
    1987   *Essai d'anthropologie de la médecine: Incompatibilities sym-
              bolique chez les fang et les beti*. Memoire, Université Libre,
              Brussels.
Hyman, L. M., and J. Voorhoeve, eds.
    1980   *L'expansion Bantoue*. 3 vols. Paris: SELAF.

Janzen, J. M.
1969   Vers une phénomènologie de la guérison en Afrique centrale.
            Etudes Congolaises 12, 2:97–115.
1977   The tradition of renewal in Kongo religion. In *African religions:
            A symposium*, ed. N. Booth, 69–114. New York, London,
            Lagos: Nok Publication.
1978*a*   *The quest for therapy in Lower Zaire.* Berkeley, Los Angeles,
            London: University of California Press.
1978*b*   The comparative study of medical systems as changing social
            systems. *Social Science and Medicine* 12, 2:121–129.
1979*a*   Deep thought: Structure and intention in Kongo prophetism,
            1910–21. *Social Research* 46, 1:106–139.
1979*b*   Ideologies and institutions in the precolonial history of Equa-
            torial African therapeutic systems. *Social Science and Medicine*
            13B:317–326.
1980   *The development of health.* Akron: Mennonite Central Commit-
            tee Monograph Series.
1981   The need for a taxonomy of health in the study of African
            therapeutics. *Social Science and Medicine* 15B, 3:185–194.
1982   *Lemba 1650–1930: A drum of affliction in Africa and the New
            World.* New York: Garland Publishing.
1983   Towards a historical perspective on African medicine and health.
            In *Ethnomedicine and medical history*, ed. J. Sterly and F. Lich-
            tenthaeler, 99–138. Berlin: Verlag Mensch u. Leben.
1985   Changing concepts of African therapeutics: An historical per-
            spective. In *African healing strategies,* ed. B. M. du Toit and
            I. H. Abdalla. Owerri, New York, London: Trado-Medic Books
            (a Division of Conch Magazine).
1986   Cults of affliction in African religion. *The encyclopedia of reli-
            gion,* ed. M. Eliade. New York: Free Press.
1987   Therapy management: Concept, reality, process. *Medical An-
            thropology Quarterly* 1:1(n.s.):68–84.
1989   Health, religion and medicine in central and southern African
            traditions. In *Caring and curing: Health and medicine in world
            religious traditions,* ed. L. Sullivan. New York: Macmillan Pub-
            lishing Co.
1990   Strategies of health-seeking and structures of social support in
            central and southern Africa. In *What we know about health
            transition,* ed. J. Caldwell, S. Findley, P. Caldwell, G. Santow,
            W. Cosford, J. Braid, and D. Broers-Freeman, 707–719. Can-
            berra, Australia: Health Transition Centre, Australia National
            University.
Johnson, T.
1977   Auditory driving, hallucinogens, and music, color, synesthesia
            and Tsonga ritual. In B. du Toit, *Drugs, rituals and altered states
            of consciousness.* Rotterdam, Netherlands: Balkan.

Junod, H.
1934   Le cas de possession et de l'exorcisme chez les Vandau. *Africa* 7, 3:270–299.

Kleinman, A.
1980   *Patients and healers in the context of culture.* Berkeley, Los Angeles, London: University of California Press.

Kuper, A., and P. Van Leynseele
1980   L'anthropologie sociale et l' "expansion bantoue." In *L'expansion bantoue,* ed. L. M. Hyman and J. Voorhoeve, 749–776. Paris: SELAF.

Lambek, M.
1981   *Human spirits: A cultural account of trance in Mayotte.* Cambridge: Cambridge University Press.

Last, M.
1981   The importance of knowing about not knowing. *Social Science and Medicine* 15B, 3:387–392.

Last, M., and G. L. Chavunduka, eds.
1986   *The professionalisation of African medicine.* Manchester, England: Manchester University Press.

Leach, E.
1966   Ritualization in man in relation to conceptual and social development. *Philosophical Transactions of the Royal Society of London,* 241, Ser. B, 772, 403–408.

1976   *Culture and communication: The logic by which symbols are connected.* Cambridge: Cambridge University Press.

Lema, G.
1978   *The Humbu.* Ph.D. dissertation, Louvain Catholic University, Belgium.

Leslie, C., ed.
1976   *Asian medical systems.* Berkeley, Los Angeles, London: University of California Press.

Lesthaege, R., and F. Eelens
1985   Social organization and reproductive regimes: Lessons from Sub-Saharan Africa and historical western Europe. Paper presented at "Fertility Transitions" Conference, East Lansing, Mich., April.

Lewis, G.
1975   *Knowledge of illness in a Sepik society.* Cambridge: Cambridge University Press.

Lewis, I.
1977   *Ecstatic religion: An anthropological study of spirit possession and shamanism.* Harmondsworth, Middlesex: Penguin Books.

1986   *Religion in context: Cults and charisma.* Cambridge: Cambridge University Press.

Lihamba, A.
1986   Health and the African theatre. *Review of African Political Economy* 36 (September).

Lokongo-Lombewo
1981   *Ilako: Essai d'analyse d'une thérapie traditionelle en sociétés Ekonda et N'tomba de Bikoro.* Thesis, University of Zaire, Lubumbashi.

Mabiala Mandela
1982   *Les rites thérapeutiques de Kinshasa.* Manuscript.

McAllister, P.
1979   *The rituals of labour migration among the Gcaleka.* Master's thesis, Rhoades University, Port Elizabeth, South Africa.

MacGaffey, W.
1977   Fetishism revisited: Kongo nkisi in sociological perspective. *Africa* 47:140–152.

1986*a*   *Religion and society in Central Africa.* Chicago: University of Chicago Press.

1986*b*   Ethnography and the closing of the frontier in Lower Congo, 1885–1921. *Africa* 56:261–279.

1988   Complexity, astonishment and power: The visual vocabulary of Kongo Minkisi. *Journal of Southern African Studies* 14, 2:188–203.

Makhubu, L.
1978   *The traditional healer.* Mbabane, Swaziland: Sebenta National Institute for the University of Botswana and Swaziland.

Marañhao, T.
1986   *Therapeutic discourse and Socratic dialogue.* Madison: University of Wisconsin Press.

Martin, S. H.
1982   Music in urban East Africa: Five genres in Dar es Salaam. *Journal of African Studies* 9, 3:155–163.

Mbepera, G. E. E. J.
1976   *Linguga: Ngoma ya Wamatergo.* Dar es Salaam. Mimeo.

Mbunga, S. B.
1963   *Church law and Bantu music: Ecclesiastical documents and law on sacred music as applied to Bantu music.* Schoeneck-Beckenried, Switzerland: Nouvelle Revue de Science Missionaire.

Meeussen, A. E.
1967   Bantu grammatical reconstruction. *Africana Linguistica* 3:79–122.

1980   *Bantu lexical reconstructions.* Tervuren, Belgium: Musée Royal de l'Afrique Centrale, Archives d'Anthropologie, 27.

Meillassoux, C.
1981   *Maidens, meal and money.* Cambridge: Cambridge University Press.

Merriam, A.
1977   Traditional music of black Africa. In *Africa,* ed. P. M. Martin and P. O'Meara, 243–258. Bloomington: Indiana University Press.

Mills, J.
1982   *Health and healing in a South African township.* Master's thesis,
            University of Cape Town.
Mitchell, J. C.
1956   *The Kalela dance: Aspects of social relations among urban Afri-
            cans in northern Rhodesia.* Manchester, England: Manchester
            University Press (Rhodes-Livingstone Papers No. 27).
Mohamed, A. K.
1976   *Ngoma ya Ndege.* Dar es Salaam: UTAFITI kwa Idara ya
            Muziki.
Morsy, S. A.
1981   Towards a political economy of health: A critical note on the
            medical anthropology of the Middle East. *Social Science and
            Medicine* 15B:159–163.
Mudimbe, V. Y.
1986   Review of *Lemba 1650–1930. Culture, Medicine and Psychiatry*
            10:277–282.
Murdock, G. P.
1959   *Africa: Its peoples and their culture history.* New York, Toronto,
            London: McGraw-Hill Book Co.
Murray, C.
1979   The work of men, women and the ancestors: Social reproduction
            in the periphery of Southern Africa. In *The social anthropology
            of work,* ed. Sandra Wallman. New York: Academic Press.
1981   *Families divided: The impact of migrant labour in Lesotho.*
            Johannesburg: Ravan Press.
Navarro, V.
1974   The underdevelopment of health or the health of underdevelop-
            ment. *International Journal of Health Services,* 4.
Needham, R.
1967   Percussion and transition. *Man* 2:606–614.
Neher, A.
1962   A physiological explanation of unusual behavior in ceremonies
            involving drums. *Human Biology* 34, 2:151–160.
Ngubane, H. *See also* Sibisi.
1977   *Body and mind in Zulu medicine: An ethnography of health.*
            New York: Academic Press.
1981   Aspects of clinical practice and traditional organization of in-
            digenous healers in South Africa. *Social Science and Medicine*
            15B, 3:361–366.
Nsiala Miaka Makengo
1979   Le Nkita, rite et thérapie. *Médecine traditionnelle au Zaire.* Spe-
            cial issue *Révue de Recherche Scientifique,* 11–36. Kinshasa:
            Institute de Récherche Scientifique.
1982   Personal communication.

Obenga, T.
1985   *Les Bantu: Langues, peuples, civilisations.* Libreville, Paris: Centre International des Civilisations Bantu; Editions Présence Africaine.

Parsons, T.
1949   *The structure of social action.* New York: Free Press.
1951   *The social system.* New York: Free Press.

Phillipson, D. W.
1975   The chronology of the Iron Age in Bantu Africa. *Journal of African History* 16, 3:321–342.
1976   Archeology and Bantu linguistics. *World Archeology* 8, 1:65–82.
1977   The spread of the Bantu language. *Scientific American* 236 (April):106–114.
1980   L'expansion Bantoue en Afrique orientale: Les temoignages de l'archéologie et de la linguistique. In *L'expansion Bantoue,* ed. L. M. Hyman and J. Voorhoeve, 649–714. Paris: SELAF.
1985   An archeological re-consideration of Bantu expansion. *Muntu* 2:69–84.

Polome, E. C.
1980   The reconstruction of proto-Bantu culture from the lexicon. In *L'expansion Bantoue,* ed. L. M. Hyman and J. Voorhoeve, 779–791. Paris: SELAF.

Prins, G.
1979   Disease at the crossroads: Towards a history of therapeutics in Bulozi since 1876. *Social Science and Medicine* 13B, 4:285–316.
1986   Review of *Lemba 1650–1930. Journal of African History* 27: 488–500.

Ranger, T. O.
1975   *Dance and society in Eastern Africa: The Beni Ngoma.* London: William Heinemann.
1985   *Peasant consciousness and guerrilla war in Zimbabwe.* London: James Currey; Berkeley and Los Angeles: University of California Press.

Riesman, P.
1985   Review of *Lemba 1650–1930. Research in African Literature,* 624–627.

Roberts, A. F.
1988   Through the bamboo thicket: The social process of Tabwa ritual performance. *The Drama Review* 32, 2:123–128.

Rouget, G.
1985   *Music and trance: A theory of the relations between music and possession.* Chicago and London: University of Chicago Press.

Salum, M. A.
n.d.   *Ngoma ya Msewe, Pemba.* Dar es Salaam. Mimeo.

Sautter, G.
1966   *De l'Atlantique au Fleuve Congo: Une geographie du sous-peuplement.* 2 vols. Paris, La Haye: Mouton.

Savage, M.
1979   The political economy of health in South Africa. In *Economics of health in South Africa*, ed. F. Wilson and G. Wescott, 140–160. Johannesburg: Ravan Press.

Schneider, D. M.
1984   *A critique of the study of kinship*. Ann Arbor: University of Michigan Press.

Shileondoa Muwisi, O.
1976   *"Mbasa," Ngoma ya Utamaduni Wetu*. Dar es Salaam: Ministry of Culture.

Shorter, A.
1974   *East African societies*. London and Boston: Routledge & Kegan Paul.

Sibisi, H. *See also* Ngubane.
1976   The place of spirit possession in Zulu cosmology. In *Religion and social change in Southern Africa*, ed. M. Whisson and M. West, 48–57. Cape Town: David Philip.

Sindzingre, N.
1985   Healing is as healing does: Pragmatic resolution of misfortune among the Senufo (Ivory Coast). *History and Anthropology* 2:33–57.

Smith, M. G.
1974   *Corporations and society*. London: Gerald Duckworth & Co.

South African Institute of Race Relations
1983   *Survey of race relations in South Africa 1982*. Johannesburg: South African Institute of Race Relations.

Spencer, P.
1985   *Society and the dance*. Cambridge: Cambridge University Press.

Spring, A.
1978   Epidemiology of spirit possession among the Luvale of Zambia. In *Women in ritual and symbolic roles*, ed. J. Hoch-Smith and A. Spring, 165–190. New York and London: Plenum Publishing.
1985   Health care systems in northwest Zambia. In *African healing strategies*, ed. B. M. du Toit and I. H. Abdalla, 135–150. Owerri, New York, London: Trado-Medic Books.

Stevens, P.
1984   Review of *Lemba 1650–1930*. *African Arts* 84:29–31.

Stock, R.
1986   "Disease and development" or "The underdevelopment of health": A critical review of geographical perspectives on African health problems. *Social Science and Medicine* 23, 7:689–700.

Stuart, C. H.
1986   Review of *Lemba 1650–1930*. *Africana Journal* 13:235–237.

Sullivan, L. E.
1986   Sound and senses: Toward a hermeneutics of performance. *History of Religions* 26, 1:1–33.

Swantz, L. W.
  1974   *The role of the medicine man among the Zaramo of Dar-es-Salaam.* Ph.D. dissertation, University of Dar es Salaam.
Swantz, M. L.
  1970   *Ritual and symbol in transitional Zaramo society.* Uppsala, Sweden: Gleerup (Studia Missionalia Upsaliensia XVI).
  1976   The spirit possession cults and their social setting in a Zaramo coastal society. *Ethnologia Fennica* 1–2:27–39.
  1977a   Dynamics of the spirit possession phenomenon in eastern Tanzania. In *Dynamics and institution,* ed. H. Biezais, 90–111. Abo, Finland: Scripta Instituti Donneriani Aboensis IX.
  1977b   Methodological notes on cultural research amidst planned development: A case study on spirit possession. *Temenos: Studies in Comparative Religion* 13:154–174.
  1979   Community and healing among the Zaramo in Tanzania. *Social Science and Medicine* 138:169–173.
Swaziland Central Statistical Office
  1979   *Swazi population census 1976.* Vol. I. Mbabane: Central Statistical Office.
Temkin, O.
  1973   Health and disease. In *Dictionary of the history of ideas,* 395–407. New York: Charles Scribner's Sons.
Thompson, R. F.
  1983   *Flash of the spirit.* New York: Random House.
Turner, V. W.
  1967   *The forest of symbols: Aspects of Ndembu ritual.* Ithaca, N.Y.: Cornell University Press.
  1968   *The drums of affliction: A study of religious processes among the Ndembu of Zambia.* Oxford: Clarendon Press.
  1975   *Revelation and divination in Ndembu ritual.* Ithaca: Cornell University Press.
Unschuld, P.
  1975   Medico-cultural conflicts in Asian settings, an explanatory theory. *Social Science and Medicine* 9:303–312.
Van Binsbergen, W.
  1977   Regional and non-regional cults of affliction in western Zambia. In *Regional cults,* ed. R. P. Werbner. London, New York: Academic Press (ASA 16).
  1981   *Religious change in Zambia.* London: Routledge & Kegan Paul (African Studies Centre Leiden).
Van Binsbergen, W., and M. Schoffeleers, eds.
  1985   *Theoretical explorations in African religion.* London, Boston, Melbourne, and Henley: Routledge & Kegan Paul.
Van Noten, F.
  1981   Central Africa. In *General history of Africa II: Ancient civilizations of Africa,* ed. G. Mokhtar. London: Heinemann Educa-

tional Books; Berkeley, Los Angeles, London: University of California Press; Paris: UNESCO (with collaboration of D. Cahen and P. de Maret).

Van Onselen, C.
1976   *Chibaro*. London: Pluto Press.

Vansina, J.
1979–80   Bantu in the crystal ball. *History in Africa* 6:287–333; 7:293–325.
1984   Western Bantu expansion. *Journal of African History* 25:129–145.
1990   *Paths in the rainforests*. Madison: University of Wisconsin Press.

Vass, W. K.
1979   *The Bantu speaking heritage of the United States*. Los Angeles: Center for Afro-American Studies, University of California, Monograph 2.

Wagner, R.
1986   *Symbols that stand for themselves*. Chicago: University of Chicago Press.

Waite, G.
1987   Public health in pre-colonial East-Central Africa. *Social Science and Medicine* 24, 3:197–208.

Webster, D.
1982   Personal communications.

Werbner, R., ed.
1977   *Regional cults*. London, New York: Academic Press (ASA Monograph 16).
1989   *Ritual passage, sacred journey*. Washington, D.C., and Manchester: Smithsonian Institution Press and Manchester University Press.
1990   Bwiti in reflection: On the fugue of gender. *Journal of Religion in Africa* 20, 1:63–91.

Wilson, M.
1936   *Reaction to conquest*. London: Oxford University Press.

World Bank
1985   *World development report*. Geneva: World Bank.

World Health Organization
1978   *Primary health care*. Geneva: World Health Organization.
1979   *Statistical annual 1978*. Geneva: World Health Organization.

Young, A.
1977   Order, analogy and efficacy in Ethiopian medical divination. *Culture, Medicine and Psychiatry* 1, 2:183–200.

Zaretsky, I., and C. Shambaugh
1978   *Spirit possession and spirit mediumship in Africa and Afro-America*. New York and London: Garland Publishing.

Zilaoneka Kaduma, G.
    1972   *A theatrical description of five Tanzanian dances* [Ngoma]. Master's thesis, University of Dar es Salaam.

Zola, I.
    1966   Culture and symptoms: An analysis of patients' presenting complaints. *American Sociological Review* 31:615–630.

Index

Designer: U.C. Press Staff
Compositor: Prestige Typography
Text: 10/13 Sabon
Display: Sabon
Printer: Thomson-Shore, Inc.
Binder: Thomson-Shore, Inc.